ENFORCEMENT OF HUMAN RIGHTS IN INDIA

DR. UPENDRA NATH DUBEY

BLUEROSE PUBLISHERS
India | U.K.

Copyright © Dr Upendra Nath Dubey 2023

All rights reserved by author. No part of this publication may be reproduced, stored in a retrieval system or transmitted in any form or by any means, electronic, mechanical, photocopying, recording or otherwise, without the prior permission of the author. Although every precaution has been taken to verify the accuracy of the information contained herein, the publisher assume no responsibility for any errors or omissions. No liability is assumed for damages that may result from the use of information contained within.

BlueRose Publishers takes no responsibility for any damages, losses, or liabilities that may arise from the use or misuse of the information, products, or services provided in this publication.

For permissions requests or inquiries regarding this publication,
please contact:

BLUEROSE PUBLISHERS
www.BlueRoseONE.com
info@bluerosepublishers.com
+91 8882 898 898
+4407342408967

ISBN: 978-93-5741-092-2

Cover design: [Muskan Sachdeva]
Typesetting: [Pooja Sharma]

First Edition: July 2023

Contents

Chapter I: Enforcement Of Human Rights In India: **17**
    An Introduction 17

Chapter II: Historical Background **25**
    Introduction 25
    The Religious Tradition 25
    The Hindu Tradition 26
    The Buddhist Tradition 28
    The Muslim Tradition 28
    Western Tradition 29
    National Freedom Movement 31
    Role of Gandhi 32
    Nehru and Indian Civil Liberties Union 35
    Human Rights after Independence 39
    Conclusion 40

Chapter III: International Standard **48**
    Introduction 48
    International Law and Human Rights 48
    Principles for Older Persons 57
    International Convention on the Elimination of All Forms of Racial Discrimination 59
    Committee on the Elimination of Racial Discrimination 60
    International Covenant on Civil and Political Rights 61
    The Covenant is divided into six major Parts: 61
    Human Rights Committee 63
    First Optional Protocol to the International Covenant on Civil and Political Rights 63
    Second Optional Protocol to the International Covenant on Civil and Political Rights 64
    International Covenant on Economic, Social and Cultural Rights 65
    Committee on Economic, Social and Cultural Rights 66
    Optional Protocol to ICESCR 67

Convention on the Elimination of All Forms of Discrimination against Women 68

Committee on the Elimination of Discrimination against Women 69

Optional Protocol to the Convention on the Elimination of All Forms of Discrimination against Women 70

Convention against Torture and Other Cruel, Inhuman or Degrading Treatment or Punishment 71

Committee against Torture 72

Optional Protocol to the Convention against Torture and Other Cruel, Inhuman or Degrading Treatment or Punishment 73

Convention on the Rights of the Child 73

Committee on the Rights of the Child 75

Optional Protocol on the Involvement of Children in Armed Conflict 75

Optional Protocol on the Sale of Children, Child Prostitution and Child Pornography 76

International Convention on Protection of the Rights of All Migrant Workers and Members of their Families 78

Committee on the Protection of the Rights of All Migrant Workers and Members of the Families ... 79

Convention on the Rights of Persons with Disabilities 80

Optional Protocol to the Convention on the Rights of Persons with Disabilities 81

International Convention for the Protection of All Persons from Enforced Disappearance 82

Key Provisions 82

Committee on Enforced Disappearances 84

Conclusion 84

Chapter IV: National Standard 85

Introduction 85

The Constitution of India 85

Directive Principles of State Policy 86

Right against Arbitrary Arrest and Problems of Custodial Violence 87

Right to Work, Right to Education and Right to Public Assistance 89

Right to Just and Humane Conditions of Work 89

Right to Living Wages for Workers 89

Right against Exploitation 89

Employment of Children 90

Right to Education (Article 21-A) 90

Right of a Citizen to admission to Educational Institutions (Article 29 (2)) 90

Compulsory Early Childhood Care & Education for Children (Article 45) 91

Promotion of Educational and Economic Interest of Weaker Sections (Article 46) 91

Article 21 of Indian Constitution and Prisoners Rights 91

Right to Free Legal Aid -Right to Appeal 91

Right to Speedy Trial 92

Right against Inhuman Treatment –Third Degree Methods 92

Right against Custodial Violence 93

Right to a fair trial /fair investigation 93

Right to Bail 93

Right against handcuffing 94

Right against Bar Fetters 94

Right against Solitary Confinement 94

Right to Personal Liberty 95

A New Dynamic Dimension-Facets of Personal Liberty 96

Right to Privacy 96

Right to Health of Women 96

Evolution of Health Care System in India 97

Changes in the global arena 97

Increase in drug prices and effect of TRIPS 99

Health Policies and Programmes in India 99

National Health Policy (NHP) 100

National Population Policy (NPP) 2000 101

National Nutrition Policy (NNP), 1993 102

National Mental Health Programme 103

Reproductive and Child Health 103

National Rural Health Mission 105

Other Programmes 105

Women and Communicable Diseases 107

Hysterectomies of Mentally Challenged Women 108

Women and Occupational Health 108

Right to Health and the Women's Movement 109

HDEP Drug issue 110

Campaign Process in Brief... 110

Campaign against Long-acting hormonal Contraceptives 111

Hazardous Effects of Depo-Provera and Depo-Provera 112

The Battle against Sex-selection and Selective Abortion of Female Foetuses 114

Challenging Population Control policies and Two-child Norm 117

Campaigning for a Rational Drug Policy 119

The Bhopal Gas Tragedy – A Sustained Campaign 120

National Campaign for Health care as a Fundamental Right 120

Monitoring NRHM: A People's Rural Health Watch 121

Decentralization of Health – An effort by Mine Workers of dalli rajhara 122

Low cost Standard Therapeutics – LOCOST 122

Federation of Medical and States Representatives' Association of India (FMRAI) 122

Search for Alternatives – a Shodhini Experience 123

Appropriate Technologies for Health – Jan Swasthy Sahayog (JSS) 123

Sadaphuli – barefoot Gynecologists of MASUM 124

Counseling of Women Victims of Violence in a Public Hospital: the DILAASA project 124

Jan Swasthya Abhiyan (JSA) 124

Care and Treatment in Mental Health Institutions 126

Conclusion 128

Chapter V: Role Of Human Rights Enforcement Agencies Of India 135

Introduction 135

Implementation of Human Rights under Covenants and First Optional Protocol 135

Implementation Provisions under the Covenants 136

Reporting Procedure 137

Optional Protocol to the International Covenant on Civil and Political Rights 138

Implementation of the Human Rights under the Covenant on Economic, Social
and Culture Rights 139

Reports 139

Remedial Fundamental Right under the Constitution of Indian 140

enforcemnt Of Fundamental Rights: Article 32 Clauses (1) & (2) 141

Who can invoke the Jurisdiction? 141

Public Interest Litigation 141

Breach of Fundamental Rights 144

Over –burdening of the Court 145

The Province of PIL: Some Illustrative Cases 146

Judicial Predicament and Public Interest Activism 146

Against Whom a Writ, etc., Lies 147

No Writ can be Issued against High Courts 148

Jurisdiction of the High Court under Article 226 150

Existence of Alternative Remedy 150

Petition Barred by Laches 150

Petition Barred by *res judicata* 151

Petition Barred on Account of Misconduct or Bad Conduct of Petitioner 152

Disputed Question of fact may Bar petition 152

A Writ will not be Issued if it would be Futile 152

Can a Remedy under Article 32 be directly pursued in the Supreme Court? 152

The Writs 153

Mandamus 154

Who can Seek Mandamus 154

Against Who Mandamus may be Claimed 155

When performance of public Duty is Discretionary, no Mandamus Lies 156

Certiorari and prohibition 156

Who can Seek these Writs 157

Against whom, Certiorari and Prohibition Lie 157

When does Certiorari or Prohibition Lies 159

Habeas Corpus 161

Who can Seek Habeas Corpus 161

Against whom Petition for Habeas Corpus Lies 162

Habeas Corpus Jurisdiction is Remedial and not Punitive 162

Preventive Detention and Habeas Corpus 162

Successive Application for Habeas Corpus 163

Appeal 163

Quo Warranto 163

Conclusion 164

Chapter VI: Role Of Judiciary In India 173

Writ Jurisdiction of the Supreme Court and the High Courts 175

Rule of Locus Standi vis-à-vis Public Interest Litigation 176

Prisoners and the Human Rights 178

Rights against Hand Cuffing 181

Rights against Inhuman Treatment of Prisoners 182

Right to have Interview with Friends, Relatives and Lawyers 184

Right to Legal Aid 186

Right to Speedy Trial 188

Care and Treatment in Mental Health Institutions 189

Compensatory Jurisprudence and Human Rights 191

Monetary Compensation and Human Rights 192

Nature of the Constitutional Remedy 194

Sovereign Immunity and Violation of Human Rights 195

Environmental Protection and Human Rights 198

Judicial Contribution to Protection of Environment 198

Response of the Judiciary on Child Labour 202

Judicial Response on Bonded Labour System 205

Conclusion 208

Table Of Cases

A

A.K. Gopalan v State of Madras, AIR 1950 SC 27

A.K. Kraipak v. Union of India, AIR 1970 SC 150

A. Nesamony v. T. M. Vasghose, (1952) Tr Co. 66

A.R. Chaudhary v. Union of India, AIR 1974 SC 532

Air Corporation Employees' Union v. D.V. Vyas, 1962 Bom 274 Amalgamated Coal – fields v. Janapade, AIR 1964 SC 1013 Amalgamated Coal – fields v. Ranade, AIR 1961 SC 964 Ambika Mills v. Bhatt, AIR 1961 SC 970

Amrit Lal v. State of W.B., AIR 1972 SC 2060 Amrit Lal v. Collector, AIR 1975 SC 538 Anand Henal v. Ram Sahav, AIR 1952 MB 31 Anwar v. State J&K, AIR 1971 SC 337

Arunachal Pradesh v. Khudiram Chakma, 1 S.C.C. (1994) p. 614 Asiad Workers Case, AIR 1982 SC 1976.

Associated Cement Co .v. P.M. Sharma, AIR 1955 SC 1595

B

B.E. Supply Co. v. The Workmen, AIR 1972 SC 330

B. R. Kapoor & others vs. Union of India, AIR 1990 SC 752, JT 1989 (2) SC 330 Bakoro and Ramgur Ltd. V. State of Bihar, AIR 1963 SC 516

Bangalore Medical Trust v. B.S.Muddappa, AIR 1991 SC 1902 Bennet Coleman & Co. v. Union of India, AIR 1973 SC 106 Bhopal Sugar Industries v. Income Tax Officer, AIR 1961 SC 182 Bishnu Charan v. State, AIR 1973 Orissa 199

Board of High School v. Ghanshyam, AIR 1962 SC 1110

Bombay Union of Journalist v. State of Bombay, AIR 1964 SC 1617 Bool Chandra v. Chancellor, AIR 1968 SC 292

Borhan Kumar v. Boruni Oil Refineries, AIR 1971 Pat 174

Burmah Construction Company v. State of Orissa, AIR 1962 SC 1320

C

C. Bhusan v. Dy. Director Cons., U.P., AIR 1967 SC 1273

C.I.T v. Raman & Co., AIR 1964 SC 49

C. Shanmugam v. SRVS, AIR 1963 SC 1926

Champalal v. CIT, AIR 1970 SC 645 Chetkar v. Vishwanath, AIR 1970 SC 1932

Chiranji Lal v. Union of India, AIR 1951 SC 42 Chotey Lal v. State of U.P., AIR1951 All 228 Commr. Of Police v. Gordhandas, AIR 1952 SC 16 Commr. of Police v. Gordhandas, (1953) SCR 135 Cox v. Hakes, (1890) 15 AC 506

D

DAV College v. State of Punjab, (1971) Supp SCR 688

D.C. Mills v. Commr. of Income Tax, AIR 1955 SC 65

D.C. Works v. State of Saurastra, AIR 1957 SC 164

D.F.O. V. Ram Sanehi, AIR 1973 SC 204.

D. K. Basu v State of West Bengal, AIR 1997 SC 610 Darva v. State of U.P., AIR 1961 SC 1457

Daulat Singh v.Dy. Commr., Karnal, AIR 1972 P & H 28

Delhi Development Horticulture Employees' Union v. Delhi Administration, Delhi and others, AIR 1992 SC 789

Devilal Modi v. STO, AIR 1961 SC 1150

Dwarka Prasad v. State of U.P., AIR 1954 SC 224

E

Electricity Board, Raj, v. Mohan Lal, AIR 1967 SC 1857

Engineering Mazdoor Sabha v. Hind Cycles, AIR 1963 SC 874 Express Newspaper v. Workers, AIR 1963 SC 569

F

F. K. Hussain v. Union of India, AIR 1990 Ker 321 Fedco v. Bilgrani, AIR 1960 SC 415

Filartiga v. Pena-Irala, 630 F 2d (1980) 876

Francis Coraile Mullin v Delhi Administration, AIR 1981 SC 746

G

G.J. Fernondez v. State of Mysore, AIR 1967 SC 1753

G. K. Karkare v. The Shived, AIR 1952 Nag 330

G. Sadanandan v. State of Ker., AIR 1966 SC 1952

Gandhinagar Motor Transport Society v. State of Bombay, AIR 1964 Bom. 202 Gangula Ashok and others v State of Andhra Pradesh, 2000 (1) SCR 468 Ghrita Mohan v. Addl. District Magistrate, AIR 1954 Cal 97

Ghulam Sarwar v. Union of India, AIR 1967 SC 1335 Gohar Begum v. Suggi, AIR 1960 SC 93

Gopalan v. Government, AIR 1966 SC 816 Govt. of A.P. v. Nersimha, AIR 1991 SC 1732 Gulab Chand v. State, AIR 1965 SC 1953

Gullapalli v. A.O. State Transport Corporation, AIR 1959 SC 388 Gullapalli I, AIR 1959 SC 308

Gullapalli II, AIR 1959 SC 1376

H

Halder v. Misakar, AIR 1973 Ori 132

Hans Muller v. Supdt. Presidency Jail, AIR 1955 SC 367 Hare Krishna v. Chief Minister, Orissa, AIR 1971 Ori 175

Haryana Electricity Board v. State of Punjab, AIR 1974 SC 2060

Hira Nath and State of J&K v. Bakshi Gulam Md, 1967 AIR 122, 1966 SCR (4) Hira Nath v. Rajendra Medical College, Ranchi, AIR 1973 SC 1216

Hussainara Khatoon & Ors vs Home Secretary, State Of Bihar, 1979 AIR 1369, 1979 SCR (3) 532

I

Indian Airlines Corporation v. Sukhdeo Singh, AIR 1971 SC 1820 In re Hastings (NO.3), 1959 KB 358

In re Prahlad Krishna Khurana, AIR 1951 Bom. 25

J

Joseph Pothen v. State of Kerela, AIR 1965 SC1514 Judges Transfer Case, (1981) Supp. SCC 87

Jyoti Prakash v. M.K. Bose, AIR 1963 SC 209

K.C. Kochuni v. State of Mad., AIR 1959 SC 725

K. K. Kochuni v. State of Mad., (1959) Supp 2 SCR 356

K.N. Guruswami v. State of Mysore, (1955) 1 SCR 305 Kalinadi v. Tata Loco & Engineering Co., AIR 1963 SC 914 Kalyan Singh v. State of U.P., AIR 1962 SC 1183 Kaminikumar v. State of W.B., AIR 1972 SC 2062

K

Kanungo v. Collector of Customs, Calcutta, AIR 1972 SC 2136 Kanu Sanyal v. Dist Magistrate, AIR 1973 SC 2684

Karnataka Public Service Commission v. B.M. Vijai, AIR 1992 SC 952 Kedar Nath v. State of Punjab, AIR 1960 Punj 122

Kharak Singh v. State of U.P., AIR 1963 SC 1295

L

Laxminappa v. Union of India, AIR 1955 SC 3; Nain Sukh v. State of U.P., AIR 1953 SC 3 U.P Lekhraj v. Dy. Custodian, AIR 1966 SC 334

Lekhraj v. Mathur, AIR 1962 Ker 152

Louis De Raedt v. Union of India, 3 S.C.C. (1991) p. 554

M

M.C.Mehta v. UOI, (1987) 4 SCC 463; see also M.C. Mehta v. UOI, (1988) 2 SCC 421

M.P. Industries v. Union of India, AIR 1966 SC 671

Maganbhai Ishwarbhai Patel v. Union of India, AIR 1969 SC 783 Mahor Chandru Bhan v. Latafat Ullah, AIR 197 SC 1814 Maneka Gandhi v. Union of India , AIR 1978 SC 597

Manek Lal v. Prem Chand, AIR 1957 SC 429 Mathew v. Union of India, AIR 1974 Ker 4 Md. Alam v. State of W.B., AIR 1974 SC 917 Miss Cama v. Banwari, AIR 1953 Nag 81

Mohini Jain v. State of Karnataka, Supreme Court Cases 3 (1992) p. 666

Mrs. Veena Sethi vs State Of Bihar And Ors, AIR 1983 SC 339, 1983 Cri LJ 675 Mukti Sangrsh Movement v. State of Mach, (1990) Suppl SCC 37

N

NMCS & Weaning Mills v. Ahmedabad Municipality, AIR 1967 SC 1801

N. Masthau v. Chief Commr., Pondicherry, AIR 1963 SC 533

Nagendra Nath Bora v. Commr . of Hill Div, AIR 1958 SC 398 Nand Kishore v. State of Orissa, AIR 1991 SC 1720 1728 Naranjan Singh v. State of Punj, AIR 1952 SC 1063

Narinder Chand v. Ly. Governor, H.P., (1971) 2 SCC 743

National Human rights Commission v. State of Arunachal Pradesh, A.I.R. Supreme Court, 1996 p. 1234

National Institute v. K.K. Raman, AIR 1992 SC 1809

O

Olga Tellis v Bombay Municipal Corporation AIR 1986 SC 180

P

P. Basant v. Eugle Rolling Mills, AIR 1964 SC 1260

P.L Lakhanpal v. Union of India, AIR 1967 SC 1507

P.L. Lakhanpal v. A.N.Roy, AIR 1975 Del 66 (FB)

P.N. Kumar v. Municipal Corporation of Delhi, AIR 1989 SC 1285 Paramanand Katara vs. Union of India, 1989 AIR 2039, 1989 SCR (3) 997 Paramjlt kaur v. State of Punjab, AIR 1999, SC, 340

Parry & Co. v. Second Industrial Tribunal, AIR 1970 SC 1334

Paschim Banga Khet Samity vs. State of West Bengal, 1996 SCC (4) 37, JT 1996 (6) 43 Pathumma v. State of Kerela, Supreme Court Cases 1 (1978)

People's Union for Civil Liberties v. Union of India, AIR 2005 SC 2419

People's Union for Civil Liberties v Union of India and others Civil write Petition No.196 of 2001.

Peoples' Union for Civil Liberties v. Union of India, SCC 3 (1997) People's Union of Democratic Rights v. Union of India, AIR 1982 SC 1976 Piara Singh v. State of Punjab, (1969) 1 SCC 379

Pillai v. Government of India, AIR 1970 Ker 110 (FB) Pioneer Traders v. C.C. Exports & Imports, AIR 1963 SC 734 Praga Tool Corporation v. Immanuel, AIR 1969 SC 1306 Pramatha Nath v. Chief Justice of Calcutta, AIR 1961 Cal 545

Prem Chand v. Excise Commr., AIR 1963 SC 996 Prem Prakash v. Punjab University, AIR 1972 SC 1408 Prem Sagar v. S.V. Oil Co., AIR 1956 SC 111

Prem Shankar Shukla v Delhi Administration, AIR 1980 SC 1535 Puran Lal v. P. C. Ghosh, AIR 1970 Cal 118

R

R.C. Cooper v. Union of India, (1970) 35 CR 530

R.D. Singh v. Bihar State Small Industries Co., AIR 1974 Pat 212

R.S. Deodhar v. State of Maharashtra, AIR 1974 SC 259 R.V, Electricy Commissioner, (1924) KB 173

R. V. Legislative Committee of the Church Assembly (1928) 1KB 411 Re H.K. (An infant), (1967) 2 KB 617

Radheshyam v. State of M.P., AIR 1959 SC 107 Rajamahundary v. State of A.P., AIR 1954 SC 201

Raj Bahadur v. Legal Remembrancer, AIR 1952 Cal 522 Rajendra Singh v. N.K. Shejwalkar, AIR 1972 MP 249

Rakesh Chandra Narayan vs. State of Bihar, 1989 AIR 348, 1988 SCR Supl. (3) 306 Raman Ltd v. State of Mad., AIR 1959 SC 694

Raman & Raman v. State of Madras, AIR 1959 SC 694 Ram Bali v. State of W.B., AIR 1975 SC 623

Ramchandaran v. Alagiriswami, AIR 1961 Mad 45 Ram Chandra v. State of Orissa, AIR 1957 SC 298.

Rameshwar Prasad v. Commr., Land Reform, AIR 1959 SC 498 Ram Manohar Lohia v. State of Bihar, AIR 1966 SC 740

Ram Narayan Singh v. State of Delhi, AIR 1953 SC 227

Rashid Ahmed v. Municipal Board, Kairana, AIR 1950 SC 163

Rashid Ahmad v. Municipal Board, AIR 1950 SC 610 Ridge v. Baldwin, (1963) 2 WLR 935.

Romesh Thapar v. State of Madras, AIR 1950 SC 124. Rukmanand v. State of Bihar, AIR 1971 SC 746

Rural Litigation and Entitlement Kendra v. State U.P, (1985) 2 SCC 481

S

S.H. Kochuni v. State of Mad., (1959) SCR 725

S. N. Mukherjee v. Union of India, AIR 1990 SC 1984

S.P Gupta v. Union of India, (1981) Supple, SCC 87 at 211

S.P. Gupta v. UOI, (1981) Suppl, SCC at 507

S. Soundarajan v. Union of India, AIR 1970 Del 29 STO v. Shiv Ratan, AIR 1966 SC 142

Sadhu Singh v. Delhi Admn., AIR 1966 SC 91 Sahngin Singh v. Desa Singh, AIR 1970 SC 672

Samarth Transport Co. v. RTV, AIR 1961 SC 932

Satish Chandra v. Rajasthan University, AIR 1970 Raj 148 Sayed Yakoob v. Radhakrishna, AIR 1964 SC 477 Shankar Lal v. Shankar Lal, AIR 1965 SC 507

Shankar v. Krishna, AIR 1970 SC 1

Shankar v. Returning Officer, AIR 1952 Bom 277 Shanngam v. SRVS, AIE 1963 SC 1963

Sharif Ahmed v. Regional Transport Authority, AIR 1978 SC 209

Sheela Barse vs. union of Indian and others, JT 1986 136, 1986 SCALE (2)230 Shri Bhagwan v. Ram Chandra, AIR 1965 SC 176

Siderman de Blake v. Argentina, (1992) 965 F zd 699

Smt. Vidhya Verma v. Shive Narayan Verma, AIR 1956 SC 108 Sohan Lal v. Union of India, AIR 1957 SC 829

Sridhar v. State of Maharastra, AIR 1967 SC 1 State of Bihar v. D.N. Ganguly, (1959) SCR 1991

State of Bihar v. Rambalak Singh, AIR 1966 SC 1441

State of Bombay v. Hospital Mazdoor Sabha, AIR 1960 SC 1960 SC 610 State of Bombay v. K. S. Advani, AIR 1950 SC 222

State of J.&K. v. A.R. Jakki, AIR 1992 SC 1546

State of Madras. v. Sundaram, AIR, 1964 SC 1103 State of M.P. v. Bhailal, AIR 1964 SC 1006

State of M.P v. Mandawar, AIR 1954 SC 493 State of M.P. v. Peer Md., AIR 1963 SC 645 State of M.P. v. Srikant, AIR 1992 SC 2303

State of Mysore v. Chandrasekharan, AIR 1965 SC 932 State of Orissa v. Binapani Devi, AIR 1967 SC 1269 State of Orissa v. Murlidhar, AIR 1963 SC 404

State of U.P. v. Nooh, AIR 1958 SC 86 Subar v. Workmen, AIR 1960 SC

Subhas Kumar v. State of Bihar, AIR 1991 SC 420

Subramanium v. Collector of Customs, AIR 1972 SC 2178 Sukhdeo Singh v. Bhahat Ram, AIR 1975 SC 1331.

Sukhdesh v. Mahadevanand, AIR 1961 AP 250

Suresh Koshy v. University of Kerela, AIR 1969 SC 1998

T

T.C. Basappa v. Nagappa, AIR 1954 SC 440

T.G. Goakar v. R.N. Shukla, AIR 1968 SC 1050;

T.G. Mudaliar v. State of T.N., AIR 1973 SC 974

T.T. Devasthanams v. Ram Chandra, AIR 1966 AP 112 Talik Hussain v. State of J. & K., AIR 1971SC 62

Toonen v Australia, Communication No. 488/ 1992, U.N. Doc CCPR/C/50/D/488/1992 Trilok Chand v. H.B. Munshi, (1969) 2 SCR 824

Trilok Chand v. H.B. Munshi, AIR 1970 SC 898

U

U.P State Warehousing Corporation v. C.K.Tyagi, AIR 1970 SC 1244 Ujjain Singh v. State of U.P, AIR 1962 SC 1621

Umakant v. State of Bihar, AIR 1973 SC 965 Union of India v. Goel, AIR 1964 SC 364

Union of India v. Nanak Singh, AIR 1968 SC 1370

Union of India v. T. R. Varma, AIR 1957 SC 882

Union of India v. Win Chadda, AIR 1993 SC 1082 University of Mysor v. Govin Rao, AIR 1956 SC 491

Upendra Baxi vs. State of Uttar Pradesh & others, (1998) 8 SCC 622

V

Vaish College Society v. Lakshmi Narain, AIR 1974 All 1

Vice Chancellor, Utkal University v. S. K. Ghosh, (1954) SCR 883 Vishal Jeet v. Union of India, (1990) 3 SCC 318

Vishwanath v. State, AIR 1967 Raj 75 Veerappa v. Raman, AIR 1952 SC 192;

Venkateswaran v. Wadhwan, AIR 1961 SC 1506 Venkataya v. Siverama, AIR 1961 AP 250

Chapter I

Enforcement Of Human Rights In India:

An Introduction

Author wants to start with a quote from Daniel Goleman "It is the paradox of our time that those with power are too comfortable to notice the pain of those who suffer, and those who suffer have no power ".

Civil society is based upon the concept of Human Rights which are essential not merely to fulfil biological needs of the mankind but as well as for the dignity of the individual. Without recognising the concept of Human Rights no polity can be a democratic one. Every democratic constitution tries to recognise the concept of Human Rights in one way or the other. The Constitution of India recognises the concept of human rights through its preamble. Human rights are implied as civil liberties (Fundamental Rights) and democratic rights (Directive Principles of State Policy) in the Constitution of India.[1]

With the evolution of human life, certain rights of men have come to be considered as basic rights, which they enjoy as human beings. These Human Rights are inalienable rights of people. From their nature, these rights can hardly be considered as having been created at any given moment; on the contrary they must have existed in however nascent form for as long as man had lived in communities. The human well being is based on enjoyment of human rights. The measure of wellbeing is the extent to which the people are able to enjoy their human rights and freedoms. Thus human rights become very important in any society.

As pointed out by Louis Henkin, "(R)ights have bedevilled legal and political philosophers for centuries. There are volumes on the meaning of rights, their source, what gives them authority. There are continuing debates about the relations of rights to duties. Most of these jurisprudential enquiries are not material to the law, the politics or the sociology of human rights in our day. For our purpose human rights are claims asserted and recognised 'as of right', not claims upon love or grace or brotherhood or charity; one does not have to earn or deserve them. They are. Not merely aspirations or moral assertions bug increasingly, legal claims under some applicable law".[2]

Human rights, in short, are statements of basic needs or interests. They are politically significant as grounds of protest and justification for reforming policies. They differ from appeals to benevolence and charity in that they invoke ideals like justice and equality. A man with a right has no reason to be grateful to benefactors; he has grounds for grievance when it is denied. The concept presupposes a standard below which it is intolerable that a human being should fall... Human Rights are the corollary, then, of the equally modern notion of social justice.[3]

Human Rights are legal rights against society as represented by government and its officials. In human rights, individual holds the status of 'tights holder' and the

State is in the position of an 'obligator'. Therefore, State by its act or omission should not hit Human Rights.[4] If it does so the state will be liable for the violation of human rights since it fails to discharge its obligation. State must protect the individual and provide legal remedies against the wrongdoer. The rights are claimed against the State. Earlier the Human Rights were thought of as limitations on what government might do to the individual; now they also include what society is deemed obliged to do for the individual.

The greatest positive contribution during the second half of the twentieth century to humanity is concretization of human right values and realisation of the need for governance with a human soul. This was an outcome of eternal vigilance which was meticulously carried out by the concerned Human Rights Organisations (international, national and local), conscious people, national leadership and active judiciary.[5] Franklin Roosevelt's famous four freedoms[6] formed the basis of the United Nations Charter and the Universal Declaration of Human Rights. When taken together, these freedoms are universal in appeal and application; only the emphasis is different in different countries.[7] Although the United Nations Charter and the Universal Declaration do not offer a comprehensive recipe for the achievement of an ideal world they do proclaim a set of values which give guidance to all nations in choosing a wide range of alternative policy options.[8] The two International Covenants of 1966- on

Civil and Political Rights as well as on Economic, Social and Cultural Rights- further provide a legal framework to the jurisprudence of human rights.

Human rights are now established in principle and are national and international law for many nations. There is common agreement that every individual has both political, civil and economic, social claims upon his society. But in a world of nation state the strength of commitment of human rights and the extent to which it is realised depends upon the particular state and its institutions, the condition of human rights thus differs markedly in different societies.[9]

Human Rights are basic rights in political and social conditions variously defined to which every individual is entitled as a human being. Originally they were called natural rights or the rights of man and included the rights to life, liberty and the pursuit of happiness cited in the US Declaration of Independence. Over the years the concept of human rights has been broadened to include rights to social benefits such as social security, rest and leisure and education. These rights are basic to human existence and hence are also called basic rights.[10]

Since the World Wars the concept of human rights which was essentially a concept found in national laws of any state, has been internationalised. The birth of United Nations marked a sea change in the growth of international law. Concern of the mankind about the rights of people led to the declaration of human rights and to subsequent covenants. Universal Declaration of Human Rights was made which includes both justifiable civil rights such as equality[11] and social or cultural rights such as right to participate in cultural life.[12] The realisation of practical inconvenience led to separate Covenants on Economic, Social and Cultural Rights apart from Civil and Political Rights. New rules were framed through treaties and conventions, wherein many such rules related to the sphere of human rights. States are bound to recognise and give effect to the human rights which axe enumerated basically in the two Covenants of 1966. However, unfortunately in majority of the cases an individual's rights are violated by his own state. In the absence of international machinery for their enforcement, the domestic institutions remain the main instruments of effective implementation.

The Universal Declaration of Human Rights, 1948, which was proclaimed after three years of United Nations Charter with an elaborate list of human rights, was a statement of intent or principle, and not a treaty or a legal agreement between countries or a binding legal document. However it influenced the constitutions and legal systems of many countries.[13] The concept of protection of human rights which emerged originally in the field of domestic legislations[14] was translated into international terms only after Second World War.[15] Keeping in view the fact that in majority of the cases an individual's rights are violated by his or her own state, in the absence of international machinery for enforcement, the domestic application of human rights norms remain the main basis for their effective implementation. The domestic courts can become the most effective means by which international conventions could be implemented and made. Effective enforcement of remedies requires that they be articulated as effectively, as impartially, and as sincerely as possible. And a real independent judiciary can be the most effective mechanism in this articulation.[16]

The characteristic feature of the development of international human rights law is the fact that the relationship between the states and their own citizens, are regulated through the international human rights conventions. No doubt, it is a desirable development but, it is equally true that these rights are guaranteed to the individuals only through the intervention of states. Thus, the position is that these Conventions on being accepted by the states become legally binding upon them, but they do not enable the individuals to present claim against their own states for the vindication of their rights or for that matter to claim compensation.[17]

Implementation mechanism is non existent and fragile in human rights. But, the requirement of effective implementation does not otherwise affect the concept of human rights since it is a requirement for the concept of the 'law' and not for the concept of 'human rights'. If the concept does not consist an 'effective implementation mechanism', it has to be explored. It cannot be a ground to disapprove the requirement of human rights.[18]

Human Rights are best protected under the national systems,[19] as most of the international instruments on the Human Rights leave the enforcement to the State Parties. State Parties are obliged to adopt measures to give effect to the Human Rights recognised under such instruments. And also before the international protection of human rights violation, the instruments require exhaustion of local remedies and states consider human rights as matters of domestic jurisdiction. The perception of Human Rights also differs depending upon the state's cultural, socio-economic and political conditions.

In India, human rights as basic or fundamental rights were recognised and demanded for even prior to the Constitution. The demand for guarantee of fundamental rights was made as early as the Constitution of India Bill, 1885.[20] The fight for civil liberties had been from the beginning an integral part of the Indian freedom movement. The Indian freedom movement also developed an internationalist outlook and visualised the Indian struggle as a part of worldwide struggle for freedom, democracy and social progress. The ideals of the freedom movement were sought to be reflected in the Indian Constitution.[21]

Further India became member of the United Nations when she had recently become independent and signed the Universal Declaration of Human Rights in 1948 when she had not yet made her Constitution. India shared the concerns of the Declaration ever since her National Movement for independence and they were reflected in the Constitution.[22] The two different but inseparable aspects of human rights, namely the civil and political rights and economic and social rights are both reflected in the Constitution of India. The realization of civil and political rights was considered as a goal within immediate reach while the economic, social and cultural rights were regarded as ideals for which the country should strive.[23] The framers of the Indian Constitution incorporated human rights into two parts, much the same way as International Covenants, civil and political rights, the justifiable human rights were included in Part III (Fundamental Rights) and non-justifiable social, economic and cultural rights were set forth in Part IV (Directive Principles of State Policy) of the Constitution.[24]

The Preamble to the Constitution, Fundamental Rights and Directive Principles which together have been described as forming the core of the Constitution[25], and which together reflect the basic principles of Universal Declaration of Human Rights and the Covenants on Civil and Political Rights and Economic Social and Cultural Rights.

The Constitution envisages a nation where the values of justice, equality, liberty and fraternity prevail. The Constitution protects not just civil and political rights, which are found in the form of justifiable fundamental rights guaranteed in Part III of the Constitution. Along with these rights, there are directive principles of state policy which elaborate social, economic and cultural rights. Apart from this, the Protection of Human Rights Act, 1993 was also enacted. Thus, human rights are guaranteed to the people of India. Now what remains to be seen is whether these guarantees alone should be sufficient to protect the Human Rights. The observations of Chief Justice Anand are apt to be quoted here:

"The Constitution though by itself is an important document, is after all a cold print on a piece of paper. What is important to remember is the system the Constitution seeks to introduce and the way that system works. The Constitution, no matter how it is drafted, it will not be able to deliver the goods unless the system which it introduces functions effectively to realise the dreams of the founding fathers of the Constitution. When we talk of the Constitution as living law it is usually understood to refer to the directives and understandings that the courts have invented, developed, spread and applied to make the constitution work in every situation. It is well settled that while a Bill of Rights (like the chapter on Fundamental Rights in the Constitution of India) is the conscience of this Constitution, an independent judiciary is the conscience keeper".[26]

The judiciary has increasingly interpreted the rights as being closely linked to fundamental rights.[27] For example Article 21 has been held as entailing a number of rights to protect life, thus making some of the directive principle justiciable fundamental rights.

In spite of having good constitution and also an independent judiciary, giving due consideration to ordinary human failings which may not be absent in the men adorning the judiciary also, there is not a substitute for an alert people. As Benjamin Franklin, one of the Constitution makers of U.S.A. observed, you can have a government that you want to have only if the people are conscious of their duties and rights and also ready to keep them up, if compelled by a struggle against those who try to derail the Constitution and the rule of law in its real sense.[28]

If people are aware about Human Rights they participate in making choices about their own lives, unleashing their own creative energies and strengthening social unity. Not only this much, living within a Human Rights protecting culture allows people to develop to the maximum of their capabilities.

Therefore, proper sensitization of Human Rights amongst the citizens and proper enforcement of Human Rights in all countries are necessary for world peace.

In India, enforcement of Human Rights is an issue complicated by the country's large size, its tremendous diversity, its status as a developing country and a sovereign, secular and democratic republic. Here, every system is available for effective enforcement of Human Rights. An independent judiciary and free media also act as checks on Human Rights Abuses and abusive practices. However, reluctance to hold public officials to account for Human Rights abuses or dereliction of duty continues to foster a culture of corruption and impunity. That is why, a thorough study regarding the enforcement of Human Rights in India is needed with an aim to find the possible ways to improve the functions of enforcement mechanisms of India.

Now, in order to understand all the chapters of this book readers must know the following in a clear way:

What are human Rights?

Ans: The U N has defined human rights as those rights which are inherent in our state of nature and without which we can not live as human beings. These are universal, undeniable and subjective.

What are human rights violations?

Ans: When Human Rights are denied to an individual, whether by the State or Non-State actors, it constitutes human rights violations.

What are human rights Abuses?

Ans: When large scale violations of human rights occur, it establishes human rights abuses. Human rights abuses in this context could refer to large scale violations of human rights committed repeatedly by State or Non-State actors to any community or group of people in their everyday lives. Further human rights abuses occur when random arrests, killings, torture, rape, oppressive legislation, discrimination, etc., are carried out methodically against any community or sections of society by the state or non-state actors with the objective of suppressing a particular group's aspiration or demand for the equal standard of living vis-à-vis other groups in that country.

What are the causes of human rights violations?

Ans: Though it may be impossible to understand the causes of every human rights violation, however, broadly speaking there are four causes of human rights violations namely:

(i) Government behaviour and structure,

(ii) Armed conflict,

(iii) Economic factors and

(iv) Psychological factors.

Difference between Enforcement and Implementation of human rights

Enforcement of human rights is the act of ensuring observance of human rights or it is the act of ensuring obedience to human rights whereas Implementation of human rights is the act of giving practical effect to actual fulfillment of human rights observance by concrete measures.

Refrences

[1] Chiranjeet Singh and M.R.Garg, " Human Rights as the Base Component of Democratic State," in B.P.Singh Sehgal (Ed), Human Rights in India-Problems and Perspectives, (New Delhi: Deep and Deep Publications, 1996), p.98.

[2] Louis Henkin The Rights of Man Today, (London: Stevens and Sons, 1979),pp 1-2.

[3] The Encyclopaedia of Philosophy, Paul, Edwards, (Ed), Vol. VII, (New York: Macmillan publishing Co, Inc. & the Free Press, London, Collier Macmillan Publishers), pp.198-199.

[4] Dr.B.L. Sharma et.al., " Human Rights; Sparse Productive Measures to Inhibit Defilements", Law Journal : Alert, vol. 1 :1,2003, p. 107.

[5] Dr. P.Ishwar Bhat, "The Role of NGOS in Protection of Human Rights, in The Changing Law", in Lectures on Current Trends in Jurisprudential Thought, Geetha Bhaskar and Sri.V.Sudhesh (Ed.), (Bangalore: Prof.V.B.Coutinho SBC Committee, 2003), p.225.

[6] i.e. freedom of speech; freedom of worship; freedom from fear and freedom from want.

[7] F.S. Nariman, " It Pays to be Free-Some Thoughts on The Fortieth Anniversary of the Universal Declaration" in Human Rights in the Changing World, Ed. Justice E.S. Venkataramiah, (New Delhi: International Law Association, 1988), p.I55.

[8] lbtdp.t56.

[9] Louis Henkin, supran.2. p.31.

[10] Indhrani Sridharan, " Practising Human Rights - A Feminist Perspective" (Ed) Chiranjivi J. Nirmal, Human Rights In India Historical, Social and Political Perspective", (New Delhi: Oxford University Press 2000), p.91.

[11] Article 7 of the Universal Declaration of Human Rights.

[12] Article 27 (t) Ibid.

[13] Dr.A.K.Pandey, "Constitutional Contours of Human Rights in India", in Ranbir Singh & Ghanshyam Singh (Eds), Human Rights Education, Lew and Society, (Hyderabad: Nalsar University, 2N4), p.t52.

[14] E.g. the MagnaCarta in England, The Bills of Rights in the US Constitution and the Declaration of Rights Man in France.

[15] E.g. Provisions of United Nations Charter; Universal Declaration of Human Rights etc.

[16] Noor Mohammed Bilal, "National Human Rights Commission-A Shackled Watchdog", KU.L.R., vol.1, Dec 1994, p.130.

[17] Dr. U. Chandra Human Rights,(Allahabad: Allahabad Law Agency Publications, 1999), p.iii.

[18] Dr. B.L. Sharma et ,al ., supra n.3, p.109.

[19] L.D. Naikar, The Law Relating to Human Rights, (Bangalore: Puliani and Puliani, 2004),p.327.

[20] D.D. Basu, Human Rights in Constitutional Law,(New Delhi: Prentice Hall, 1994), p.49.

[21] Human Rights: A Source Booft- NCERT, p.129

[22] S.P. Sathe "Human Rights and Natural Law Thought: From the National Movement to The Constitution- An Indian Experience", in Human Rights in the Changing World, supra n.7, p.222. [23] L.D. Naikar, supra n, 19, pp. 332-333.

[24] Ibid, pp.333-334.

[25] Human Rights: A Source Book, NCERT, p.130

[26] Justice Anand, "Justice N. D. Krishna Rao Memorial Lecture," (1997) AIR (Jour) I 1.p.24.

[27] Sujata Manohar, "Human Right Agenda: A perspective for Development," Vol.45, J.I.LJ., (2003), p.169

[28] T. Chandrasekharan Menon, "Protection of Human Rights in India",(2000) C.U.L.R., XXIV, p.5.

Chapter II

Historical Background

Introduction

The belief that individual people in society should have the right to make their own decisions, etc; rather than be controlled by the Government, the idea of individual human rights is commonly associated with the various forms of liberal individualism as they developed in the West particularly in Britain, France and America in the seventeenth and eighteenth centuries,[1] it is often argued by scholars like Robertson that "human right have been cherished through the centuries in many lands ... it is always apparent in the endeavour to protect the individual against the abuse of power by the monarch, the tyrant or the state."[2] It is thus important to look at the historical development of the ideas of human rights for "the attitudes and values of nations are as much conditioned as by history as by modern political theory or ideology"[3]. As some of the major rights issues are inseparable from religious and cultural traditions, this chapter examines the development of the idea of human rights n India from a historical perspective.

In looking at the historical development of the ideas of Human Rights in India, Sections 1 of this chapter focus on the main tendencies of the Hindu, Buddhist and Muslim traditions. Section 2 examines the influence of Western ideas in the context of British rule in India, and the major factors that led to the emergence of notions of social equality and freedom. The next section outlines the phases of the national freedom movement in relation to growth of these ideas. The contradictory ideologies of two leading national figures, Gandhi, the Father of the Nation, and Ambedkar, the architect of the Constitution of India, are examined. The nature and contribution of the first human rights organization in India, founded by Jawaharlal Nehru, a leader of the Congress party (and later, independent India's first Prime Minister), is discussed in detail. The final section briefly looks at some of the organizations in Post-Independent India till the end of the 1960s.

The Religious Tradition

India is a land of many cultures and religious traditions and has significant minority groups, but it would be fair to say that the Indian society is based largely on Hindu patterns of thought and ways of life. Buddhism emerged as an important heterodox tradition in ancient India and made an impact on Hinduism but its current relevance lies in the acceptance of some of its ideals by leaders of modern India. For example, Gandhi, who led the Indian freedom movement, made ahimsa (non-violence) an integral part of his life and work; and Ambedkar, a champion of the rights of the low castes and architect of the Constitution of Indian, converted to Buddhism towards the end of his life. The Islamic tradition came to India about eight hundred years age. Today, Muslims constitute the largest and most significant minority in the country.

The Hindu Tradition

Hinduism, within which there exists a wide diversity of practice, emerged in India around 3,500 years ago.[4] It is characterized by continuity: new ways of thought and behavior do not replace the old ways, which persist in slightly modified forms.[5]

Scholars of Hinduism have noted that to understand the notion of rights in actual social institutions, it is useful to focus on the law books and historical sources rather than metaphysical aspects. Among the law books, *Manu's Manava Dharma Sutra* (The Treatise on Human Duties), compiled between 200 BC and 200 AD, and *Kautilya's Arthashastra* (The Treatise on Political Economy), written in third century BC stands out as being the most popular.[6] These are also relevant in the present context for many of the ideas contained there have survived to the present day.[7]

Two characteristics of Hindu tradition stand out and are relevant here: the caste system and the concept of *dharma*. The caste system came about as the ancient Hindu society and institutions were concerned with "a purposeful ordering of life" or "order in the universe" -- both cosmic and social. While cosmic order was characterized by individualism and tolerance in the pursuit of spiritual advancement, social order was characterized by conformism and social rigidity[8]. This obsession with order led to organized groups, which crystallized into caste system by about 200 BC and 200 AD (or the time when Manu's wrote his Code). The caste system seems wholly incompatible with the ideas of human rights,[9] and is often seen as the chief cause of human rights abuse in India.

The Indian society suffers from the vilest and the most persistent form of discrimination known to mankind.... The caste system, the most ingenious social structure of social deprivation and discrimination, has persisted for the last five thousand years and more. The Vedas hint at it, the Bhagvad Gita talks about it, the Ramayana and Mahabharata present its agonising illustrations, the Manu Smruti (sic) justifies it.[10]

The caste system refers to the fact that the society was divided into four castes or *varnas*: the *brahmins* or priestly caste; the *kshatriyas* or warrior caste; the *vaisyas* or trading caste; and the *shudras* or serving caste. A later development was the category of outcastes or the Untouchables.[11] An important feature of the caste system is that it recognizes fundamental differences between members of different castes. Thus they cannot be governed by a single norm. each caste must do its duty or dharma.[12] Individual salvation or *moksha* lies in the balanced pursuit of *dharma* (laws of the social order), *artha* (economic activity and prosperity), and *kama* (pleasure). Dharma is the most important of these activities: it refers to duties of each individual in accordance with his or her caste and age as articulated in the theory of *varnashrama dharma*.[13]

Religious texts such as the *Bhagvad Gita* tell people to perform their caste duties, and that perfection and *moksha* can only be attained by those who do their duty; indeed, it advises that it is better to do one's won duty poorly than doing another's duty well.[14]

As the rules of dharma were formulated by the brahmins, they expounded the superiority of their caste and formulated a system of social hierarchy where social, economic and legal privileges increased or decreased according to one's caste. Rights were extended primarily to the upper castes; the *shudras* and the untouchables, at the lowest rung of the caste system had absolutely no rights.[15]

One implication was that there was no equality before the law as far as individuals were concerned. Judicial process had to take the caste of the offender into consideration. There was an "extraordinary lack of universality" in Hindu thought. "To be moral, for Manu, is to particularize – to ask who did what, to whom and when." Ramanujan quotes Manu: " A Kshatriya, having defamed a Brahmin, shall be fined one hundred (panas); a Vaisya one hundred and fifty; a Sudra shall suffer corporal punishment.[16]" Thus the codes were not universal: they were different for different castes.

The *varna* dharma theory had an in-built system of caste discrimination. For example, only the three upper castes were entitled to education. In reality only the Brahmins and aristocracy received any formal education as the content of the education dept the non- brahmins away. And the *shudras* had no right to education anyway – they were barred from reading the *Vedas* or any other holy scriptures. Other kinds of rights such as of free thought and expression or to assembly were non-existent.[17]

As dharma gradually became the most important and significant concept in the Hindu tradition, it was elevated to divine status, higher than that of the king or the government. But dharma basically meant maintenance of *varna* dharma: it enjoined the king, state or government to uphold and maintain the caste system, and the people not to deviate from it. If there was deviation from dharma, the state was supposed to enforce it at any cost – including the use of *danda* (a rod or a stick, signifying punishment). In both, Manu and Kautilya's political system, *dandaniti* (the policy of using danda) was primary.[18]

While the scholars referred to above point out that Manu detailed the duties of individuals according to their caste positions, and Kautilya's pragmatic view of the purpose of government and reinforcement of the caste system had little use for individual human rights, some authors have advanced the view that ancient Hindu tradition was sympathetic to the ideas of human rights.

They point out that references occur as early as in the *Rig Veda* to the three rights of *tana* (body), *skridhi* (dwelling place) and *jibasi* (livelihood); that Kautilya's *Arthashastra*, not only affirmed and elaborated the civil and legal rights first formulated by Manu but also added a number of economic rights; that the epic Mahabharata described the rights of the individual in a political state; that the concept of dharma covered the basic principles involved in the theory of rights, duties and freedoms; and further that the policy of dandaniti was to enforce legal rights.[19] These authors however, fail to demonstrate that a system of rights was either a prevalent or accepted norm in the ancient Hindu society. What was perhaps more relevant to human rights was the existence of certain heterodox traditions.

Brahminical orthodoxy inherent in the Hindu tradition was opposed by heterodox traditions. These traditions – which can be divided into three broad trends – drew their following mostly from the lower castes, advocated the equality of all human beings, and encouraged the acceptance of a higher status for women.[20] The first trend was the offer of alternate religions like Buddhism and Jainism in the fifth century BC.[21] The second trend was the offer of non-religious alternatives like that of the *Loakayatas,* who denied any ultimate meaning for human existence; the *Charavakas*, who lived a life n pursuit of pleasure; or the *Ajivakas,* who lived a life of asceticism. The third trend was of reformist groups like the Bhakti movements which propagated devotion and denied the caste system. *Chaitanya* (1485-1533), a Hindu revivalist in Bengal, can be seen as a representative of the *Bhakti* movement.[22] Though he rejected the caste system, his teaching was directed more towards piety and mysticism rather than any conceptions of human rights.[23]

Though these aspects are perhaps relevant to human rights in as much as they present an alternative way of life, it seems clear nonetheless that in the overall framework of Hindu Society, emphasis was on duties, and access to rights was limited to the privileged few of the upper castes.

The Buddhist Tradition

Buddhism originated during a period of political awareness and broke away from the orthodox *brahminical* tradition. It can be seen as political philosophy, opposed to *brahminical* views which were inimical to the "tribal democratic institutions" of the time; and Buddha's "middle path" can be seen essentially as a technique to protect the tribal traditions.[24]

Its earliest supporters came from the republican tribes of north India. Soon it became popular amongst the commercial classes with their preferred emphasis on contractual arrangements. Unlike the Hindu tradition, according to which government was formed due to divine intervention (and caste too had divine origins), according to the Buddhist tradition, government was formed by the people themselves. The republican background – especially the absence of monarchical authoritarianism and the idea of divinity in the political sphere – emphasized rights of the individual in the society.[25]

Buddhist tradition protested against the caste system and embraced the concept that all human beings are equal. It was in favour of equality before the law, and sought to punish offences without reference to caste immunities or privileges. It also showed greater liberality towards women.[26]

The Buddhist *sanghas* community of monks or monasteries was democratic institutions. There was an elaborate system of individual rights and duties within the *sanghas*, such as right to free speech. But there were duties too -- political, social and economic. In fact, it would be correct to say that there was more stress on duties than on rights.[27]

Buddhism's greatest contribution to Indian tradition was the concept of ahimsa (non- violence), which recognized the most fundamental human right: the right to life -- thought it is not of as extreme or absolute form as that of the Jain tradition.[28] As already pointed out, in the twentieth century, Gandhi borrowed this concept and in making it a central part of his philosophy, popularized it. Ambedkar, an arch-rival and critic of Gandhi, embraced this religion as a way out of the Hindu caste system.

The Muslim Tradition

The Muslim tradition came to India following the Arab conquest of Sind in the eighth century. Muslim rule was consolidated over the next two centuries and lasted well into the eighteenth century.[29] Today Muslims constitute the largest religious group after the Hindus.

Its codes and principles are embodied in the *Quran*, the *Sunna,* the *Hadith*, and the *Shariya*. In the ideal-typical sense, its scriptures and law books may be said to contain some tenets supportive of rights of the individuals such as right to life, to dignity, to justice, to freedom, to equality, to privacy and other rights. But these rights are recognized more as legal rights than as "human rights" belonging to all humans as "natural due." According to this tradition, human existence is not sufficient condition for rights, but submission to the Creator, and obedience to the government as well. The idea of rights is applicable to God, rather than to men who have only duties (*farud*).[30]

The tradition of Islam was founded on a non-hierarchical world-view, but by the time it came to India, the Muslim population was stratified into various classes. It soon absorbed some of the structural and cultural characteristics of the Hindu society, including elements of the caste system.[31]

Islamic holism or notions of equality are based on the unity of the Muslim *umma*, the collectivity of the faithful. The tradition speaks of a nation of believers, the *millat*. The elements of equality or egalitarianism are only meaningful within this concept. Thus, a sharp line is drawn between the community of believers and others. "A society in which the latter have preponderance could under some circumstances be declared *Dar-ul-harb*, or a war zone, antithetical to *Dar-ul-Islam*, or the land of Islam. *Jihad* or holy war against such a society is religiously sanctioned."[32] In a society ruled by the Muslim, the *jazia* (a tax for non-believers) may be imposed on them.[33]

Islam is a proselytizing both in the religious and cultural sphere. The *ulemas* have a dominant role to play in the Muslim world as "religion, politics and society are united into one single principle." In India, during the period of Muslim rule, this tradition was perpetuated on orthodox lines through the administrative organization, financial policies and machineries of law and justice. For example Muslims held all the important positions of *qazis* (judges), *muftis* (preachers). *Faujdars* (district administrators), and they held all political power. During a large part of the Muslim rule in India, persons of other religions, especially Hindus, had to pay the *jazia tax*.[34]

Just as the *Bhakti* movement tried to reform Hinduism, the Sufi movement made an attempt to reform Islam -- again with little success. It preached the universal brotherhood of man and denounced the narrow sectarianism of priests. Just as Ashoka (third century BC) is taken as an example of a just and noble king, exemplifying the best of Hindu and Buddhist traditions, so among the Muslim rulers, it is Akbar (1526-1605). He sought to remove the political and religious discrimination from which the Hindus suffered. He also tried to introduce a new religion, *Din-e-ilahi* (combining some of the teachings of both Hinduism and Islam), which was not very popular and was forgotten after his death.[35]

With the coming of the British, the Muslims gradually lost all political power. One of the consequences of this was that there was a decline in whatever liberal tendencies there were. As Yogendra Singh has noted, "The emergence of the orthodox cultural patterns dates back to the eighteenth century, soon after the decline of the Muslim power started."[36] Later, this tendency led to fear and suspicion which was accentuated by Hindu communalism and the exhortations of nationalist leaders like Tilak, Lajpat Rai and Gandhi who used Hindu symbolism. This finally culminated in the creation of Pakistan.[37] From a human rights point of view, it is important to note that the mistrust and insularity between Hinduism and Muslim tradition still continues and is a source of many human tragedies, including communal riots which have become a common feature of Indian society.

Western Tradition

India's interaction with Western ideas first began through contact with Europe in the late fifteenth century, but as the British consolidated their power in the early eighteenth century and established British rule in India for about two hundered years, the Western impact (at least up to national independence in 1947) can be said to be primarily British.[38] The spread of liberal Western ideas was mainly through modern education. These ideas were further embedded through civil and judicial administration.

There was change in the organizational structure of education. Unlike in the Hindu tradition, where the *guru* (teachers) was a Brahmin, modern education was impacted by teachers appointed on the basis of educational record. The nature and literary content of Western education was both modernizing and liberal. Drawn from the literature of the European Renaissance, Reformation and Enlightenment, it enabled Indians to learn of struggles for rights in other parts of the world.

John Stuart Mill's essay "On Liberty" soon after its publication became a text in Indian colleges. Indians came to know about Magna Carta, and the struggle for liberty and equality in Europe and America.[39]

Western influence was reinforced by the indigenous literary tradition, first in Bengal and later, in other parts of the country. This created a medium for the transmission of Western values to the Indian people.[40]

The integration of the Western values and ideologies among the members of the new educated class also contributed to the rise of social and cultural reformation movements in the eighteenth and nineteenth centuries. These were reform movements within Hinduism largely due to the encounter with Western individualistic values. Vivekananda (1863-1902), founder of Ramakrishna Movement without denouncing Manu advocated equality on the basis of *Vedanta,* arguing that the essence of all humans is divine. Raja Rammohan Roy (1772-1833), founder of Brahama Samaj Movement, denounced the caste system, and advocated equality of all individuals basing his arguments on the revealed texts of Hinduism, the *Vedas* and *Upanishads*, as opposed to the Code of Manu which was based on tradition. These movements advocated the eradication of certain Hindu social customs such as *sati* (widow immolation), female infanticide and child marriage. Even though these movements were localized, their importance in the context of rights trends lies in the fact they made an impact on British policy makers.[41]

The British also sought to extend their version of social rights in India by introducing legal measures, particularly before the British government took over the interests of the British East India Company in 1858. Many of these measures had the support of the educated elite in India. Various laws were passed: infanticide was banned (1774); claims on legal rights on slaves (1843) were abolished; *sati* (widow immolation) was abolished on the initiative of Ram Mohan Roy in 1829 in Bengal, and later in other parts of the country; Caste Disabilities Removal Act of 1850 prevented religious conversions resulting in the forfeiture of inheritance; and Widow Remarriage Act of 1856 was passed. Many of these legal measures -- based on the principles of humanism, universalism and individualism -- introduced by the British, were contradictory to the traditional Hindu practices. Recognition of the individual rather than groups as the primary unit at least in all civil and legal matters and the establishment of the principle of individual equality led to the creation of a consciousness of positive rights. Another significance of the growth of the "rule of law" was "that even the governmental executive decisions were now contestable in civil courts, thus providing a foundation for the rule of law and the right of liberty and justice."[42]

The spread of modern education, growth of a universalistic legal system, and influence of Western ideas -- particularly the writings of liberal thinkers like Mill, Hume, Paine and Bentham, "enthused them with a feeling of nationhood and quest for freedom and liberty."[43] In a nation that was under colonial rule, this led to the mobilization of people's aspirations for freedom and found expression in political demands of equality.

National Freedom Movement

The demand for equality and freedom or the national freedom movement can be said to have broadly three phases from a rights point of view. The *first phase* was directed towards gaining some kind of equality with the British. This was the central theme of the demands articulated by most of the organized interest groups throughout the nineteenth century. The *zamindars* or landlords were by and large supportive of the British rule, and formed associations like the Zamindars Association (1837) to protect their interests. The peasants and the economically weaker sections initiated some localized movements but with little success. It was, however, the new urban middle class formed with the introduction of Western education that raised its voice for some kind of racial equality, especially in relation to opportunities in employment. This phase culminated in the formation of the Indian National Congress (INC) in 1885 and continued till the beginning of the rise of the extremist wing in the Congress. The INC during this period (the early phase or moderate phase), demanded representative political institutions, the repeal of such laws as the Arms Act of 1878, which prohibited any Indian from carrying arms, and sedition laws, especially the Seditious Meeting Act of 1911. It must, however, be said that the moderates who dominated the INC in its early phase, supported much of the government legislation as "temporary measures" in the interest of "law and order." Additionally, the INC did not have any coherent policy on rights -- either in relation to peasants or factory and mine workers.[44]

The *second phase* can be said to begin with Gandhi's Rowlatt Satyagraha of 1919 -- which added a new dimension to the struggle for equality and freedom by providing a framework for "direction action" against the state. The Anarchical and Revolutionary Crimes Bill was enacted on 18 March 1919, and came be known popularly as the Rowlatt Act. As this was meant to tackle the growing revolutionary activities, it provided for special courts with no provisions of appeal, trial in camera, extraordinary powers of search, etc. Gandhi started a *satyagraha* (satya - truth; agraha = to ask politely) to campaign against this Act on 6 April but called it off on 18 April following loss of lives and destruction of public property. Sitharamam sees this as "the first popular movement for a civil rights cause" for up till this time Congress protest had been merely in the form of passing resolution, issuing appeals and submitting petitions to the government.[45]

Earlier, in a special session of the INC held in Bombay in 1918 to discuss the Bill, a Declaration of Rights had been adopted for the first time, setting out a comprehensive list of civil liberties, such as freedom of speech, expression and association, equality before the law, trial by jury, etc. The INC demanded its incorporation in a new constitution of India.[46] Events in 1919 led S. Satyamurty, a Congress leader from Madras to write a book, '*The Rights of Citizens.*' One of the themes was the demand for *swaraj* (self-rule) within the British dominion as a prerequisite for the protection of citizen's rights. Dutta has observed,

The book makes it clear that the contemporary discussions on civil liberty did not originate, as many scholars would like us to believe, in an abstract intellectual exercise with the work of Western liberal philosophers. The objective situation created by the onslaught on peoples' right during the First World War, and more profoundly, the threat of the draconian Rowlatt Act, called for the new awareness.[47]

The *third phase* can be seen to begin with the rise of Jawaharlal Nehru to the leadership of the INC in the early 1930s, and his definition of civil liberties as "the right to oppose the government." In 1927, the INC in its Madras session had asked its working committee to draft a constitution based on a Declaration of Rights. The Committee headed by Motilal Nehru -- the father of Jawaharlal Nehru -- prepared a draft (Nehru Report of 1928) incorporating nineteen "fundamental rights," including the right to life and liberty, freedom of speech and expression, and right to organize and assemble. The 1933 Karachi Resolutions adopted by the Congress emphasized both individual and group rights. It sought to secure for every citizen a comprehensive set of fundamental rights.[48] These were later incorporated in the constitution of free India. This phase can be said to culminate in the eventual independence of India in 1947.

Role of Gandhi

The role of Gandhi in the national freedom movement can hardly be overemphasized, but what was his ideology as far as human rights are concerned? As the leader of the national freedom movement, Gandhi's objective was to attain independence -- but his other objective was to save Indian society, and more specifically, Hinduism. He insisted that India should show her capacity to reform herself even while asking for freedom. His method of integrating nationalist aspirations within the framework of social reform, explains his extraordinary tactics -- for example, his manner of suddenly calling off a movement when the nature of the movement turned violent.[49]

An important aspect of Gandhi's reform was that it had to take place absolutely within Hinduism. This was illustrated in Poona in 1931 when he fasted to exact from Ambedkar his renunciation of a separate electorate for the Untouchables.[50] His thrust was that of a social reformer campaigning amongst the higher castes of the Hindu community, propagating social acceptance of the Untouchables by the community. In this process, he renamed the Untouchables "Harijans" (sons of God). Hindu temples had been closed for entry to the Untouchables. Through various campaigns, Gandhi sought to bring about temple entry, and their acceptance in hotels and restaurants, etc.[51]

Gandhi's programme of social reform was based on duties rather than rights. He said very clearly that he did not care for rights, but for duties. If all simply insist on rights and no duties, there will be utter confusion and chaos. If instead of insisting on rights everyone does his duty, there will immediately be the rule of order established among mankind.[52] Not only did he value duties more than rights, but went further to say that the assertions of rights might even be harmful:

While it is true that . . . hereditary inequalities must go as being injurious to the well-being of society, the unabashed assertion of rights of the hitherto down-trodden millions is equally injurious, if not more so to the same well-being. The latter behavior is probably calculated to injure the millions rather than the few claimants of divine or other rights. They could but die a brave or cowardly death but those few dead would not bring in the orderly life of blissful contentment.[53]

He argued that if there were any rights at all, it could only be the result of well-performed duties:

It is therefore necessary to understand the correlation between rights and duties. I venture to suggest that rights that do not flow directly from duty well-performed are not worth having. They will be usurpations sooner discarded the better.[54]

But what happens in case someone does not perform his duty in relation to someone else? Gandhi takes the example of the princes and the *ryot* (peasant). He says that if the princes, whose duty is to act as servants of the people, fail to perform their duty, "the *ryots* not only owe no return duty, but the duty devolves on them of resisting the princely usurpation. It may be otherwise said that *ryots* earn the right of resisting the usurpation or misrule." This resistance must however be peaceful, in keeping with the doctrine of *ahimsa* (non-violence): "The resistance will become a crime against man in terms of duty if it takes the form of murder, rapine and plunder."[55]

When H. G. Wells[56] sought Gandhi's opinion on the "Rights of Man" drawn up by him, Gandhi argued for a "Charter of Duties" instead. The text of the cable that Gandhi sent to Wells sets out his views regarding rights and duties in no uncertain terms.[57]

Received Your Cable. Have Carefully Read Your Five Articles. You Will Permit Me To Say That Yur Are In The Wrong Track. I Feel Sure That I Can Draw Up A Better Charter of Rights Than You Have Drawn Up. But of What Good Will It Be? Who Will Become Its Guardian? If You Mean Propaganda Or Popular Education You Have Begun at the Wrong End. I Suggest The Right Way. Begin With A Charter of Duties of Man (Botrh M And D Capitals) And I Promise The Rights Will Follow As Spring Follws Winter. I Write From Experience. As A Young Man I Began Life By Seeking To Assert My Rights And I Soon Discovered I Had None Not Even Over My Wife. So I Began By Discovering And Performing My Duty By My Wife My Children Friends Companions and Society And I Find Today That I Have Greater Rights Perhaps Than Any Living Man I Know. If This Is Too Tall A Claim Then I Say I Do Not Know Anyone Who Possesses Grater Rights Than I.

Gandhi takes the attitude of a social reformer calling upon the higher castes to accept the Untouchables. He does not say that the Untouchables have rights, but says that upper castes have a duty towards them. When he advocates resistance, it must be done in the manner of *satyagraha* -- that is, not by asking for rights, but by showing the other person what his duty is. This is obvious that Gandhian notions are not sympathetic to human rights unless they are products of duties well performed. Yet the relevance of Gandhi today lies in the fact that many rights activists identify themselves as "Gandhians" or followers of Gandhi. By this, they primarily mean that they follow his strategy of non-violent protest. The views of Gandhi can be contrasted with those of Ambedkar (1892-1956). Though both championed the cause of the Untouchables, their approaches differed widely.

Gandhi's work for the Untouchables was mainly done through the Harijan Sevak Sangh, of which Ambedkar was one of the early members, but later resigned and became one of the foremost critics of both the Sangha and Gandhi.[58]

What is the object of this Harijan Sevak Sangha? Is it to prepare the Untouchables to win their freedom from their Hindu masters, to make them their social and political equals? Mr. Gandhi had never had any such object before him and he never wants to do this. This is the task of a democrat and a revolutionary. Mr. Gandhi is neither. He is a Tory by birth as well as by faith. The work of the Harijan

Sevak Sangha is not to raise the Untouchables. His main object, as every self-respecting Untouchable knows, is to make India safe for Hindus and Hinduism. He is certainly not fighting the battle of the Untouchables. On the contrary by distributing through the Harijan Sevak Sangh petty gifts to petty Untouchables he is buying, benumbing and drawing the claws of the opposition of the Untouchable which he knows is the only force which will disrupt the caste system and will establish real democracy in India. Mr. Gandhi wants Hinduism and the Hindu caste system to remain intact. Mr. Gandhi wants Hinduism and the Hindu caste system to remain intact. Mr. Gandhi also wants the Untouchables to remain as Hindus. But as what? Not as partners but as poor relations of the Hindus. Mr. Gandhi is kind to the Untouchables. But for what? Only because he wants to kill, by kindness, them and their movement for separation and independence from Hindus. The Harijan Sevak Sangh is one of the many techniques which has enabled Mr. Gandhi to be a successful humbug.[59]

These are indeed strong words. But it must be remembered that Ambedkar never forgave Gandhi for his "fast unto death" rather than consenting to the demands of the Untouchables for a separate electorate.[60]

The Untouchables were designated as Scheduled Castes under the Government of India Act of 1935 -- and this is a term still in use. Gandhi had started and popularized the term Harijan for the Untouchables (though many saw it as being patronizing). Ambedkar, however, continued to use the term Untouchables.[61] The term now being increasingly used for them is "dalit" denoting "the oppressed."[62]

Ambedkar characterized the national movement led by Gandhi as the "struggle for power distinguished from freedom" and accused all political parties of showing no concern for the cause of the Untouchables. He argued that the freedom movement was merely a movement by the Hindu to restore traditional Hindu India, and saw the Indian Congress primarily as a Hindu body." A body of middle class Hindu supported by the Hindu capitalists whose object is not to make India free but to be independent of British control and to occupy places of power now occupied by the British." He further said that if freedom were achieved, it would bring no benefit to the Untouchables: "If the kind of Freedom which the Congress wants was achieved there is no doubt that the Hindus would do to the Untouchables exactly what they have been doing in the past.[63]

He firmly believed that the caste Hindus would not accede any rights to the Untouchables due to the very nature of Hinduism itself: "The Hindus have animate and inveterate conservatism and they have a religion which is incompatible with liberty, equality and fraternity, i.e. with democracy."[64] It might be said that he simply did not trust the Hindus.

Why should the Untouchables entrust their fate to such people? How the Untouchables could be legitimately asked to leave their interests into the hands of a people ... who in all certainty deny justice to them and discriminate against them and who by reason of the sanction of their religion have not been and will not be ashamed to practice against the Untouchables any kind of inhumanity. The only safety against such people is to have the political rights which the Untouchables claim as safeguards against the tyranny of the Hindu Majority defined in the Constitution.[65]

His position thus led him to assert that the Hindus and Untouchables were "not merely different but antagonistic," and demand that the Untouchables ought to be treated as distinct from the Hindus. He advocated a separatist policy, including radical changes in the village system that is, forming separate Schedule Caste villages, with land and money for settlement to be provided by the government. He called this the "New Life Movement," whose object was to "free the Untouchables from the thralldom of the Hindus."[66]

Thus, he advocated reservations in government and legislatures, in public services, judiciary, revenue and police services for Untouchables on the basis of "minimum qualification" -- not on the bases of "highest qualification" -- for he argued that "self government is better than good government" and that "good government based on highest qualification will be a communal government."[67]

While dismissing the idea of a purely territorial constituency, which would "only enable the Hindus to collect and concentrate all political power in their hands," and mixed electorates, where the representative would at best only be a "nominal representative" not a "real representative" of the Untouchables, Ambedkar argued that there should be separate electorates, that is, an electorate composed exclusively of Untouchable voters who would elect an Untouchable as their representative to the legislature. His argument was that the caste basis of Hindu society required this kind of political structure. He believed that only constitutional provisions could guarantee rights to the Untouchables. To his critics, he could point out that these measures were necessary due to the caste basis of the Hindu society.[68]

Zelliot has aptly summarized the relative positions of Gandhi and Ambedkar. Gandhi sought to change the heart of the caste Hindu by moral pressure within the framework of Hindu tradition. Ambedkar continued to work in the fields of education and politics in an attempt to gain legal rights for the Untouchables in the secular world.[69]

Ambedkar's methods and solutions for the advancement of Untouchables, through legal and constitutional measures seems more in tune with the realities of Indian social order than Gandhi's attempt "to change the hearts of caste Hindus." It is not surprising, therefore, that the guiding ideology of the Untouchables, scheduled castes and other backward castes in modern India is that of Ambedkar rather than that of Gandhi.

Nehru and Indian Civil Liberties Union

Indian Civil Liberties Union (ICLU), the first civil liberties organization in India, emerged in the background of unprecedented repression on the Indian National Congress and was formally inaugurated on 24 August 1936.

Laws enacted by the British primarily to curb the "revolutionary and terrorist struggles" began to be used to suppress the Congress-led civil disobedience movement which had begun in May 1930 to achieve the goal of complete independence. But even after the movement was called off in April 1934, and the Congress party decided to take part in the elections to the legislatures, there seemed to be little change in government attitude. The general secretary of the Congress party in his annual report complained that the government "preferred to coerce the people into submission by further curtailing their civil liberties rather than make an honorable peace with them."[70]

By mid-1935, about 55,000 Congress activists were still in prison. In his presidential address to the Congress Socialist Party in Calcutta (1935), Jayaprakash Narayan (popularly known as JP) noted the government design to make any "national and mass activities impossible" through various "acts of high handedness and unlawful victimization." He then went on to suggest a possible solution: the formation of an organization to highlight such instances:

Most of these acts would not be committed if the public were a little vigilant and if there were some organization, the task of which was to bring such acts to light and put up a flight against them through the law courts, the legislature, the press and the platform (which should be composed) not of political workers but of leading jurists of the country, eminent publicists, and journalists, women workers, social workers…"[71]

This was a time when various organizations were being formed for protecting the interests of particular sections of the society -- for example, the All India Kisan Sabha (All India Peasants Conference), All India Students federation and the Progressive Writers' Association.[72] This seemed like an opportune moment to form a civil liberties organization. But it was not JP who founded the first such organization in India. It was Jawaharlal Nehru.

Nehru visualized a crucial role for a civil liberties organization in India. He had earlier met leaders of the American Civil Liberties Union (ACLU) in the US and the National Council for Civil Liberties (NCCL) in Britain[73], observed their work and was impressed with what he saw.

In America, England and France powerful civil liberties unions, of a purely non-party character, have been established to resist all such encroachments and their activities have borne substantial fruit. In India the necessity for such a joint effort embracing all groups and individuals, who believe in civil liberties, is obviously even more necessary than elsewhere.[74]

Additionally, during his European tour in 1935, he found "amazing ignorance" among people and members of parliament in England about the condition of political prisoners and civil liberties in India and was eager to rectify this. But, perhaps most importantly, government repression was at its worst at this time in history, as noted by Nehru:

This suppression has been progressively getting more widespread and intensive and has now become the normal feature of the administration at no time since the revolt of 1857 have civil liberties in India been suppressed to the extent they are today.[75]

It is not surprising therefore that on his return from Europe in 1936, he seized this opportunity and proposed the formation of ICLU, which would "collect data give publicity to it." He proposed that it would consist of individuals from all political parties and professions, and would be open to all who believed in the values of civil liberties, but it was not meant to be a mass organization. Nehru was specific: "The Union is not meant to be a mass organization, though there is no restriction on anyone becoming a member."[76] He accordingly sent letters to 150 prominent individuals.[77]

Only a few individuals really responded to Nehru's letter with enthusiasm[78]. There were many who refused to join the organization. The members of the Congress Working Committee felt that "there is no meaning if both the organizations have the same members." They wanted non-Congressmen to enroll. But members of other political parties feared that the new organization would merely be a "second string to the Congress bow" and opposed it on the grounds that the Congress itself was responsible for the civil liberties situation and that it could be improved with the change in Congress strategy[79]. Even Gandhi did not join ICLU on the pretext that it was a "political organization." He wrote to Nehru, If you will not misunderstand me, I would like you to keep me free of the (work of the) Union. I do not like for the time being to join any political institution. . . .[80]

Nehru, however, went ahead with the formation of ICLU -- and managed to attract some widely respected individuals to the organization – including Rabindranath Tagore (a poet and Nobel laureate), and Sarojini Naidu (a poetess who later also held many important public offices including that of governorship). They were appointed honorary president and working president respectively, and headed a national council of "prominent persons," the supreme body of ICLU. Later, a twenty-one member executive committee was formed – for day to day functioning of the organization – which had its own president, chairperson, and general secretary.[81]

On the very day that ICLU was inaugurated (24 August 1936) as a national body, a branch (the Bombay Civil Liberties Union) was also established. Later other branches in madras and Calcutta were established. ICLU organized public meetings and issued appeals to mobilize public opinion. According to Dutta, ICLU "investigated cases of political imprisonment, police brutalities, government bans and restrictions, etc." – but as an organization, it did not make any significant impact[82]. Tarkunde, who was then a member of the Bombay branch holds the same opinion.

The CLU did not really become a force in the country at any stage. It has historical importance in that it was thought of at that time. But in the day to day affairs of the country, it hardly mattered . . . Domestically; a separate presence of the CLU was not felt as it took up the same issues as the nationalist movement.[83] While the country was under British rule, it did not matter if ICLU and the Congress party were raising similar issues. Nehru envisaged the scope of civil liberties organizations as primarily preventing the government "from becoming too autocratic." He said: It is obvious that questions of civil liberties only arise when there is a conflict between the public or certain sections of it, and the executive government ... A democracy can only function properly if public opinion constantly checks government and prevents it from becoming too autocratic .. . This does not and must not mean approval of the methods of any political party, nor does it mean that the Congress or any group should be allowed by government to carry on revolutionary activities or civil disobedience without check or hindrance. But there are certain fundamental principles governing civil liberties which apply whatever the activities of political parties might be.[84]

The scope is narrow in the sense that it focuses purely on the functioning of the government. The idea of civil liberties is advanced as the right to oppose the government. Dutta makes the same point when he says that the conception "was that the civil liberties movement was in fact an anti-state movement."[85] Though the role of civil liberties is seen as political, it is interesting to note that Nehru makes an implicit distinction between civil liberties and political groups. He seems to be saying that while political parties may and do resort to questionable methods, or engage in "revolutionary activities," a civil liberties group must be above this. This particular understanding of civil liberties later led to conflict between ICLU and the Congress party.

Even before the formation of the ICLU, the liberals and some others had refrained from joining ICLU as they feared that it would be a "second string to the Congress bow." To this Nehru has said "that the Congress bow was a hefty bow and had many strings to it and many more would be added to it." He never doubted the role of the Congress in civil liberties. He emphasized: "The Congress is the largest organization in the country. The Congress has been fighting for the civil liberties of the Indians."[86]

Nehru obviously did not see any contradiction in the roles of the Congress and civil liberties activities. He was in fact proud of the achievements of the Congress ministries when they were eventually formed in 1937, after elections were held in the Provinces (or states):

The acceptance of ministerial office by the congressmen in six provinces, and later in one more province, brought about a rapid and marked change in all these provinces. The change was especially noticeable in regard to civil liberties. The bans imposed by the Governments on hundreds of organizations were removed, a large number of political prisoners were released, securities taken from newspaper were returned, the continuous shadowing of and spying on people engaged in public work became less obvious. Public meetings and demonstrations were not interfered with. It seemed as if a heavy burden had been taken away and people in towns and villages alike breathed more freely.[87]

In spite of Nehru's claims, problems still remained, such as banning of political parties and censorship. For this he blamed the governor-general, the governors, central government legislations and the permanent services.[88]

However, within a year (1938), there was conflict between the Congress and ICLU, especially in Bombay. ICLU passed a resolution criticizing the Bombay government for continuing surveillance activities and the implication of labour leaders in fresh cases and their arrest. Replying to the criticism, K. M. Munshi, the then Home Minister of Bombay said: "You cannot have civil liberty in an atmosphere surcharged with violence and excitement such as a breach of the peace." The all India Congress Committee (AICC) passed a resolution does not cover acts of or incitement to violence or promulgation of palpable falsehoods." Nehru wrote to K. B. Menon, the secretary general of ICLU not to be "anti-Congress," and disassociate himself from the public demonstrations organized by the ICLU.[89]

Thus the changing tone and emphasis of the Congress party – and even Nehru – on civil liberties is evident. Before the elections leading to the formation of ministries, the tone was radical; in the first year of the functioning of ICLU and Congress ministries, Nehru was proud of the civil liberties record; but as soon as criticism began to be directed at Congress-led provincial governments, the tone was evidently lukewarm, if not almost hostile.

This made ICLU's task even more difficult. Sarojini Naidu resigned in 1938, and its work almost came to a halt. The demands of the national movement stunted the growth of any movement for civil liberties. As Tarkunde notes,

In the nationalist movement, persons who were committed to civil liberties in a broad sense were very few . . . There was little broad-minded agreement on the necessity of individual freedom ... from the beginning my feeling has been that the nationalist assertion had submerged the movement for social and individual freedoms.[90]

Finally, after independence, Nehru, contradicting his earlier perspective, said that the idea of an independent organization for disseminating information relating to violations of civil liberties was redundant. He withdrew from ICLU and urged that it be dissolved. It had anyway long been defunct.[91]

Human Rights after Independence

After the advent of independence, the Congress party, which had earlier been in the forefront of the national movement and raised some issues concerning civil liberties, became the "ruling party." Nehru became the first prime minister of the country. The focus shifted to "development." It is now generally accepted that the development policies pursued by successive governments after independence did not lead to any significant rise in living standards, or as harsher critics would say, it led to the "continuing impoverishment and marginalization of millions of people ... distributive justice, popular participation, 'wars' on poverty – all still remain, by and large, pious intentions."[92]

Additionally, immediately after the independence, the government was faced with the primary task of holding the country together, which "often involved armed repression of rebellious groups and forced annexation of political units that were unwilling to join the new republic."[93] The government had to use the same institutions that the Congress had been so critical of in the past: the civil service, army and the police – armed with similar "repressive powers."

In these circumstances, the Communist party (which had been formed in 1925), emerged as a major critic of government policies.[94] It also became vigilant about issues dealing with people's rights. There were instances of public firing on peasants, political activists, students and trade union leaders in the first two years of independence, and in the following two decades.[95] A communist party worker wrote about police repression:

In 1947, the Congress Government used bullets to silence the widespread mass movements that had begun in west Bengal against this black Act 9Internal Security Act). The young social worker Sisir Mandal was the first to only his life before their bullets. After that, regime of naked terror was brought about in west Bengal from 1948 by the indiscriminate application of this hated Act.[96] A lawyer, A. K. Pillai, bemoaned the absence of any civil liberties in the initial year's after independence. The all-too limited liberties which the subject had under the British regime have themselves become the first casualty in the wake of the advent of national independence.[97]

As far as organized response to human rights violations in concerned, the issue was taken up by a few intellectuals, political leaders, and lawyers in different parts of the country. There were efforts to form organizations of the lines of ICLU.

Organizations were formed in Madras, Calcutta, Bombay and Assam. The Madras Civil Liberties Union (MCLU) was revived in the latter part of 1947. It supported the local peasant movement against Madras government's reluctance to adopt land reform policies. It was also concerned with repression on regional political parties and other national parties like the Rastrya Swayamsevak Sangh (RSS) and the Communist Party of India (CPI) after they were banned in 1948. This organization was led by S. Krishanmoorthy, mostly as a one-man organization (with additional help from a few lawyers) until his death in 1976.[98]

The Bombay Civil Liberties Union (BCLU) was revived by S. G. Waze and v. M. Tarkunde, who were earlier, associated with the ICLU. This organization, like the one in

Madras, took up detention cases of RSS and CPI party workers,[99] but could not sustain its activities for more than a few years.

The Calcutta Civil Liberties Union (CCLU) was established in 1948 by some well-known intellectuals and left-wing political activists to highlight mass detention and torture of Communist activists, especially as they were leading a peasant movement called the Tebhaga movement.[100] The organization issued a bitter note on 22 October 1949.

For the last twenty-one months, the Roy Ministry ... have been submerging in bloodbath the worker's demands for bread and the peasants' demand for land ... The barbaric torture of the political prisoners by the fascist government has surpassed that of the days of Anderson (British officer who ordered the police to fire and kill participants at a public meeting in Jallianwalls Bagh, Amritsar, in 1919.)[101] Its secretary and two joint secretaries were arrested, and the president was prevented from making public speeches. However, after the general elections were announced in 1952 and political prisoners released, the organization lost the support of political parties and became inactive.[102]

These regional organizations made an attempt to form a national level organization. The Bombay Civil Liberties Union organized an All India Civil Liberties Conference in Bombay on 1-2 January 1949; later the same year, another Conference was organized in Madras on 16-17 July 1949 by the Madras Civil Liberties Union. This led to the establishment of an All India Civil Liberties Association (AICLA), which remained largely inactive. An effort was made to rejuvenate it in an All India Civil Liberties Conference held in Calcutta in 1954, but it was a fruitless exercise.[103]

After the enactment of preventive detention laws in 1951, some lawyers got together and organized a Convention on Civil Liberties in Guwahati in June-July 1951. The All Assam Civil Liberties Union (AACLU) was born at this Convention, and was affiliated to the All India Civil Liberties Association. But it had a very short life-span: it became defunct as soon as political prisoners were released in 1952 after the general elections.[104] In the wake of Sino-Indian war in 1962, there was large scale arrest of CPI activists. In 1964, members of the newly formed Communist Party of India (Marxist) were arrested indiscriminately. This led to the establishment of another national level organization, the All India Civil Rights Organization (AICRO), following a Convention held in Bombay on 13 June 1965. It became inactive when Communist leaders were released and elections declared in 1967.[105]

Conclusion

The ancient Indian traditions were not sympathetic to notions of individual freedom and human rights as understood today. They did not carry the conception of "equality" or the conception that all humans are born free and equal in dignity. Rights, if any, were extended only to elite groups. The emphasis was on duty. The heterodox traditions struggled against caste discrimination, and preached religious tolerance, but did not advocate any notion of human rights. Similarly, the Muslim tradition and social reality can hardly be said to present a notion of the rights of the individual. Human rights with their modern attributes are a development more or less parallel with the growth of constitutional government and parliamentary institutions from the time of the British rule in India. The demand for civil and political rights was first raised by the Western educated elite. It grew as a response to changes in the political system, and was incorporated in the nationalist ideology, championed by the Congress party. The efforts of Nehru led to the formation of the first human rights organization in 1936. This became a model for various organizations that were formed n the post-independence period, when Congress-led governments became their primary target. These organizations were highly informal and limited in their scope. Their central (and perhaps, only) concern was to focus on repressive laws, and arrest of political activists. Each of these organizations (with the exception of the Madras Civil Liberties Union) became defunct once political prisoners were released or elections announced. The faith in parliamentary democracy was still firm. This faith began to be shaken towards the end of the 1960s, and gave rise to the current human rights movement.

Refrences

[1] Richard E. Flathman, *The Practice of Rights*, Cambridge: Cambridge University Press, 1976, pp.2-3.

[2] A. H. Robertson, *Human Rights in the World: An Introduction to the International Protection of Human Rights*, 2nd edition, Manchester: Manchester University Press, 1982, p. 9.

[3] Ralph Buultjens, "Human Rights in India Political Culture," in *The Moral Imperative of Human Rights: A World Survey*, edited by Kenneth W. Thompson, Washington D.C.: University Press of America, 1980, p. 109.

[4] Buultjens, op. cit., pp. 110-111.

[5] This view is taken by a number of Scholars. For example, see A. K. Ramanujan, "*Is There an Indian Way of Thinking?*" in India Through Hindu Categories, edited by McKim Marriott, New Delhi: Sage Publications, 1990, pp. 41-57; A. B. Shah, Religion and Society in India, Bombay and New Delhi: Somaiya Publicaitons, 1981, pp. 23-24; and K. R. Jadhav, "Foreword" in The State and Repressive Culture: The Andhra Experience by Kancha Ilaiah. Hyderabad: Swecha Prachuranalu, 1989, pp. iv-v.

[6] There is some doubt as to whether Manu was an actual person. However, this need not concern us here. What is relevant is that the *Manava Dharma Sutra* is commonly attributed to him, and that this document is accepted to reflect the era it was compiled in, which is about 200 BC to 200 AD.

[7] Romila Thapar, *"The Hindu and Buddhist Traditions,"* in International Social Science Journal, vol. 18, no. 1, 1966, p. 31; Kana Mitra, *"Human Rights in Hinduism,"* in Journal of Ecumenical Studies, vol.19, no. 3, Spring 1982, p. 77; Kancha Ilaiah, *The State and Repressive Culture: The Andhra Experience,* Hyderabad: Swecha Prachuranalu, 1989, p. 130.

[8] Buultjens, op. cit., p. 111; Romila Thapar, op. cit., p. 32.

[9] Buultjens, op. cit., p. 111; Mitra, op. cit., pp. 79-80.

[10] Jadhav, op. cit., p. iv.

[11] In actual practice, these four castes have numerous sub-castes. For more details, see Mitra, op. cit., pp. 79-80. For an analysis of the concept of untouchability, see Simon R. Charsley, *"Untouchable': What is in a name?"* in *Journal of the Royal Anthropological Institute*, incorporating Man, New Series, vol. 2, no. 1, 1996, pp.1-23.

[12] Buultjens, op. cit., p. 112.

[13] This refers to four stages into which a man's life was divided: *bramacharya* or being a student, *grihasthya* or duty as householder, *vanaprastha* or duty to detach from worldly pursuits and retirement from professional and domestic duties and preparation for the next stage, and finally, *sanyasa* or ascetic, wherein all caste barriers are transcended. Mitra, op. cit, p. 80; Romila Thapar, op. cit., p. 35.

[14] Romila Thapar, op. cit., p. 34.

[15] Romila Thapar, op. cit., p. 35; The Sanskrit word *adhikara* (just claim or right) was used by Manu only in reference to the Brahmins. Mitra, op. cit., pp. 78-79.

[16] Ramanujan, op. cit., p. 46.

[17] Romila Thapar, op. cit., p. 36; Kancha Ilaiah, "Buddhism as political Philosophy," Ph.D Thesis, Osamnia University, Hyderabad, 1993, p. 246

[18] Romila Thapar, op. cit., p. 35; Ilaiah, "Buddhism,," op. cit., pp. 152 and 178-80.

[19] P.B. Mukharji, *Civil Liberties: Ramananda Lectures* (1965) of the *Calcutta University,* Bombay: N.M. Tripathi Private Ltd., 1968, pp. 19 – 28;Subhas C. Kashyap, *Human Rights and Parliament*, New Delhi: Metropolitan, 1978, pp. 19 – 20; Nagendra Singh, *Human Rights and the Future of Mankind*, Delhi: Vanity Books, 1981, p. 9; Satish Kumar, "Human Rights and Economic Development," in *Human Rights Quarterly,* vol. 3, no. 3, Summer 1981, pp. 47 – 48.

[20] For reasons why heterodox tradition failed to over through the brahmanical tradition, see Romila Thapar, op. cit., p. 37, note 4.

[21] Another religion that emerged much later was Sikhism in the sixteenth century. The founder was Guru Nanak (1469-1538), and the last guru was Govinda Singh (1675-1708). See Khushwant Singh, *A History of the Sikhs,* 2 vols., Princeton: Princeton: Princeton University Press, 1936-66.

[22] Mitra, op. cit., p. 80.

[23] Buultjens, op. cit., p. 115.

[24] Ilaiah, "Buddhism," op. cit., pp. 136-140 and 147-48.

[25] Romila Thapar, op. cit., p. 33.

[26] Ibid, pp. 36-37; Ilaiah, "Buddhism," op. cit. pp. 210 and 245.

[27] Ilaiah, "Buddhism," pp. 213 and 247-68; see also Kenneth K. Inada, "The Buddhist Perspective on Human Rights," in *Journal of Ecumenical Studies*, vol 19, no. 3, Spring, 1982, pp. 66-76. He has argued that in Buddhism, the question of human rights is secondary to the question of human nature for human rights is merely a legal matter. Buddha's doctrine of *anatman* or non-self refers to going beyond self and therefore individual human rights are meaningless.

[28] Ilaiah, "Buddhism," op. cit., p. 245; Romila Thapar, op. cit., p. 37.

[29] The most significant period of Muslim rule was during what is known as the Mughal dynasty founded By Babur in 1526; the last "Great Mughal" emperor was Aurenzed (1658-1707). The last nominal Mughal emperor was formally deposed in 1958. See Ishwari Prasad, A Short History of Muslim Rule in India; From the Conquest of Islam to the Death of Aurangzeb, third edition, Allahabad: 1933; Percival Spear, A history of India, volume 2, Harmondsworth: Penguin Books, 1985 (first published 1965), pp. 15-80.

[30] For details, see Riffat Hassan, "On Human Rights and the Quranic Perspective," in Journal of Ecumenical Studies, vol. 19, no. 3, Spring 1982, pp. 55-66. See also James P. Piscatori, "Human Rights in Islamic Political Culture," in The Moral imperative of Human Rights: A World Survey, edited by Kenneth

W. Thompson. Washington D.C.: University Press of America, 1980, p. 142-43.

[31] The original tribal egalitarian system was soon transformed into religion-oriented egalitarianism; with foreign conquests (which were provided with moral and religious justifications by the *ulemas* or Muslim priests) this was further transformed into feudal-authoritarian structure. Yogendra Singh, Modernization of Indian Tradition, Jaipur: Rawat Publication, 1986, pp. 64-68 and 74-76.

[32] Ibid., pp. 63-64; see also Prasad, op. cit.

[33] Piscatorial, op. cit, p. 145-46.

[34] Y. Singh, op. cit., pp. 64, 71 and 79-81; Prasad, op. cit., 664-708.

[35] Om Gautam, *"Human Rights in India,"* in *Towards a Human Rights Framework*, edited by Peter Schwab and Admantia Pollis. New York: Praeger Publishers, 1982, pp. 170-71; See also Spear, op. cit., pp. 26-39.

[36] Y. Singh, op. cit., pp. 69-70.

[37] Ibid., p. 71. For an account of relations between the Hindus And Muslims, see Gardner Murphy, " The Insecurity of the Muslims," in *In the Minds of Men; A Study of Human Behavior and Social Tension in India* by Gardner Murphy, new York; Basic Books, 1953, pp. 117-165.

[38] The earlier contacts – first with the Portuguese in the fifteenth and sixteenth centuries, and later with the Dutch and the French in the seventeenth and eighteenth centuries – did not result in any significant influence. See L. S. S. O'malley, *"The Impact of European Civilization,"* in *Modern India and the West: A Study of the Interaction of their Civilizations*, edited by L. S. S. O'Malley, London: Oxford University Press, 1941, pp. 44-50; K. P. Karunakaran, *Religion and Political Awakening in India,* Meerut: Meenakshi Press, 1969, pp. 19-34.

[39] Shanti S. Tangri, "Intellectuals and Society in Nineteenth-Century India," in *Comparative Studies in Society and History,* vol 3, 1960-61, pp. 272-73. Quoted in Y. Singh, op. cit., p. 103.

[40] Y. Singh, op. cit., p. 91; D. P. Singhal, *A History of the Indian People,* London: Methuen, 1983, pp. 307- 326; J. C. Ghosh, et al., *"Literrature and Drama,"* in *Modern India and the West: A Study of the Interaction of their Civilizations*, edited by L. S. S. O'Malley, London: Oxford University Press, 1941, pp. 487-528.

[41] Mitra, op. cit., p. 81; Gautam, op. cit., pp. 170-171; Y. Singh, op. cit., pp. 90-92. See also J. T. F. Jordens, :"Hindu Religious and Social Reform in British India," in *A Cultural history of India,* edited by A. L. Basham, Oxford: Clarendon Press, 1975, pp. 365-382.

[42] Y. Singh, op. cit., pp. 92-101; Buultjens, op. cit., pp. 117-118; Jordens, op. cit.; Singhal, op. cit.; see also Benjamin Lindsay, "Law" in *Modern India and the West: A Study of the Interaction of their Civilizations,* edited by L. S. S. O'Malley, London: Oxford University Press, 1941, pp. 107-137; Srinivas, M. N. *Social Change in India*. Berkley and Los Angles: University of California Press, 1966, 48-50.

[43] Y. Singh, op. cit, p. 97.

[44] A. R. Desai, *Social Background of Indian Nationalism,* 5th edition, Bombay: Popular Prakashan, 1976, chapters 3, 4 and 7; Spear, op. cit., 158-180.

[45] K. Sitharamam, "Civil Rights Movement in India." PhD Thesis. Centre for Social Studies, South Gujarat University, Surat, 1993, pp. 18-19.

[46] Ibid., p. 19.

[47] Nilanjan Dutta, "With Little Victories and Big Defeats," in *Civil Rights: Past and Present,* Calcutta: Sujato Bhadra for APDR, 1986, pp. 41-42.

[48] International League for the Rights of Man (ILRM), "The Violation of Human Rights in India," in *Case Studies on Human Rights and Fundamental Freedoms,* edited by Willem A. Veenhoven, et al., The Hague: Martinus Nijhoff, 1975 vol. 5, p. 509; Subhash C. Kashyap, op. cit., p. 20; Gautam, op. cit., p. 173-174.

[49] An Excellent example is calling off the Civil Disobedience or Non Cooperation movement in February 1922 after a crowd attacked a police station in Chauri Chaura, killing 22 policemen. See Desai, *Social Background,* op. cit., p. 352.

[50] Louis Dumont, "Nationalism and Communalism," in *Religion, Politics and History in India: Collected Papers in Indian Sociology,* Paris: Mouton Publishers, 1970, p. 104.

[51] S. R. Mohan Das, "Discrimination in India," in Case Studies on *Human Rights and Fundamental Freedoms,* edited by Willem A. Veenhoven, et al. The Hague: Martinus Nijhoff, 1975, vol. 2, p. 164.

[52] M. K. Gandhi, "Rights and Duties," in *The Moral and Political Writings of Mahatma Gandhi,* edited by Raghavan Iyer. Oxford: Clarendon Press, 1986, vol. 3, p. 496. (First published in *Harijan*, 6 July 1947).

[53] Ibid.

[54] Ibid.

[55] Ibid., p. 498.

[56] Herbert George Wells (1886-1946), English novelist, and historian; author of the *Time Machine, The War of the Worlds, The Shape of Things to Come, The Outline of History, The Invisible Man,* and various other works.

[57] Gandhi quoted in Iyer, op. cit., vol. pp. 492-493. First published in *The Hindustan Times,* 16 April 1940.

[58] For details, see Eleanor Zelliot, "Gandhi and Ambedkar – A Study in Leadership," in the *Untouchables in Contemporary India* edited by Michael J. Mahar, Tuscon, Arizona: The University of Arizona Press, 1972, pp. 87-88.

[59] B. R. Ambedkar, *Emancipation of the Untouchables,* Bombay: Thacker and Co., Ltd, 1972, pp. 55-56. (First published in 1943).

[60] Ibid., pp. 20-21.

[61] Ibid., p. 15; For a discussion of various terms for the Untouchables, see Harold R. Isaces, "The Ex-Untouchables," in *The Untouchables in Contemporary India,* edited by Michael J. Mahar, Tuscon, Arizona: The University of Arizona Press, 1972, pp. 383-91.

[62] The term "dalit" popularized by the protest movements since the 1970s. It includes all backward sections, and at times, specifically the Untouchables. See Barbara R. Joshi, editor, *Untouchable ! Voices of the Dalit Liberation Movement*, London: Zed Boods and The Minority Rights Group, 1986, pp. 3-4.

[63] Ambedkar, op. cit., pp. 13-14.

[64] Ibid., pp. 52-53.

[65] Ibid., pp. 46-47.

[66] Ibid., pp. 15-18, 32-33, 37 and 40.

[67] Ibid., pp. 16 and 31.

[68] Ibid., pp. 15-16 and 24-30.

[69] Zelliot, op. cit., p.86.

[70] Sitharamam op. cit., p. 22.

[71] Yusuf Meherally, editor, *Towards Struggle: Selected Manifestos, Speeches and Writing of Jayaprakash Narayan,* Bombay: Padma Publications, 1946, p.. 108-9.

[72] Nilanjan Dutta, *"With Little Victories and Big Defeats,"* in APDR. *Civil Rights: Past and Present,* Calcutta: Sujato Bhadra For APDR, 1986, p. 42.

[73] For a historical account of NCCL, see Mark Lilly, *The National Council for Civil Liberties: The First Fifty Years,* London and Basingstoke: Macmillan, 1984.

[74] Jawaharlal Nehru, "Circular Proposing the Setting up of ICLU, 22 April 1936," in APDR, Two Decade of APDR, *Two Decade* of APDR and Human Rights, Calcutta: Sujato Bhadra for APDR, 1991, p. 20.

[75] Nehru, "Circular," op. cit., p. 19.

[76] Jawaharlal Nehru. :"The First Declaration: speech at the Inauguration of ICLU, 24, Aug 1936," in APDR, *Two Decade* of APDR *and Human Rights,* Calcutta; Sujata Bhadra for APDR, 1991, p. 22.

[77] Dutta, "With Little Victories," op. cit., p. 42; Sitharamam, op. cit., pp. 22-23.

[78] Amrit Kaur was one. She was an enthusiastic supporter of this organization, asked question and suggested measures. But it seems that she was not too happy with the organization as it functioned. In one of her letters, she deplores "the fact that a woman has not been appointed a member of the Working Committee"; in another, she wrote: "no apology is necessary regarding the omission of my name form the list of members of the civil liberties organization." See Amrit Kaur, "Letters to Jawarharlal Nehru (from Simla)," four letters: dated 9 May 1936, 28 May 1936, 30 May 1936, and 6 September 1937, New Delhi: Nehru Memorial Museum and Library. Holograph.

[79] Sitharamam, op. cit., p. 24.

[80] M. K. Gandhi, Letter to Jawaharlal Nehru, Dated 15 July 1936, New Delhi: Nehru Memorial Museum and Library. Holograph.

[81] The 21 – member executive committee included Nehru, Abdul Kalam Azad, Sharat Bose, Ramananda Chattopadhya, Bhulabhai Desai, Zakir Hussain, Amrit Kaur, Jayaprakash Narayan, Sardar Pate and Rajendra Prasad, among others. Sitharamam, op. cit., p. 24-25.

[82] A branch in Punjab was also established, but its details are not available. The regional branches and their own executive committees. Though there was some communication between regional organizations and ICLU, it is not clear if they functioned independently or under the direction of ICLU. The relation between the national council and executive committee of ICLU is also not clear due to lack of data. Sitharamam, op. cit., pp. 24-25; Dutta,"With Little Victories," op. cit., p. 43.

[83] Smitu Kothari, "An Interview with V. M. Tarkunde." *In Rethinking Human Rights: Challenges for Theory and Action,* edited by Smitu Kothari and Harsh Sethi. New York: New Horizons Press and Delhi: Lokayan, 1989, p. 136.

[84] Nehru quoted in Sitharamam, op. cit., pp. 25-26.

[85] Dutta, "With Little Victories," op. cit. p. 43.

[86] Nehru, "The First Declaration," op. cit., pp. 21-13.

[87] Jawaharlal Nehru, "Message to Indian Civil Liberties Conference to be held in London on 17 Ocotber 1937," 4 Ocotber 1937. New Delhi: Nehru Memorial Museum and Library, p. 2. Holograph.

[88] Ibid., pp. 3-4.

[89] Sitharamam, op. cit., pp. 28-30; see also Desai, *Social Background*, op. cit., pp. 375-76.

[90] Smitu Kothari. "An Interview with V. m. Tarkunde," op. cit., p. 137.

[91] Ibid.

[92] Smitu Kothari, "The Human Rights Movement in India: Crisis and Challenges," in *Human Rights and Development: International Views*, edited by David P. Forsythe, 1989, p. 94; See also A. R. Desai, "Rural Development and Human Rights in Independent India, In *Economic and Political Weekly,* 1 August 1987,

pp. 1291-96. Desai has argued that the concept of rural development underwent a change n 1950s, to further enrich the better-off at the cost of the rural poor.

[93] Atul kohli, *Democracy and Discontent: India's Growing Crisis of Governability,* Cambridge: Cambridge University Press, 1990.

[94] Sumit Sarkar, *Modern India*, 1885-1947, Basingstoke: The Macmillan Press, 1989, pp. 247-51 and 411-13.

[95] Nilanjan Dutta, *Violation of Democratic Rights in West Bengal since Independence,* edited by A. r. Desai, Bombay: C. G. Shah memorial Trust. 1985, pp 4-9. Reprinted in *Expanding Governmental Lawlessness and organized Struggle*, edited by A. R. Desai. Bombay: Popular press, 1991, pp. 236-256.

[96] Quoted in Nilanjan Dutta, *Violation of Democratic Rights,* op. cit., pp. 4-5.

[97] A. K. Pillai, quoted in Dutta, "With Little Victories," op. cit., p. 45.

[98] P. V. Ramanajunam, "A Brief Outline of the History of the Democratic Movement in Tamil Nadu," in *Civil Rights: Past and Present,* Calcutta: Sujato Bhadra for APDR, 1986, pp. 26-27; also Sitharamam, op. cit., pp. 38-39.

[99] Sitharamam op. cit., pp. 40-41.

[100] See Dutta, Violation of Democratic Rights, op. cit., pp. 236-256; also Sitharamam, op. cit., 39-40.

[101] Quoted in Dutta, *Violation of Democratic Rights,* op. cit., p. 7.

[102] See Dutta, *Violation of Democratic Rights,* op. cit., pp 5-7; also Sitharamam op. cit., pp. 39-40.

[103] Dutta, *Violation of Democratic Rights,* op. cit., pp, 4-9; Dutta, "Little Victories," op. cit., p. 45; Sitharamam, op. cit., pp. 39-41.

[104] D. K. Kakti, "The Civil Liberties Movement in Assam," in *Civil liberties: Past and Present,* Calcutta: Sujato Bhadra for APDR, 1986, pp. 33-34; also Sitharamam, op. cit., p. 41.

[105] Sitharamam, op. cit., pp. 43.

Chapter III

International Standard

Introduction

The transformation of the position of the individuals after the Second World War has been one of the most remarkable developments in contemporary International Law. While a few rules are directly concerned with regulating the position and activities of individuals, a few others, indirectly affect them. For instances, national of the Allied and Associated Powers were empowered to bring cases against Germany before the Mixed Arbitral Tribunal in their own names for compensation in accordance with Article 304(b) of the Treaty of Versailles of 1919. Further, Treaty of 1907 between five Central American States establishing the Central American Court of Justice provided for individuals to bring cases directly before the Court. Human right is one of such rights which have been conferred to individuals by the States in the modern International Law. Human beings are rational beings. They by virtue of their being human possess certain basic and inalienable rights which are commonly known as human rights. Presently, the vast majority of legal scholars and philosophers agree that every human being is entitled to some basic rights. Thus, there is universal acceptance of human rights in principle in domestic and international plane. Human Rights are a generic term and it embraces civil rights, civil liberties and social, economic and cultural rights.

International Law and Human Rights

Human Rights are those rights which belong to an individual as a consequence of being human as a means to human dignity. These are the rights which all men everywhere at all times ought to have, something so which no one may be deprived without a grave affront to justice.[1] They are based on elementary human needs as imperatives. Some of these human needs are elemental for sheer physical survival and health. Human rights being essential for all-round development of the personality of the individuals in the society, be necessarily protected and be made available to all the individuals. The need for the protection has arisen because of inevitable increase in the control over men's action by the government which by no means can be regarded as desirable. The consciousness on the part of the human beings as to their rights has also necessitated the protection by the States. It has been realized that the functions of all the laws whether they are the rules of municipal law or that of international law should be to protect them in the interest of the humanity.

Presently, there is a widespread acceptance of the importance of human rights in the international structure. However, one will not hesitate to admit that there is a confusion prevailing as to its precise nature and scope and the mode of International Law as to the protection of these rights. Civil Rights or liberties are referred to those rights which are related to the protection of the right to life and personal liberty. They are essential for a person so that he may live a dignified life. Such rights include right to life, liberty and security of persons, right to privacy, home and correspondence, right to own property, freedom from torture, inhuman and degrading treatment, freedom of thought, conscience and religion and freedom of movement.

Political Rights may be referred to those rights which allow a person to participate in the Government of a State. Thus, right of vote, right to be elected at genuine periodic elections, right tjo take part in the conduct of public affairs, directly or through chosen representatives are instances of political rights. Economics, social and cultural rights (also called 'freedom to') are related to the guarantee of minimum necessities of the life to human beings. In the absence of these rights the existence of human beings is likely to be endangered. Right to adequate food, clothing, housing and adequate standard of living and freedom from hunger, right to work, right to social security, rights to physical and mental health and right to education are included in this category of rights of rights. These rights are included in the International Covenant on Economic, Social and Cultural Rights.

Promotion and encouragement of respect for and observance of human rights and fundamental freedoms is one of the purposes of the United Nations. The Charter of United Nations mentions the term promotion of human rights seven times, but makes no reference to "protection" of "human rights". The protection of human rights in international level is a difficult problem because of a variety of reasons. Firstly, the International Court of Justice is open to States only. It implies that individuals have no access to the Court. Thus, it has always refused to entertain the petitions and requests which have often seen addressed to it by individuals. Secondly, the jurisdiction of the International Court of Justice depends upon the consent of the States involved, and this has been done by few States to disputes involving human rights. Thirdly, even if the International Court in a few cases is able to render judgments against the State, which violates human rights, there is no international police to enforce the decisions of the court.

The idea for the protection for human rights and fundamental freedoms was conceived in the Atlantic Character (1941) and in the Declaration of the United Nations (1942).When the founders of the United Nations met at San Francisco Conference in 1945 to draft the Charter of the United Nations, Latin American States, in particular, wanted the Conference to discuss an International Bill of Human Rights. After the United Nations Charter came into force, the most important task before the United Nations was the implementation of the principles of the universal respect for and observance of human rights and fundamental freedoms for all without distinction as to race, sex, language or religion as laid down under Article 55 of the U.N. Charter.

The Universal Declaration of Human Rights was adopted in 1948 and two International Covenants were adopted in 1966 codifying the two sets of rights outlined in the Universal Declaration. International Covenant on Civil and Political Rights and the International Covenant on Economic, Social and Cultural Rights entered into force in 1976.

The Generally Assembly also adopted two Optional Protocols to the International Covenant on Civil and Political Rights: Optional Protocol to the International Covenant on Civil and Political Rights in 1966 which came into force on March 23, 1976 and the Second Optional Protocol to the International Covenant on Civil and Political Rights Aiming at the Abolition of Death Penalty in 1989 which came into force of July 11, 1991. The International Bill of Human Rights represents a milestone in the history of human rights, a veritable Magna Carta marking mankinds arrival at a vitally important phase: the conscience acquisition of human dignity and worth.

The draft of the Declaration was prepared by the Drafting Committee which was appointed by the Commission on Human Rights after having received comments from the governments. The Council adopted a resolution without vote and submitted it before the General Assembly. The General Assembly adopted it (after the examinations of its Third Committee) on December 10, 1948 through a resolution known as the Universal Declaration of Human Rights. The resolution was adopted without dissent by 48 votes with 8 States abstaining. The Declaration consisted of 30 Articles besides a Preamble.

The Declaration has exercised a profound influence upon the minds of men. It is a primary proclamation of the international community's commitment to human rights as a common standard of achievement for all peoples and for all nations. Its message is one of hope, equality, liberation and empowerment. Article 1, 2 and 7 express the fundamental right of equal treatment and non-discrimination with respect to guaranteed human rights without distinction of any kind.

Article 4 of the Declaration provided that no one shall be held in slavery or servitudes; slavery and slave trade shall be prohibited in all their forms. The prohibition against slavery is universally held to form part of customary law. It has been prohibited by a number of widely ratified conventions. International Court of Justice has regarded protection from slavery as included in the basic rights of the human person which give rise to obligations which States owe erga omnes.

The prohibition against "torture or cruel, inhuman or degrading treatment or punishment" provided under Article 5 of the Declaration has been widely regarded as a customary rule of International Law. In *Filartiga v. Pena-Irala,* the issue was whether torture was a breach of international law.

Article 9 of the Declaration stipulated that no one shall be subjected to arbitrary arrest, detention or exile. International Court of Justice in United States Diplomatic and Consular Staff in Tehran observed that "wrongfully to deprive human beings of their freedom and to subject them to physical constraint in conditions of hardship is in itself manifestly incompatible with the principle of the Charter of the United Nations, as well as with the fundamental principles enunciated in the Universal Declaration of Human Rights."

The Commission of Human Rights in 1947, while considering the preliminary draft of an International Bill of Human Rights prepared by the drafting Committee, decided to draw up a separate Covenant which would be a Covenant on such specific rights as would lend themselves to blinding legal obligations. The document was to be known as International Covenant on Human Rights. In order to prepare it, a Working Group was established which parts. The first part described the obligations of states which adhered to the Covenant; the Second part defined some of the rights and freedoms listed in accession to the Covenant would be affected and how amendments would come into force.

In 1950, the General Assembly recommended the inclusion of the economic, social and cultural rights in the Covenant. Accordingly, the Commission at its 1951 Session proceeded to draft the articles on economic, social and cultural rights. When the draft was being considered by the Economic and Social Council, a number of objections were made by many countries as to having both the categories of rights in one Covenant. The argument advanced by them was that the economic, social and cultural rights are different in nature and they are secondary rights. It was a misunderstanding which was further spread by a terminology which grouped these rights into different 'generation'. The economic and social rights were meant for second generation. Later, in 1952, the General Assembly, on the recommendation of the Economic, and Social Council, decided that the two Covenants shall be drawn up and directed to the Commission on Human Rights to prepare two drafts, one dealing with civil and political rights, the other with economic, social cultural rights. However, it was stated that each Covenant should contain as many of the provisions as possible 'to stress the unity of the aim in view'.

On the recommendation of the Third Committee, the General Assembly on December 16, 1966 adopted the two Covenants: International Covenant on Civil and Political Rights and International Covenant on Economic, Social and Cultural Rights. It also adopted an Optional Protocol to the International Covenant on Civil and Political Rights. The General Assembly on December 15, 1989 adopted the Second Optional Protocol to the International Covenant on Civil and Political Rights Aiming at the Abolition of the Death Penalty. The Second Optional Protocol came into force on July 11, 1991 in accordance with Article 8, Para 1. With the adoption of the two Covenants and two Optional Protocols, the United Nations completed the task of formulating the international standard of human rights of the individuals. They together along with the Universal Declaration of Human Right is regarded to have constituted international Bill of Human Rights. Thus, the United Nations fulfilled one of the main objects which it had cherished in 1947.

The Covenant on Civil and Political Rights consists of 53 Articles and is divided into six parts. While in Parts I, II various rights and freedoms are enumerated, the other three parts are devoted with implementation procedures for effective realization of these rights along with the final clauses.

The two Covenants have been criticized by the authors on different grounds which are as follows:

It has been asserted that human rights cannot be universal in character. They differ from one State to another depending upon the different economic, social and political conditions of the States. According to them, the rights of the individuals of developed, developing and least-developed countries cannot be identical. But this aspect has not been taken into consideration by the drafters of the Covenants.

It is submitted that neither human rights can be different for Eastern countries to Western countries nor they can be different for developed countries and for the Third World countries. Human rights are colour blind and direction blind. They know neither right nor left, but only the human. The universality and indivisibility of human rights have come to be particularly emphasized recently. It is human dignity which gives substance to human rights. Human beings carry human dignity wherever they are and whatever the circumstances. The Human Rights therefore are not place and time relative. Further, there cannot be several categories of the rights of human beings because they all are equal.these criticisms are made mainly because of the different systems of law, and also because of different ideologies and policies of the government of the States. In fact, there is much of substantial benefit in the covenant and they can help to ensure human dignity, worth and freedom throughout the World.

The Charter of the United Nations had expressed the desirability of promoting and encouraging respect for human rights and fundamental freedoms for all without distinction as to race, sex, language or religion. The term genocide has derived from the Greek term 'genos' (race) and the Latin word 'cide' (killing).

The General Assembly, as early as in 1946, began the process of formulating a convention on genocide. It adopted a resolution in 1946 wherein it unanimously declared that genocide- the killing of a group of human beings – is a crime under International Law.

The Universal Declaration of Human Rights had stated that all human beings are born free and are equal of dignity and rights, and that everyone is entitled to all the rights, and freedoms set forth in the Declaration, without distinction to any kind, such as race, colour or national origin. Racial segregation and apartheid were condemned by the International Convention on the Elimination of All Forms of Racial Discrimination.

The crime of apartheid has been defined under Article II which states that the crime of apartheid shall include similar policies and practices of racial segregation and discrimination as practiced in Southern Africa shall apply to the following inhuman acts

(a) denial to a member or members of a racial group or groups of the right to life and liberty of person (i) by murder of members of a racial group or groups; (ii) by the infliction upon the members of racial group of serious bodily or mental harm, by the infringement of their freedom or dignity, or by subjecting them to torture or to cruel, inhuman or degrading treatment or punishment; (iii) by arbitrary arrest and illegal imprisonment of the members of racial group or groups; (b) deliberate imposition on a racial group or groups of living conditions calculated to cause its or their physical destruction in whole or in part; (c) Any legislative measures and other measures calculated to prevent a racial group or groups from participation in the political, social, economic and cultural life of the country and the deliberate creation of conditions preventing the full development of such a group or groups (d) any measures, including legislative measures, designed to divide belonging to a racial group or groups or members thereof; (e) exploitation of labour of members of a racial group or groups in particular by submitting them to forced labour; (f) persecution of organization and persons, by depriving them of fundamental rights and freedoms because they oppose apartheid.

Torture is widely spread across all continents but the methods adopted by the States are quite different. Some common forms of physical and psychological torture are: isolation, falanga (blows to the soles of the feet), electric shocks, suffocation (for instance, victim's head forced into water filled with excrements), pulling out teeth, burning by cigarettes or red-hot iron bars, mutilation (nails pulled of our parts of body amputated), sexual torture, mock execution, letting detained torture each other, pharmacological torture. Torture is done to criminals, innocent persons trapped by law enforcement agencies, spies, prisoners of war, refugees, opposition leaders, journalists, ethnic minority leaders and others, including their family members, both adult and children. Torture of children is performed for putting pressure on their parents, or forces them to beg. Torture is also used often as a political weapon.

The Universal Declaration of Human Rights under Article 5 and the International Covenant on Civil and Political Rights under Article 7 had provided that no one shall be subjected to torture or to cruel, inhuman or degrading treatment or punishment, but neither the term torture was defined therein nor it was elaborated that how the torture and other inhuman or degrading treatment or punishment shall be prevented.

Slavery which has been in practice throughout the ages in some form or the other is a blot on humanity. In ancient days slavery could mean the total dominance and personal control by the master but is presently limited to the economic bondage.

The Convention under Section II made provisions for the Slave Trade. Article 3 laid down that the act of conveying or attempting to convey slaves from one country to another by whatever means of transport shall be a criminal offence under the laws of the states Parties and persons convicted thereof shall be liable to very severe penalties.

Section III of the Convention stated that in those States where the slavery has not been abolished or where the institutions or practices similar to slavery has not yet completed, the act of mutilating, branding or otherwise marking a slave or a person of servile status in order to indicate his status, or as a punishment, or for any other reason, or of being accessory thereto, shall be criminal offence and persons convicted thereof shall be liable to punishment.

Meaning of the term forced labour has been elaborated by the Supreme Court in *People's Union for Democratic Rights v. Union of India,* by stating that where labour is forced upon a person irrespective of the payment factors shall be deemed as forced labour. If a person has been forced or compelled to perform work against this wishes, i.e., if he has been force to do work, it shall be a case of forced labour even if he has received remuneration for the work done. It was observed by the Court that a person may be compelled to do work because of 'physical force' or legal force (i.e., where a person is forced to work because of the provision of the punishment for not providing labour or service) or economic force.

The prostitution and the accompanying evil of the traffic in persons for the purpose of prostitution are incompatible with the dignity and worth of the human person. The United Nations in 1949 consolidated in a single Convention a series of international instruments which were adopted under the auspices of the League of Nations. These included (1) International Convention for the Suppression of the Traffic in Women and Children of September 30, 1921; (2) International convention for the Suppression of the Traffic in Women of Full Age of October 11, 1933 aimed at ending what had been known as the "white slave trade." It is estimated that more than two million people World-wide are being trafficked each year, the majority of whom are women and children.

The Convention came into force on July 25, 1951 in accordance with Article 24 of the convention. As on February 2, 2002, the Convention had 74 States Parties. The parties to the present Convention also agreed to take or to encourage, through their public or private educational, health, social and other related services, measures for the prevention of prostitution and for the rehabilitation and social adjustment of the victims of prostitution.

The Universal Declaration of Human Rights under Article 2 laid down that the rights and freedoms provided in the Declaration shall be available to all the persons irrespective of race, colour, sex and religion. In 1963, the Assembly proclaimed the Declaration on the Elimination of All Forms of Racial Discrimination. The Declaration affirmed the fundamental equality of all persons and confirmed that discrimination between human beings on the grounds of race, colour or ethnic origin is a violation of the human right and is an obstacle to friendly and peaceful relations among nations and people.

The Convention under Article 1 defines the term 'racial discriminating' by stating that racial discrimination shall mean any distinction, exclusion, restriction or preference based on race, colour, descent or national or ethnic origin which has the prupose or effect of nullifying or impairing the recognition, enjoyment or exercise, on an equal footing, of human rights and fundamental freedoms in the political, economic, social, cultural or any other field of public life.

Death penalty involves inevitable element of suffering and humiliation. In those cases especially where delay occurs in the execution of the death penalty. Sentenced person's mental anguish of anticipating the violence which is to be inflicted upon him is cruel and inhuman, and therefore, it is a violation of human rights – the right to life and the right not to be subjected to cruel, inhuman or degrading treatment. Further, the execution of death sentence is an act of torture.

Article 6 of the Covenant on Civil and Political Rights had referred the desirability of the abolition of death penalty as it is one of the measures for the enjoyment of the right to life. Abolition of death penalty contributes to enhancement of human dignity and progressive development of human rights.

The advancement of women has been a focus of the work of the United Nations since its creation. The Preamble of the charter of the United Nations sets as a basic goal to reaffirm faith in fundamental human rights, in the dignity and worth of the human person, in the equal rights of men and women. Furthermore, Article 1 of the Charter proclaims that one of the purposes of the United Nations is to achieve international cooperation in promoting and encouraging respect for human rights and fundamental freedoms for the people without distinction as to race, sex, language or religion.

The General Assembly on November 7, 1967 adopted a Declaration on the Elimination of Discrimination against Women, and in order to implement the principle set forth in the Declaration, a Convention on the Elimination of All Forms of Discriminating against Women was adopted by the General Assembly on December 18, 1979.

The Convention under Article 1 defines the term discrimination against women as any distinction, exclusion or restriction made on the basis of sex which has the effect or purpose of impairing or nullifying the recognition, enjoyment or exercise by women, irrespective of their marital status, on a basis of equality of men and women, of human rights and fundamental freedoms in the political, economic, social, cultural, civil or any other field.

The Convention under Article 10 provides that women shall be provided same conditions for careers and vocational guidance as to that of men. They shall be provided same access to studies for the achievement of diplomas in educational establishments of all categories in rural as well as in urban areas.

The Convention under Article 11 provided that States Parties shall take all appropriate measures to eliminate discrimination against woman in the field of employment providing same rights in particular, (a)_ the right to work; (b) right to same employment opportunities; (c) right to free choice of profession and employment; (d) right to equal remuneration including benefits and to equal treatment in respect of work of equal value as well as equality of treatment in ht evaluation of the quality of work; (e) the right to social security particularly in cases of retirement, unemployment, sickness, invalidity and old age and other incapacity to work, as well as the right to paid leave; (f) right to protection of health and to safety in working conditions. There shall be no discrimination against women on grounds of marriage or maternity.

The Convention under Article 12 provides that Sates Parties shall take steps to eliminate discrimination against women in the field of health care, access to health care services, including those related to family planning.

Article 13 of the Convention provides that discrimination against women shall be eliminated in other areas of economic and social life. They shall be provided, the same rights as to that of men in particular.

Article 14 provided elimination of discrimination against rural areas.

Article 15 of the Convention provides that 'States Parties shall accord to women equality with men before the law'. Women shall have equal rights to conclude contracts and to administer property and States Parties shall treat them equally in all stages of procedure in courts and tribunals

Article 16 provides that States Parties shall take all measures to eliminate discrimination against women in all matters relating to marriage and family relations.

Child Labour is one of the most pressing social problems which th einternaitonal community has been facing. According to the International Labour Organization (ILQ) estimates in 2000 some 211 million children between 5 to 14 years of age work in developing countries, with about half working full time. Another ILO survey shows that some 141 million children between the ages of 15 to 17 worldwide are engaged in economic activities and a majority of them are working in worst forms of exploitive jobs which endanger their physical, mental or moral well-being. The goals of the United Nations, in terms of child labour, are to protect working children from exploitation and hazardous conditions that endanger their physical and mental developments, to ensure children's access to at least minimum levels of education, nutrition and health achieve the progressive elimination of child labour.

The Constitution of India under Article 24 provides that no child below the age of fourteen years shall be employed in any factory or mine or engaged in any other hazardous employment.

In India, the Employment of Children Act of 1938 was the first statutory enactment dealing with child labour. The Act had prohibited employment of children below 14 years of age in the railways and other means of transport.

A number of legislative enactments enacted after independence are in force which prohibit employment of child labour in different occupations. They are: Indian Factories Act (1948); Indian Mines Act (1952); Motor Transport Workers Act (1961); Beedi and Cigar Workers (conditions of Employment) Act, (1966) and the Apprentices Act (1961). Shop and Commercial Establishment Acts under different nomenclatures in various States also prohibit the employment of children.

The Supreme Court in *M.C. Mehta v. State of Tamil Nadu,* laid down exhausting guidelines so that State authorities may protect economic, social and humanitarian rights of the millions of child who are working either in hazardous or non-hazardous jobs. The Court directed that for the hazardous jobs the employer of the factory where children are working must be asked to pay compensation for every child employed in contravention of the Act a sum of Rs. 20000 which would be deposited in a fund to be known as Child Labour Rehabilitation-cum-Welfare Fund. The fund so generated shall form corpus whose income shall be used only for the concerned child. The Court also directed that the liability of the employer would not cease even if he would desire to disengage the child previously employed.

Migrants are a particular vulnerable group and they find their rights routinely violated. In order to eliminate widespread discrimination against the migrant workers and members of their families a Convention was adopted by the General Assembly on December 18, 1990 which is known as the International Convention on the Protection of the Rights of All Migrant Workers and Members of Their Families.

A migrant worker has been defined under Article 2 of the Convention as a person who is to be engaged or has been engaged in a remunerated activity in a State of which he or she is not a national. The expression members of the family has also been defined under Article 4 as persons married to migrant workers or having with them a relationship that, according to applicable law, produces effects equivalent to marriage, as well as their dependent children and other dependent persons who are recognized as members of the family by applicable legislation or applicable bilateral or multilateral agreements between the States concerned.

Refugees are referred to those persons who leave their States in which they have permanent residents to escape persecution or military action. Any person who owing to well founded fear of being persecuted for reasons of race, religion, nationality, membership of a particular social group or political opinion, is outside the country of his nationality and is unable, or owing to such fear, is unwilling to avail himself of the protection of that country, or who not having a nationality and being outside the country of this former habitual residence as a result of such events, is unable or, owing to such fear, to unwilling to return to it.

The General Assembly on December 14, 1950 adopted the Statute of the Office of the United Nations High Commissioner for Refugees (UNHCR) UNHCR came into existence on January 1, 1951. UNHCR was set up initially for a period of three years.

India is neither a party to the Refugee Convention of 1951 nor its Protocol of 1967. It has not enacted any domestic law relating to refugees despite the fact that it has invariably provided refugee to the people fleeing mostly from Tibet, Bangladesh, Sri Lanka and Afghanistan.

The Supreme Court of India in *Louis De Raedt v. Union of India,* held that Article 21 of the Constitution protects life and personal liberty to all persons and therefore aliens in Indian territory shall not be deprived of those rights except according to procedure established by Law.

In *Arunachal Pradesh v. Khudiram Chakma,* it was stated that *Chakmaas* are foreigners in accordance with the Citizenship Act of 1955 and therefore they are not entitled to all the fundamental rights enshrined in Part III of the Constitution.

The decision of the Supreme Court given in *National Human Rights Commission v. State of Arunachal Pradesh,* is relevant regarding the protection of some of the rights to refugees and is worth mentioning.

More than 500 million persons – 10 per cent of the World's population, an estimated 80 per cent of them living in the developing World – suffer from either mental or physical disability. They are often denied basic educational opportunities and often given menial or poorly paid jobs. Social attitudes exclude them from cultural life and normal social relationship. Rights of disabled persons have been proclaimed in different instruments which are as follows:

After recalling the Principles of the Universal Declaration of Human Rights, the General Assembly on December 20, 1971 proclaimed the Declaration on the Rights of Mentally Retarded Persons and called for national and international action to ensure that it will be used as a common basis and frame of reference for the protection of these rights.

The Declaration affirmed that the mentally retarded persons shall have the rights as other human beings and wherever possible, should live with his or her family. Rights provided to such persons included rights to proper medical care and physical therapy and to education, training, rehabilitation and guidance; a right to economic security and a decent standard of living; a right to a qualified guardian to protect his personal well-being and interests and a right to protection from exploitation, abuse and degrading treatment. If prosecuted for any offence, he shall have a right to due process of law with full recognition being given to his degree of mental responsibility.

The General Assembly on December 17, 1991 laid down the Principles for the Protection of Persons with Mental Illness and the Improvement of Mental Health Care.

A Declaration on the Rights of Disabled Persons was adopted by the General Assembly on December 9, 1975. The term disabled person was defined in the Declaration as any person unable to ensure by himself or herself, wholly or partly, the necessities of a normal individual and or social life. The Declaration asserted that disabled persons shall have the same fundamental rights as their fellow citizens and are entitled to measures designed to enable them to become as self-reliant as possible. They have the inherent right to decent level of living; right to live with their families or with foster parents and shall be protected against all exploitation, all regulations and all treatments of a discriminatory, abusive or degrading nature.

The United Nations is concerned not only with the equality of the life of human beings, but it is also equally concerned with the longevity of the human beings. As a result of the gradual decline in death rates and rising life expectancy, it is expected that all countries of the world during the next two decades will witness an increase in the proportion of their population aged 60 or over. By the year 2020 more than 1000 million people aged 60 years and above will be living in the World. The United Nations is committed to help those countries which are facing the challenge for the needs of elderly persons and using effectively their contribution to development.

Principles for Older Persons

The General Assembly on December 16, 1991 by a resolution adopted a set of 18 Principles for Older Persons. These principles were related to the independence, participation, care, self-fulfilment and the dignity of the older persons. Some of the Principles are as follows:

1. Older Persons should have the opportunity to work and determine when to leave the work force.

2. Older Persons should remain integrated in society and participate actively in the formulation of policies which effect their well-being.

3. Older Persons should have access to health care to help them maintain the optimum level of physical, mental and emotional well-being.
4. Older Persons should be able to pursue opportunities for the full development of their potential and have access to educational, cultural, spiritual and recreational resources of society.
5. Older Persons should be able to live in dignity and security and should be free from exploitation and mental and physical abuse.

In *Mohini Jain v. State of Karnataka*, the Supreme Court has rightly observed that –

Right to life is the compendious expression for all those rights which the Courts must enforce because they are basic to the dignified enjoyment of life. It extends to the full range of conduct which the individual is free to pursue.

The attempts of the courts should be to expand the reach and ambit of the fundamental rights rather than accentuate their meaning and content by process of judicial constitution. In Peoples' union for Civil Liberties v. Union of India it was stated by the Supreme Court that –

For the present, it would suffice to state that the provisions of the Covenant which elucidate and go to effectuate the fundamental rights guaranteed by our Constitution can certainly be relied upon by Courts as facets of these fundamental rights and hence enforceable as such.

Whatever rights are available to a person under the Indian Constitution are neither absolute nor unlimited. Rights have been provided subject to certain restrictions. The framers of the constitution had realized that the fundamental rights were not absolute, and therefore, they provided for restrictions upon the exercise of these rights to be imposed by law. But the restrictions are not contrary to the provisions of the Covenant. Rights provided in the Covenant on Civil and Political Rights are also not absolute. The rights and freedoms enshrined therein are restricted, controlled and regulated. Thus the restrictions stipulated in the Constitution on the fundamental rights are not inconsistent with the Covenant on Civil and Political Rights.

India while acceding the Covenant on Civil and Political Rights had made certain reservations which are laid down in the Instrument of Accession by way of 'Declaration'. They specify the conditions of its willingness to become a party to the Covenant. Thus, they restrict the application of the Covenant on it.

Right of self-determination is collective human rights which is available to a group of individuals. It is an established principle of international law which is applied to the colonial peoples. These are the peoples of trust territories and of non-self-governing territories. While the trust territories are those which are administered by other States under the supervision of the United Nations, non-self-governing territories are those which were of colonial type at the time of the adoption of the Charter of the United Nations.

The Covenant under Article 9 provides various safeguards against the arbitrary arrest and detention of a person. For instance, no one shall be deprived of his liberty except on such grounds and in accordance with such procedure as are established by law. Further, anyone who is arrested shall be informed, at the time of arrest, of the reasons for his arrest and shall be promptly informed the time of arrest, of the reasons for his arrest and shall be promptly informed of any charges against him.

Article 13 of the Covenant lays down that an alien lawfully in the territory of a State Party any be expelled there from only in pursuance of a decision reached in accordance with law and shall, except where compelling reasons of national security otherwise require, be allowed to submit the reasons against his expulsion and to have his case reviewed by, and be represented for the purpose before the competent authority or a person or persons especially designated by the competent authority.

Article 19(1) of the Constitution of India provides various rights to a person which includes the freedom of speech and expression, right to assemble peacefully, right to form associations or unions, and the right to move freely throughout the territory of India.

It is to be noted that India while acceding to the Covenant on Economic, Social and Cultural Rights had made certain reservations in the application of certain provisions. Such provisions, of course, would not apply to it. For instance article 1 of the Covenant which lays down as to the right of self-determination shall apply only to the peoples under foreign dominating and not to sovereign independent States or to a sections of a people or nation – which is the essence of national integrity. Further, article 4 and 8 of the Covenant shall be so applied as to be in conformity with the provisions of Article 19 of the Constitution. Article 7 © of the Covenant shall be so applied as to be in conformity with the provisions of Article 16(4) of the Constitution. The effect of the reservations would be that the Government is not required to take any step beyond that what is guaranteed in the Constitution.

It is shocking that in India, economic and social rights have not been given right that much importance which the civil and political rights have, perhaps because the former are not enforceable before the courts of law. But this attitude is not justifiable in view of the great importance given to them by the Founding Fathers. It was their aspiration to provide these rights to the individuals in a welfare State based on social, political and economic justice.

International Convention on the Elimination of All Forms of Racial Discrimination

The International convention on the Elimination of All Forms of Racial Discrimination defines and condemns racial discrimination, and commits state parties to change their national laws and policies which create or perpetuate racial discrimination. It is regarded among the most important UN Conventions for it is aimed at the achievement of one of the purpose of the United Nations which is to promote and encourage universal respect of rand observance of human rights and fundamental freedoms for all, without distinction as to race, sex, language or religion.

The Convention was the first human rights instrument to establish an international monitoring system. One of the main objectives of the Convention is to promote racial equality, which allows the various racial, ethnic, and national groups to enjoy the same social development.

The Convention follows the structure of the Universal Declaration of Human Rights, International Covenant on Civil and Political Rights, and International Covenant on Economic, Social and Cultural Rights, with a preamble and twenty-five articles, divided into three parts.

Part I (Article 1-7) commits parties to the elimination of all forms of racial discrimination and to promoting understanding among all races (Article 2). Parties are obliged to not discriminate on the basis of race, not to sponsor or defend racism, and to prohibit racial discrimination within their jurisdictions. They must also review their laws and policies to ensure that they do not discriminate on the basis of race, and commit to amending or repealing those that do. Specific areas in which discrimination must be eliminated are listed in Article.

The Convention imposes a specific commitment on parties to eradicate racial segregation and the crime of apart hid within their jurisdictions (Article 3). Parties are also required to criminalize the incitement of racial hatred (Article 4), to ensure judicial remedies for acts of racial discrimination (Article 6), and to engage in public education to promote understanding and tolerance (Article 7).

Part II (Article 8-16) governs reporting and monitoring of the Convention and the steps taken by the parties to implement it. It establishes the Committee on the Elimination of Racial Discrimination, and empowers it to make general recommendations to the UN General Assembly. It also establishes a dispute-resolution mechanism between parties (Article 11-13), and allows parties to recognize the competence of the Committee to hear complaints from individuals about violations of the rights protected by the Convention (Article 14).

Part III (Article 17-25) governs ratification, entry into force, and amendment of the Convention.

The Convention contains a non-exhaustive long list of rights and freedoms in the enjoyment of which racial discrimination is prohibited and sought to be eliminated. The list includes certain rights not expressly contained in the Universal Declaration of Human Rights (UDHR), such as the right to inherit and the right of access to any place or service intended for use by the general public. It also includes rights in regard to which racial discrimination is prohibited, such as the right to work, the right to join trade unions and the right to housing.

The principle of non-discrimination, according to Article 1, Paragraph 1, of the Convention, protects the enjoyment on an equal footing of human rights and fundamental freedoms "in the political, economic, social cultural or any other field of public life". The list of human rights to which the principle applies under the Convention is not closed and extends to any field of human rights regulated by the public authorities in the State party.

Committee on the Elimination of Racial Discrimination

The Committee on the Elimination of Racial Discrimination (CERD) is the body of independent experts that monitors the implementation of the provisions of the International Convention on the Elimination of All Forms of racial Discrimination (ICERD) by its state parties.

All states parties are obliged to submit regular reports to the CERD on how the rights contained in the Convention are being implemented. States are initially required to report a year after acceding to the Convention and then every two years. The Committee examines each report and informs the State party of its recommendations and concerns in the "concluding observations".

Some of the core functions of the CERD include:

- Considering the periodic reports submitted by the States on how they how they are implementing the obligations they have assumed by ratifying the Convention.

CERD examines each report and addresses its concerns and recommendations to the State party in the form of "concluding observations".

- Receiving and considering individual complaints, also known as "communications", made by individuals who claim violations of their Convention rights by a State party.
- Considering certain complaints made by a State party that another State party is not abiding by the obligations assumed under the Convention.
- Making general recommendations and comments.
- Informing the General Assembly of its activities.

CERD also includes in its regular agenda 'preventive measures', which include early- warning aimed at preventing existing situations escalating into conflicts and urgent procedures to respond to problems requiring immediate attention to prevent or limit the scale or number of serious violations of the Convention.

International Covenant on Civil and Political Rights

The International Covenant on Civil and Political Rights (ICCPR) is a multilateral treaty adopted by the United Nations General Assembly on 16 December 1966 and opened for signature at New York on 19 December 1966. It commits its parties to respect the civil and political rights of individuals, including the right of self-determination, right to life, freedom of religion, freedom of speech, freedom of assembly, electoral rights and rights to due process and a fair trial. The Covenant elaborates further the civil and political rights and freedoms listed in the Universal Declaration of Human Rights.

The Covenant is divided into six major Parts:

Part I (Article 1) recognizes the rights of all people to self-determination, including the right to 'freely determine their political status, pursue their economic, social and cultural goals and manage and dispose off their own resources. It recognizes the right of people not to be deprived of means of subsistence, and imposes an obligation on those parties still responsible for non-self governing and trust territories (colonies) to encourage and respect their self-determination.

Part II (Articles 2 – 5) obliges parties to legislate where necessary to give effect to the rights recognized in the Covenant, and to provide an effective legal remedy for any violation of those rights. It also requires the rights be recognized "without distinction of any kind, such as race, colour, sex, language, religion, political or other opinion, national or social origin, property, birth or other status," and to ensure that they are enjoyed equally by women.

The rights can only be limited "in time of public emergency which threatens the life of the nation", and even then no derogation is permitted from the rights to life, freedom from torture and slavery, the freedom from retrospective law, the right to personhood, and freedom of thought, conscience and religion.

Part III (Article 6 -27), often described as the heart of the Covenant, it lists the substantive rights and fundamental freedoms guaranteed by the Convention. These provisions also stipulate the narrow confines within which the death penalty may legitimately be imposed in States parties where that penalty has not been abolished.

Specific prohibition are set out concerning torture, unauthorized medical experimentation, and slavery and forced labour. The rights of a person in the context of deprivation of liberty, commonly by arrest, and in detention are also covered. These include:

- **Right to physical integrity**, in the form of the right to life and freedom from torture and slavery (Article 6, 7, and 8);
- **Liberty and security of the person**, in the form of freedom from arbitrary arrest and detention and the right to habeas corpus (Article 9 -11)
- **Procedural fairness in law**, in the form of rights to due process, a fair and impartial trial, the presumption of innocence, and recognition as a person before the law (Article 14, 15 and 16);
- **Individual liberty**, in the form of the freedoms of movement, thought, conscience and religion, speech, association and assembly, family rights, the right to a nationality, and the right to privacy (Article 12, 13, 17 – 24);
- **Prohibition of any propaganda for war** as well as advocacy of national or religious hatred that constitutes incitement to discrimination, hostility or violence by law (Article 20);
- **Political participation**, including the right to join a political party and the right to vote (Article 25);
- **Non-discrimination, minority rights** and **equality before the law** (Article 26 and 27);
- **Part IV** (Article 28 – 45) governs the establishment and operation of the Human Rights Committee, the body of independent experts that monitors implementation of the International Covenant on Civil and Political Rights by its State parties. It also allows parties to recognize the competence of the Committee to resolve disputes between parties on the implementation of the Covenant (Article 41 and 42).
- **Part V** (Article 46 -47) clarifies that "nothing in the (present) Covenant shall be interpreted as impairing the provisions of the Charter of the United Nations and of the constitutions of the specialized agencies which define the respective responsibilities of the various organs of the united Nations and of the specialized agencies in regard to the matters dealt with in the present Covenant" or "the inherent right of all peoples to enjoy and utilize fully and freely their natural wealth and resources".
- **Part VI** (Articles 48 -53) has provisions with regard to the ratification, entry into force, and amendment of the Covenant.

Human Rights Committee

The Human Rights Committee is the body of independent experts that monitors implementation of the International Covenant on Civil and Political Rights by its State parties.

All States Parties are obliged to submit regular reports to the Committee on how the rights are being implemented. States must report initially one year after acceding to the Covenant and then whenever the Committee requests (usually every four years). The Committee examines each report and addresses its concerns and recommendations to the state party in the form of "concluding observations".

In addition to the reporting procedure, Article 41 of the Covenant provides for the Committee to consider inter-state complaints. Furthermore, the First Optional protocol to the Covenant gives the Committee competence to examine individual complaints with regard to alleged violations of the Covenant by States parties to the Protocol.

The HRC's task is to supervise and monitor the implementation of Covenant obligations by States parties. One of the great strengths of the Committee is the moral authority it derives from the fact that its membership represents all parts of the world. In carrying out its monitoring and supervisory functions, the Committee has four major responsibilities.

First, the Committee receives the States parties on the steps they have taken to give effect to the rights spelled out in the Covenant.

Second, the Committee elaborates so-called general comments, which are designed to assist States parties to give effect to the provisions fo the Covenant by providing greater detail regarding the substantive and procedural obligations of States parties.

Third, the Committee receives and considers individual complaints, also known as "communication", under the Optional Protocol made by individuals who claim violations of their Covenant rights by a State Party.

Fourth, the Committee has jurisdiction to consider certain complaints made by a State party that another State party is not abiding by the obligations assumed under the Covenant.

All states that have ratified or acceded to the Covenant undertake to submit reports to the Committee on the measures they have adopted to give effect to the rights the Covenant establishes and on the progress made in the enjoyment of those rights. This obligation is contained in Article 40 of the Covenant.

First Optional Protocol to the International Covenant on Civil and Political Rights

The First Optional Protocol is a supplementary treaty to the International Covenant on Civil and Political Rights (ICCPR). It is procedural and provides a mechanism for the Human Rights Committee, set up by the ICCPR, to receive and consider individual complaints against alleged breaches of the Covenant by a state party.

Thus individuals who claim that their rights and freedoms have been violated, may call the State in question to account for its actions, provided it is a party to the optional protocol to the ICCPR.

Under Article 1 of the Optional Protocol, a State party to the Covenant that becomes a party to the Protocol "recognizes the competence of the human rights committee to receive and consider communications from individuals subject to its jurisdiction who claim to be victims of a violation by that State Party of any of the rights set forth in the Covenant." Individuals who make such a claim, and who have exhausted all available domestic remedies, are entitled to submit a written communication to the committee for its consideration (Article 2).

In additional to Article 2, Article 3 and 5 (2) lay down conditions for admissibility of complaints / communications by individuals. Complaints admitted by the Committee are then brought to the attention of the State party alleged to have violated a provision of the Covenant. The concerned State is required to submit to the committee within six months, written explanations or statements clarifying the matter and indicating the remedy, if any, that it may have applied (Article 4).

Subsequently, the Human Rights Committee considers these individual complaints in the light of all the information made available to it by the individual and the State party concerned. It then forwards its views to the concerned State party and individual(s) (Article 5).

As its name makes clear, the Protocol is not compulsory, but once a State party to the Covenant becomes a party to the Protocol, any person subject to the jurisdiction of the State party may lodge a written complaint with the Human Rights Committee (subject to permissible reservations).

Article 6 requires that the Committee report annually to the General Assembly on its activities concerning complaints, while Article 7 through 14 contain technical provisions on the mechanics of states becoming party to the Protocol, entry into force, notification, amendment, denunciation and the like.

Article 10, like the parent Covenant, provides that the Protocol extends without exception to all parts of federal States. Article 12 provides for a State party to denounce the Optional protocol.

Second Optional Protocol to the International Covenant on Civil and Political Rights

The purpose of the Second Optional Protocol is revealed by its full title, "aiming at the abolition of the death penalty". It was adopted by the General Assembly by its resolution 44/128 of 15 December 1989.

The Preamble to the Second Optional protocol reinforces the view that abolition of the death penalty is a desirable and progressive human rights measure that enhances human dignity and enjoyment of the right to life.

The second Optional Protocol creates an unqualified human right of an individual not to be executed and prohibits the execution of anyone under the domestic law of a ratifying state. Its single substantive provision, Article 1, states that no person within a state party's jurisdiction shall be executed, and that each state party shall take all necessary measures to abolish the death penalty. However, it is subject to any reservations made by a state party under Article 2 of the Protocol.

Article 2 permits. Subject to certain procedural requirements, only one reservation, namely reserving the death penalty in times of war, pursuant to a conviction for the most serious crimes of a military nature committed during wartime.

This is the only exception to the rule of abolition of the death penalty under the protocol. A state Party can only make a reservation at the time of ratifying the Protocol; otherwise it is bound to total abolition with no exceptions. Article 2.2 & 2.3 set out the procedure for a State Party to make a reservation and to notify the UN of its exercise of the reservation. Article 3 of the Optional Protocol places reporting obligation on the state parties (in accordance with Article 40 of the ICCPR), to inform the Human Rights Committee on the measures adopted to give effect to the second Optional Protocol.

Article 4 provides for a State Party to make a complaint to the UN Human Rights Committee against another State Party which it believes is violating the Protocol. Article 5 provides for individuals to make complaints to the Human Rights Committee against a State party. However, it only applies to nations that have ratified the First Optional Protocol to the ICCPR. At the time of signing the Protocol, a State Party can opt-out of this complaints procedure.

International Covenant on Economic, Social and Cultural Rights

The ICESCR is a multilateral treaty adopted opened for signature, ratification and accession by the United Nations General Assembly on 16 December 1966 and in force since 3 January 1976. Like the ICCPR, it develops the corresponding rights in the UDHR in considerable detail, specifying the steps required for their full realization.

The covenant contains some of the most significant international legal provisions establishing economic, social and cultural rights, including rights relating to work in just and favourable conditions, to social protection, to an adequate standard of living, to the highest attainable standards of physical and mental health, to education and to enjoyment of the benefits of cultural freedom and scientific progress.

The Covenant follows the structure of the Universal Declaration of Human Rights (UDHR) and ICCPR, with a preamble and thirty-one articles, divided into five parts.

Part I (Article 1) recognizes the right of all peoples to self-determination, including the right to "freely determine their political and dispose of their own resources. It recognizes a negative right of a people not to be deprived of its means of subsistence, and imposes an obligation on those parties still responsible for non-self governing and trust territories (colonies) to encourage and respect their self-determination.

Part II (Article 2 -5) establishes the principle of "progressive realization", which acknowledges that some of the right (for instance, the Right to health) may be difficult in practice to achieve in a short period of time, and that states may be subject to resource constraints, but requires them to act as best they can within their means. It also requires the rights be recognized "without discrimination of any kind as to race, colour, sex, language, religion, political or other opinion, national or social origin, property, birth or other status". The rights can only be limited by law, in a manner compatible with the rights can only be limited by law, in a manner compatible with the nature of the rights, and only for the purpose of "promoting the general welfare in a democratic society".

Part III (Article 6 -15) lists the rights themselves. These include the right to:

- Work, under "just and favourable conditions", with the right to form and join trade unions (Article 6, 7 and 8)

- Social security, including social insurance (Article 9)
- Family life, including paid parental leave and the protection of children (Article 10)
- An adequate standard of living, including adequate food, clothing and housing, and the "continuous improvement of living conditions" (Article 11)
- Health, specifically "the highest attainable standard of physical and mental health" (Article 12)
- Education, including free universal primary education, generally available secondary education and equally accessible higher education. This should be directed to "the full development of the human personality and the sense of its dignity", and enable all persons to participate effectively in society (Article 13 and 14)
- Participation in cultural life (Article 15)

Part IV (Article 16 -25) requires all States parties to report regularly to the Economic and Social Council. In 1985, the Council crated the Committee on Economic, Social and Cultural Rights to carry out the functions of monitoring implementation of the Covenant's provisions (ECOSOC Res. 1985/17). It also allows the monitoring body to make general recommendations to the UN General Assembly on appropriate measures to realize the rights (Article 21)

Part V (Article 26 -31) governs ratification, entry into force, and amendment of the Covenant.

The fundamental obligation of States under the ICESCR is to "take steps … with a view to achieving progressively the full realization of the rights" (Article 2(1)). This concept was clarified by the *Committee on Economic Social and Cultural Rights* in its General Comment 3 – "the concept of progressive realization constitutes a recognition of the fact that full realization of all economic, social and cultural rights will generally not be able to be achieved in a short period of time, … Nevertheless, the fact that realization over time, or in other words progressively, is foreseen under the Covenant should not be misinterpreted as depriving the obligation of all meaningful content (The Covenant) imposes an obligation to move as expeditiously and effectively as possible towards that goal.

The *obligation to protect* requires measures by the State to ensure that third parties (individual, armed groups, enterprise, etc.) do not deprive right-holders of their rights. Under the obligation to protect, the state could be held liable for violations of the rights outlined in the ICESCR, committed by non-State actors. Indeed, several judgments and reports issued by international human rights bodies (with regard to human rights) held Stated responsible "because of the lack of due diligence to prevent the violation (committed by non-State actors) or to respond it".

Committee on Economic, Social and Cultural Rights

The Committee on Economic, Social and Cultural Rights is a body of human rights experts tasked with monitoring the implementation of the International Convention on Economic, Social and Cultural Rights (ICESCR). Unlike the other human rights treaty bodies, the committee on Economic, Social and Cultural Rights was not established by its corresponding instrument. Rather, the Economic and Social Council (ECOSOC) created the Committee under originally assigned to the council under Part IV of the Covenant.

Under Article 16 and 17 of the Covenant, States parties undertake to submit periodic reports to the Committee, within two years of the entry into force of the Covenant for a particular State party, and thereafter, once every five years, outlining the legislative, judicial, policy and other measures which they have taken to ensure the enjoyment of the rights contained in the Covenant, as also difficulties faced in this respect.

The Committee has emphasized that reporting obligations under the Covenant fulfill seven key objectives. In its General Comment No. 1 (1988), the Committee outlined these objectives as follows:

1. To ensure that a State party undertakes a comprehensive review of national legislation, administrative rules and procedures, and practices in order to assure the fullest possible conformity with the Covenant;

2. To ensure that the State party regularly monitors the actual situation with respect to each of the enumerated rights in order to access the extent to which the various rights are being enjoyed by all individuals within the country;

3. To provide a basis for government elaboration of clearly stated and carefully targeted policies for implementing the Covenant;

4. To facilitate public scrutiny of government policies with respect to the Covenant's implementation, and to encourage the involvement of the various sectors of society in the formulation, implementation and review of relevant policies;

5. To provide a asis on which both the State party and the Committee can effectively evaluate progress towards the realization of the obligation contained in the covenant;

6. To enable the State party to develop a better understanding of problems and shortcomings impeding the realization of economic, social and cultural rights; and,

7. To facilitate the exchange of information among States parties and to help develop a fuller appreciation of both common problems and possible solutions in the realization of each of the rights contained in the Covenant.

Optional Protocol to ICESCR

The Optional Protocol to the International Covenant on Economic, Social and Cultural Rights, adopted in December 2008, is an international treaty establishing complaint and inquiry mechanisms for the International Covenant on Economic, Social and Cultural Rights. It enables victims to complain about violations of the rights enshrined in the Covenant at the international level.

The Optional Protocol reiterates the equal importance of economic, social and cultural rights with civil and political rights. It is designed to enable victims to seek justice for violations of their economic, social and cultural rights at the international level through the submission of communications before the Committee on Economic, social and Cultural Rights, which is the Treaty Body that governs the implementation of the Covenant by State Parties.

The Optional Protocol provides for a "communications procedure" (that is, a complaints mechanism), in the same way that the Optional protocols to the International Covenant on Civil and

Political Rights and the Convention on the Elimination of All Forms of Discrimination against Women do. The communication procedure allows victims of violations of their economic, social, and cultural rights to present complaints before the Committee, which can in turn, review individual complaints in a way similar to that of traditional human rights courts.

The procedure provides for the possibility of a friendly settlement and of so-called 'interim measures' which the State may be requested to take to avoid possible irreparable damage to the victims of the alleged violations, the Optional Protocol also provides for an "inquiry procedure," allowing the Committee to initiate an investigation if it receives reliable information indicating grave or systematic violations of the ICESCR by a State Party. The inquiry procedure only comes into operation if States make a specific declaration to be bound by it ('opt in' clause).

Convention on the Elimination of All Forms of Discrimination against Women

In 1979, the international community adopted a new treaty which addressed a specific phenomenon: discrimination against women on the basis of sex. Sex discrimination, like racial discrimination, is proscribed under the two covenants (ICCPR and ICESCR) in general terms. However, the CEDAW sets out in more detail what is meant by the prohibition of sex discrimination from the perspective of equality between men and women. It addresses a range of programmatic and policy aspects of the specific problem.

Consisting of Preamble and 30 articles, it defines what constitutes discrimination against women and sets up an agenda for national action to end such discrimination. By accepting the Convention, Sates commit themselves to undertake a series of measures to end discrimination against women in all forms, including:

- Incorporating the principle of equality of men and women in their legal system, abolish all discriminatory laws and adopt appropriate ones prohibiting discrimination against women;

- Establishment tribunals and other public institutions to ensure the effective protection of women against discrimination; and

- Ensuring elimination of all acts of discrimination against women by persons, organizations or enterprises.

The Convention provides the basis for realizing equality between women and men through ensuring women's equal access to and equal opportunities in political and public life – including the right to vote and to stand for election – as well as education, health and employment, States parties agree to track all appropriate measures, including legislation and temporary special measures so that women can enjoy all their human rights and fundamental freedoms.

Aside from civil rights issues, the Convention also devotes major attention to a most vital concern of women, namely their reproductive rights; it is perhaps the only human rights treaty which affirms the reproductive rights of women and the impact of culture and tradition as influential forces in the shaping of gender roles and family relations. It affirms women's rights to acquire change or retain their nationality and the nationality of their children. The Convention also obligates State parties to take appropriate measures against all forms of trafficking in women and exploitation of women.

The Convention begins by defining discrimination on the basis of sex. The initial articles oblige States both to refrain from sex-based discrimination in their own dealings and take measures towards achieving factual as well as legal equality in all spheres of life, including by breaking down discriminatory attitudes, customs and practices in society.

Article 6 explicitly requires States suppress all forms of trafficking in women and exploitation of prostitution, even though these phenomena may implicitly fall within the prohibitions of slavery and forced labour contained in other instruments. While Article 7 and 8 detail obligations to ensure equal participation of women with men in public and political life, Article 9 and 10 expand on equality in nationality and education.

Articles 11, 12 and 13 elaborate on women's rights to employment, health and other areas of economic and social life. Applying general principles to a particular phenomenon, Article 14 is the only provision in the treaties to address the particular problems faced by women in rural areas. Article 15 and 16 expand upon rights to equality before the law and in the area of marriage and family relations.

The Convention, in Part V, requires all States parties to report regularly to the Committee on the Elimination of Discrimination against Women, established to monitor implementation of the Treaty's provisions. Countries that have ratified or acceded to the Convention are legally bound to put its provisions into practice. They are also committed to submit national reports, at least every four years, on measures they have taken to comply with their treaty obligations.

States are also enquired to establish Tribunals and public institutions to guarantee women effective protection against discrimination and take steps to eliminate all forms of discrimination practiced against women by individuals, organizations, and enterprises.

Committee on the Elimination of Discrimination against Women

The United Nations Committee on the Elimination of Discrimination against Women, an expert body established in 1982, is composed of 23 experts on women's issues from around the world. The Committee's mandate is very specific: it watches over the progress for women made in those countries that are states parties to the Convention on the Elimination of All Forms of Discrimination against Women (CEDAW) and monitors the implementation of national measures to fulfill this obligation.

The committee has certain responsibilities as the body of experts charged with the consideration of periodic reports submitted to it. The Committee in its examination of States reports, enters into constructive dialogue with the State party and makes concluding comments, routinely expressing concern at the entry of reservation, in particular to Article 2 and 16, or the failure of States parties to withdrawal or modify them.

Countries which have become party to the treaty (States Parties) are obliged to submit regular reports to the Committee on how the rights of the Convention are being implemented. During its sessions the Committee considers each State party report and addresses its concerns and recommendations to the State party in the form of concluding observations.

The committee also makes recommendations on any issue affecting women to which it believes the states parties should devote more attention. For example at the 1989 session, the Committee discussed the high incidence of violence against women, requesting information on this problem from all countries.

In 1992, the Committee adopted general recommendation 19, which required the national reports to the Committee to include statistical data on the incidence of violence against women, information on the provision of services for victims, and legislative and other measures taken to protect women against violence in their everyday lives, such as harassment at the workplace, abuse in the family and sexual violence.

The 23 members of CEDAW, acknowledged as experts "of high moral standing and competence in the field covered by the Convention", are elected by the States parties. These elections have to meet the Convention's demands for equitable geographical distribution in membership and the requirement that CEDAW members represent "different forms of civilization as well as principal legal systems". Their terms last four years, with only half of the Committee members replaced each time elections take place. The meeting of States parties is convened every other year by the Secretary-General at UN headquarters in New York.

In accordance with the Optional Protocol to the Convention, the Committee is mandated to: (1) receive communications from individuals or groups of individuals submitting claims of violations of rights protected under the Convention to the Committee and (2) initiate inquiries into situations of grave or systematic violations of women's rights. These procedures are optional and are only available where the State concerned has accepted them.

The committee also formulates general recommendations and suggestions. General recommendations are directed to States and concern article or themes in the Convention.

Optional Protocol to the Convention on the Elimination of All Forms of Discrimination against Women

The convention on the Elimination of all Forms of Discrimination against Women outlaws discrimination on the basis of gender, and obliges its parties to repeal discriminatory laws and guarantee equality in the fields of health, employment, and education. The Optional Protocol to the Convention on the Elimination of All Forms of Discrimination against Women is a subsidiary agreement to the Convention. It does not establish nay new rights, but allows the rights guaranteed in the Convention to be enforced.

By ratifying the Optional Protocol, a State recognized the competence of the *Committee on the Elimination of Discrimination against Women* the body that monitors States parties' compliance with the Convention – to receive and consider complaints from individuals or groups within its jurisdiction.

The protocol contains two procedures:

1. A communications procedure which allows individual women, or groups of women, to submit claims of violation of rights protected under the Convention to the Committee. The Protocol establishes that in order for individual communications to be admitted for consideration by the Committee, a number of criteria must be met, including that domestic remedies must have been exhausted before approaching the Committee.

2. The Protocol also creates an inquiry procedure enabling the committee to initiate inquiries into situations of grave or systematic violations of women's rights, in either case, states must be party to the convention and the protocol. The Protocol includes and "opt-out clause", allowing Sates, upon ratification or accession, to declare that they do not accept the inquiry procedure. Article 17 of the Protocol explicitly provides that no reservations may be entered to its terms.

The Optional protocol entered into force on 22 December 2000, following the ratification of the tenth State party to the Convention. The entry into force of the Optional Protocol puts the CEDAW on an equal footing with the International Covenant on Civil and Political Rights, the Convention on the Elimination of All Forms of Racial Discrimination, and the Convention against Torture and other Forms of Cruel, Inhuman or Degrading Treatment of Punishment, which all have communications procedures. The inquiry procedure is the equivalent of that under the Convention against Torture.

Convention against Torture and Other Cruel, Inhuman or Degrading Treatment or Punishment

The Convention provides for each State to take effective measures to prevent torture and other similar treatment or punishment from being practiced within its jurisdiction; criminalize all acts of torture or those which constitute participation, complicity, incitement or an attempt to commit torture; recognize rights of persons who allege that they have been subjected to torture or similar treatment to complain to, and to have their cases impartially examined by the competent authorities of the State concerned; redress and compensate victims of torture; and prohibition of using as evidence any statement made as a result of torture or of other cruel, inhuman or degrading treatment or punishment.

The CAT contains a range of obligations for States Parties allied at prohibiting and preventing torture. It is important first and foremost because it contains an internationally recognized definition of torture and requires States Parties to ensure that acts of torture and made a criminal offence under their national law.

Part I (Article 1 -16) defines torture (Article 1), and commits parties to taking effective measures to prevent any act of torture in any territory under their jurisdiction (Article 2). These include ensuring that torture is made a criminal offense (Article 4), establishing jurisdiction over acts of torture committed by or against a party's citizens (Article 5), ensuring that torture is an extraditable offense (Article 8), and establishing (universal jurisdiction) to try case of torture where an alleged torturer cannot be extradited (Article

5). Parties must promptly investigate any allegation of torture (Articles 12 and 13), and victims of torture must have an enforceable right to compensation (Article 14).

Parties must also ban the use of evidence produced by torture in their courts (Article 15), and are barred from deporting, extraditing or refueling people where there are substantial grounds for believing they will be tortured (Article 3).

Parties are also obliged to prevent other acts of cruel, inhuman or degrading treatment or punishment, and to investigate any allegation of such treatment within their jurisdiction (Article 16).

Part II (Article 17 – 24) governs reporting and monitoring of the Convention and the steps taken by the parties to implement it. It establishes the Committee Against Torture (Article 17), and empowers it to investigate allegations of systematic torture (Article 20).

It also establishes an optional dispute-resolution mechanism between parties (Article 21) and allows parties to recognize the competence of the Committee to hear complaints from individuals about violations of the convention by a party (Article 22).

Part III (Article 25 – 33) governs ratification, entry into force and amendment of the Convention. It also includes an optional arbitration mechanism for disputes between parties (Article 30).

Committee against Torture

The UN Committee against Torture (hereafter "the CAT" or "the Committee") is the body created by the UN Convention against Torture to monitor the observance of the specific obligations established under the Convention. The committee was established pursuant to Article 17 of the Convention and began to function on 1 January 1988.

The Committee is entrusted with the specific supervision of a multilateral instrument for protection against torture and other forms of inhuman treatment. The Convention sets out a number of obligations designed to strengthen the sphere of protection of human rights and fundamental freedoms, while conferring upon the Committee Against Torture broad powers of examination and investigation to ensure its effectiveness in practice. At their initial meeting held at Geneva in April 1988, the members of the Committee against Torture adopted rules of procedure and defined the Committee's working methods, in conformity with the provisions of the Convention.

All State Parties are obliged under the convention to submit regular reports to the CAT on how rights are being implemented. Upon ratifying the Convention, states must submit a report within one year, after which they are obliged to report every four years. The Committee examines each report and addresses its concerns and recommendations to the State party in the form of "concluding observations." Under certain circumstances, the CAT may consider complaints or communications from individuals claiming that their rights under the Convention have been violated.

The Committee normally holds two regular sessions each year. Special sessions, however, may be convened by decision of the Committee itself at the request of a majority of its members or of a State Party to the Convention.

By virtue of Article 20 of the Convention, the Committee is empowered to receive information and to institute inquiries concerning allegations of systematic practice of torture in the States Parties. The procedure set out in Article 20 of the Convention, is marked by two features: its confidential character, and the pursuit of cooperation with the States Parties concerned.

The Competence conferred upon the Committee by this Article is optional, which means that, at the time of ratifying or acceding to the Convention, a State may declare that it does not recognize it. In that case, and so long as that reservation has not been withdrawn, the Committee may not exercise the powers conferred upon it under Article 20 in respect of that State Party.

Optional Protocol to the Convention against Torture and Other Cruel, Inhuman or Degrading Treatment or Punishment

The Optional Protocol is an addition to the Convention against Torture. It was drafted to strengthen the "protection of people deprived of their liberty" on the background "that further measures are necessary to achieve the purpose of the Convention against Torture".

Like the CAT itself, it is only binding for States that accede to it. The UN Convention against Torture provides a legal framework to combat the practice of torture, while the UN Committee against Torture is a competent body to oversee that States Parties respect their obligations to prohibit, prevent and punish torture. In addition, various norms and mechanisms against torture and ill-treatment also exist at a regional level. Nonetheless, these practices still persist and are widespread throughout the world. For this reason, an entirely new approach was needed to effectively prevent these violations.

This new approach, enshrined in the Optional Protocol to the UN Convention against Torture, is based on the premise that the more open and transparent places of detention are, the less abuse will take place.

Since places of detention are by definition closed to the outside world, persons deprived of their liberty are vulnerable and particularly at risk of torture and other forms of ill-treatment as well as other human rights violations. Furthermore, respect for their fundamental rights depends exclusively upon the authorities in charge of the place of detention and they are dependent upon others for the satisfaction of their most basic needs. Violations of the rights of people deprived of liberty can arise from a policy of repression as well as inadequate systems of oversight.

The novelty of the Optional Protocol to the UN Convention against Torture, compared to existing human rights mechanisms, lies in two factors. Firstly, the system to be established by the Optional Protocol places emphasis on preventing violations rather than reacting to them once they have already occurred. The preventive approach foreseen in the Optional Protocol is based on the regular and periodic monitoring of places of detention through visits to these facilities conducted by expert bodies in order to prevent abuses. In contrast, most existing human rights mechanisms, including the UN Committee against Torture, monitor the situation a *posteriori,* once they receive allegations of abuse.

The other novelty of the Optional Protocol is that it is based on a premise of collaboration with the States Parties to prevent violations, rather than on public condemnation of States Parties for violations already committed. While existing human rights mechanisms, including the CAT, also seek constructive dialogue, they are based on the public examination of States' compliance to its obligations thought the reporting or individual communications system described above. The system foreseen in the Protocol is based more on a process of long-term sustained cooperation and dialogue in order to assist States Parties to implement any necessary changes to prevent torture and ill-treatment in the long term.

Convention on the Rights of the Child

The United Nations Convention on the Rights of the Child is a human rights treaty setting out the civil, political, economic, social, health and cultural rights of children. The Convention generally defines a child as any human being under the age of eighteen, unless an earlier age of majority is recognized by a country's law.

The Convention on the Rights of the Child is the main international instrument for the protection of children's rights, including from all forms of abuse, violence, neglect and exploitation.

The Article of the Convention may be grouped into three categories of rights and a set of guiding principles. Additional provisions of the Convention (article 43 to 54) discuss implementation measures for the Convention, explaining how governments and international organizations like UNICEF will work to ensure children are protected in their rights.

Guiding Principles: The guiding principles of the Convention on the Rights of the Child represent the underlying requirements for any and all rights outlined in the Convention to be realized.

Survival and Development Rights: these are rights to the resources, skills and contributions necessary for the survival and full development of the child. They include rights to adequate food, shelter, clean water, formal education, primary health care, leisure and recreation, cultural activities and information about their rights. These rights require not only the existence of the means to fulfill the rights but also access to them. Specific article address the needs of child refugees, children with disabilities and children of minority or indigenous groups.

The basic rights to life, survival and development of one's full potential under this category include Freedom of thought, conscience and religion (Article 14); Social security (Article 26); Right to Education (Article 28); Leisure, Play and Culture (Article 31); Adequate Standard of Living (Article 27); health and Health Services (Article 24); Rights of Children with Disabilities (Article 23), Refuges Children (Article 22); Preservation of Identy (Article 8); and the Right to Survival and Development (Article 6), among others.

Protection Rights: These rights include protection from all forms of child abuse, neglect, exploitation and cruelty, including the right to special protection in times of war and protection form abuse in the criminal justice system. The CRC is the first international treaty to place a comprehensive legal obligation on States Parties to protect children from all forms of sexual exploitation and abuse. This obligation is an important landmark because it implicitly recognizes that sexual exploitation of children is likely to occur n every country in the world.

The rights under this category include protection against Kidnapping (Article 11): Protection from all forms of violence (Article 19); Child labour (Article 32); Drug abuse (Article 33); Sexual exploitation (Article 34); Abduction, sale and trafficking (Article 35); Detention and punishment (Article 37); and War and armed conflicts (Article 38), among others.

Participation Rights: Children are entitled to the freedom to express opinions and to have a say in matter affecting their social, economic, religious, cultural and political life. Participation rights include the right to express opinions and be heard, the right to information and freedom of association. Engaging these rights as they mature helps children bring about the realization of all their rights and prepares them for an active role in society.

The rights under this category include Respect for the views of the child or the Right to be heard (Article 12); Freedom of expression (Article 13); Freedom of association (Article 15); Right to privacy (Article 16); Access to information and mass media (Article 17); and Freedom of thought, conscience and religion (Article 14), among others.

The equality and interconnection of rights are stressed in the Convention. In addition to government's obligation, children and parents are responsible for respecting the rights of others – particularly each other. Children's understanding of rights will vary particularly each other. Children's understanding of rights will vary depending on age and parents in particular should tailor the issues they discuss, the way in which they answer questions and discipline methods to the age and maturity of the individual child.

Committee on the Rights of the Child

The Committee on the Rights of the Child (CRC) is a body of independent experts that monitors and reports on implementation of the United Nations Convention on the Rights of the Child by governments that ratify the Convention. The Committee also monitors implementation of the Optional Protocol on the involvement of Children in Armed Conflict and the Optional Protocol on the Sale of Children, Child Prostitution and Child Pornography.

States that have ratified the Convention are required to submit initial and periodic reports on the national situation of children's rights to the Committee for examination. The Committee examines each report and raised concerns or makes recommendations to the State party. It also issues occasional 'General Comments' on the interpretation of particular CRC obligations. The Committee cannot consider individual complaints, although child rights may be raised before other committees with competence to consider individual complaints.

In fulfilling its role, the Committee examines reports submitted by the State Parties, also taking into account information from other sources, including information provided by the United Nations (UN) agencies, non-governmental organizations (NGOs, which sometimes submit alternative reports) and occasionally by ombudsmen, human rights commissions and other competent bodies.

Governments of countries that have ratified the Convention are required to report to, and appear before, the United Nations Committee on the Rights of the Child periodically to be examined on their progress with regards to the advancement of the implementation of the convention and the status of child rights in their country.

Optional Protocol on the Involvement of Children in Armed Conflict

According to UNICEF, worldwide, an estimated 300,000 children are engaged in armed conflicts. They are often forcibly recruited or abducted to join armies, some under the age of 10. Many of them have witnessed or taken part in acts of unbelievable violence, often against their own families or communicates. With a view to strengthen implementation of the Convention on the Rights of the Child and increase the protection of children during armed conflicts, the Optional Protocol on the Involvement of Children in Armed Conflict was adopted by resolution A/RES/54/263 of 25 May 2000 at the fifty- fourth session of the General Assembly of the United Nations.

The Protocol requires governments to ensure that children under the age of eighteen are not recruited compulsorily into their armed forces, and calls on governments to do everything feasible to ensure that members of their armed forces who are under eighteen years of age do not take part in hostilities.

The protocol requires that ratifying governments ensure that while their armed forces can accept volunteers below the age of 18, they cannot be conscripted and "State Parties shall take all feasible measures to ensure that members of their armed forces who have not attained the age of 18 years do not take a direct part in hostilities". Non-state actors and guerrilla forces are also forbidden from recruiting anyone under the age of 18 for any purpose. Accordingly, States parties are also required to take legal measures to prohibit independent armed groups from recruiting and using children under the age of 18 n conflicts.

The Optional Protocol obligates states to "take all feasible measures to prevent such recruitment and use, including the adoption of legal measures necessary to prohibit and criminalize such practices" (Article 4).

Likewise, the Optional Protocol requires states to demobilize children within their jurisdiction who have been recruited or used in hospitalities, and to provide assistance for their physical and psychological recovery and social reintegration (Article 6(3)).

The Optional Protocol thus, represents a leap forward in international law to protect children from the harmful effects of recruitment and use in hostilities.

When ratifying the Protocol, States are required to make a declaration regarding the age at which national armed forces permit voluntary recruitment, as well as the steps that States will take to ensure that such recruitment is never forced or coerced. This requirement is particularly important because the Optional Protocol does not establish age 18 as a minimum for voluntary recruitment into the armed force, but only for direct participation in armed conflict.

Optional Protocol on the Sale of Children, Child Prostitution and Child Pornography

The Optional Protocol on the Sale of Children, Child Prostitution and Child Pornography is a protocol to the Convention on the Rights of the Child and criminalizes specific acts relating to the sale of children, child prostitution and child pornography, including attempt to engage in and complicity in such acts. It lays down minimum standards for protecting child victims in criminal justice processes and recognizes the right of victims to seek compensation.

The main premised of the Protocol are that all children must be protected, that such exploitation is criminal in nature, and that the perpetrators must be identified and punished. It encourages strengthening of international cooperation and assistance and the adoption of extra-territorial legislation, but does not provide for exemption from the dual criminality principle.

Since the Optional Protocol applies to specific forms of sexual exploitation, it is important to bear in mind that Article 34 of the Convention on the Rights of the Child (CRC) gives children the right to protection from all forms of sexual exploitation and abuse including the right to recovery and social reintegration under Article 39.

Article 1 of the Optional Protocol declares that states must protect the rights and interests of child victims of trafficking, child prostitution and child pornography, child labour and especially, the worst forms of child labour.

The remaining article in the protocol outline the standards for international law enforcement covering diverse issues such as jurisdictional factors, extradition, mutual assistance in investigations, criminal or extradition proceedings and seizure and confiscation of assets.

The protocol builds on and enhances both the general principles of the CRC and its specific rights, such as those dealing with separation of children from parents, illicit transfer of children and the issue of non-return. It also obliges nations to pass laws within their own territories return; it also obliges nations to pass laws within their own territories against these practices "punishable by appropriate penalties that take into account their grave nature."

Article 8 of the Protocol requires that States Parties "adopt appropriate measures to protect the rights and interests of child victims of the practices prohibited under the present Protocol at all stages of the criminal justice process." This detailed Article contains provisions on the treatment to which child victims are entitled and the rights of those who work with child victims. There is also a final paragraph safeguarding the rights of accused persons to a fair and impartial trial.

Article 8 contains specific rights for children and duties for States. It gives children the right to:

- Procedures that recognize children's vulnerability and special needs, as witnesses and in general (Article 8.1(a));
- Be informed of their rights, their role, the scope, timing and progress of the proceedings and of the disposition of their cases (Article 8.1(b));
- Have their views, needs and concerns presented and considered in proceedings where their personal interests are affected in a manner consistent with the procedural rules of national law (for child victims) (Article 8.1(c));
- Appropriate support services throughout the legal process (Article 8.1(d));
- Privacy and the confidential of information concerning their identity (Article 8.1(e));
- Safety and protection against intimidation and retaliation (Article 8.1(f));
- Procedures free from unnecessary delays (Article 8.1(g)).

In addition, Article 8 assigns States the duty to:

- Investigate, even when the age of the victim needs to be clarified (article 8.2);
- Consider the best interests of the child victim as a primary consideration (article 8.3);
- Provide appropriate training to all those who work with child victims (article 8.4);

The global concern with child exploitation that led to the adoption of this Protocol also led the nearly simultaneous adoption of two other important instruments: the International Labour Organization Convention concerning the Prohibition and Immediate Action for the Elimination of the Worst Forms of Child Labour ('Worst Forms of Child Labour Convention' No. 182 of 17 June 1999) and the Protocol to Prevent, Suppress and Punish Trafficking in Persons, Especially Women and Children, supplementing the United Nations Convention against Transnational Organized Crime (the 'Palermo Protocol' of 15 November 2000).

International Convention on Protection of the Rights of All Migrant Workers and Members of their Families

The United Nations Convention on the Protection of the Rights of All Migrant Workers and Members of Their Families (ICMRW) is the only UN convention devoted specifically to safeguarding the fundamental rights of undocumented migrants and addressing their needs. The ICMRW defines migrant workers as follows:

"The term "migrant worker" refers to a person who is engaged or has been engaged in a remunerated activity in a State of which he or she is not a national."

According to UNOHCHR, an estimated 214 million people currently live and/or work outside their country of origin as migrant workers and since they are outside the legal protection of their home countries, migrants are often vulnerable to abuse and exploitation. In December 1990 therefore, the UN General Assembly adopted the International Convention on the Protection of the Rights of All Migrant Workers and Members of their Families.

The Convention is by far the most comprehensive international instrument for the protection and promotion of the fundamental rights of migrants. The strength of the

Convention lies in enabling all those persons, who quality as migrant workers under its provisions, to enjoy their human rights regardless of their legal status.

Thus, the Convention protects both documented and undocumented workers by setting human rights standards that individual States must guarantee. Indeed, when a State rectifies or accedes to the Convention, it undertakes to adopt the legislative and other measures that are necessary to implement the provisions of the Convention. Furthermore, States undertake to ensure that migrants whose rights have been violated may seek judicial remedy.

In order for the Convention to become a binding instrument of international law, it must be ratified by 20 States. Thirteen years after its adoption by the UN General Assembly, on 14 March 2003, Guatemala became the 20th ratifying State, followed by EI Salvador on the same day, thus making it a legally binding international human rights instrument.

The rights of migrant workers as established by the Convention can be divided into two broad categories:

- **Part III:** Rights of Migrant Workers and Members of their Family; Applicable to All Migrant Workers (including the 'undocumented' ones)

- **Part IV:** Specific Rights of Migrant Workers and Members of their Families; Applicable only to Migrant Workers in a Regular Situation.

Migrant workers experience among the lowest incomes, poorest working conditions, and fewest benefits from social services, yet contribute significantly towards strengthening the economics of the states where they work. The lack of citizenship and resident status are key factors in understanding the conditions that migrant workers experience, for without a vote they are unable to make politicians accountable. Consequently, it is difficult to enact to make politicians accountable. Consequently, it is difficult to enact legislation or to enforce extant laws offering protection, leaving migrant workers particularly vulnerable to exploitation by employers and without the benefit of social services provided by the state.

The countries from which these workers come and those in which they work have a shared responsibility to lessen the burdens on them by protecting and promoting their rights. This can be done by increasing and engaging in international cooperation in the interest of promoting their rights and preventing abusive conditions.

The Convention applies to the entire migration process, including preparation for migration, departure, transit and the entire period of stay and remunerated activity in the state of employment as well as return to the state of origin or of habitual residence. The majority of the rights are relevant to the receiving state, though there are also obligations specifically placed upon the sending state.

The Convention begins with the familiar prohibition of discrimination in the enjoyment of the Convention's rights. The Convention then sets out in two separate parts the rights, firstly, of all migrant workers and members of their families, irrespective of their migration status and, secondly, the additional rights of documented migrant workers and their families. In defining he civil and political rights of migrant workers, the Convention follows very closely the language of the ICCPR. Some article restate the rights taking into account the particular situation of migrant workers, such as consular notification rights upon arrest and specific provisions concerning breaches of migration law and destruction of identity documents and prohibition of collective expulsion. In addition, the right to property, originally protected in the Declaration but not contained in the ICCPR, is specifically enumerated for migrant workers.

The convention defines the economic, social and cultural rights of migrant workers in the light of their particular situation. Thus, for example, at a minimum urgent medical care must be provided, as it would be provided to a national, and the children of migrant workers have the basic right of access to education irrespective of legal status. Additional rights exist for workers who are properly documented, and to particular classes of migrant workers such as frontier, seasonal, itinerant and project-tied workers.

Committee on the Protection of the Rights of All Migrant Workers and Members of the Families

The Committee on the Protection of the Rights of All Migrant Workers and Members of their Families (CMW) is the body of independent experts that monitors implementation of the International Convention on the Protection of the Rights of All Migrant Workers and Members of Their Families by its State parties.

All States parties are obliged to submit regular reports to the Committee on how the rights are being implemented. States must report initially one year after acceding to the Convention and then every five years. The Committee will examine each report and address its concerns and recommendations to the State party in the form of "concluding observations".

The Committee will also, under certain circumstances, be able to consider individual complaints or communications from individuals claiming that their rights under the Convention have been violated once 10 States parties have accepted this procedure in accordance with Article 77 of the Convention.

Members of the Committee are elected by states parties by means of a secret ballot, with due regard to fair geographical distribution, including both States of origin and States of employment of migrant workers, and to representation of the world's main legal systems. These independent experts are persons of "high moral character, with recognized competence in the field covered by the International Convention on the Protection of the Rights of All Migrant Workers and Members of their Families.

States parties accept the obligation under Article 73 to report on the steps they have taken to implement the Convention within one year of its entry into force for the State concerned, and thereafter every five years. The reports also are expected to indicate problems encountered in implementing the Convention, and to provide information on migration flows. After examining the reports, the Committee transmits such comments as it may consider appropriate to the State party concerned.

Under Article 77, a State party may make a declaration recognizing the competence of the committee to receive and consider communications from or on behalf of individuals within the State's jurisdiction who claim that their rights under the Convention have been violated. Such communications may be received only if they concern a State party which has so recognized the competence of the Committee.

If the Committee is satisfied that the matter has not been, and is not being examined by another procedure of international investigation or settlement, and that all domestic remedies have been exhausted, it may request written explanations and express its views after having considered all the available information. The individual communication procedure requires 10 declarations by States parties to enter into force.

Convention on the Rights of Persons with Disabilities

The United Nations Convention on the Rights of Persons with Disabilities (CRPD) was adopted by the UN General Assembly on 13 December 2006 and came into force on 3 May 2008. The purpose of the Convention is to promote, protect and ensure the full and equal enjoyment of all human rights and fundamental freedoms by all persons with disabilities, and to promote respect for their inherent dignity.

The CRPD consists of 50 articles addressing the full array of civil, political, economic, social, and cultural rights. The Convention does not seek to create new rights for disabled persons, but rather elaborates and clarifies existing obligations for countries within the context of disability.

The Preamble clearly endorses a social approach to disability referred to as the social model of disability - by recognizing that "disability is an evolving concept and that disability results from interaction between persons with impairments and attitudinal and environmental barriers that hinders their full and effective participation in society on an equal basis with others".

It establishes a committee of experts to monitor its implementation at the international level and also provides for the operation of independent national-level monitoring mechanisms. The CRPD also has an Optional Protocol that recognizes "the competence of the Committee on the Rights of Persons with Disabilities to receive and consider communications from or on behalf of individuals or groups of individuals subject to its jurisdiction who claim to be victims of a violation by the State Party of the provisions of the convention." The CRPD is therefore, comprehensive not only in terms of its substantive content, but also in the manner in which monitoring and implementation at all levels is addressed.

The convention is intended as a Human Rights instrument with an explicit, social development dimension. It adopts a broad categorization of persons with disabilities and reaffirms that all persons with all types of disabilities must enjoy all human rights and fundamental freedoms. It clarifies and qualifies how all categories of rights apply to persons with disabilities and identifies areas where adaptation have to be made for persons with disabilities to effectively exercise their rights and areas where their rights have been violated, and where protection of rights must be reinforced.

The Convention was adopted as a response to the fact that although pre-existing human rights conventions offer considerable potential to promote and protect the rights of persons with disabilities, such persons continued being denied their human rights and were kept on the margins of society across the world.

Principally, the Convention recognizes that persons with disabilities have inherent rights, and that they are capable of claiming those rights and making decisions for their lives based on their free and informed consent as well as being active members of society.

Article 3 of the Convention identifies a set of overarching and foundational principles. These guide the interpretation and implementation of the entire Convention, cutting across all issues. They are the starting point for understanding and interpreting the rights of persons with disabilities, providing benchmarks against which each right is measured.

The Convention is intended as a human rights instrument with an explicit, social development dimension. It adopts a broad categorization of persons with disabilities and reaffirms that all persons with all types of disabilities and reaffirms that all persons with all types of disabilities must enjoy all human rights and fundamental freedoms. It clarifies and qualifies how all categories of rights apply to persons with disabilities and identifies areas where adaptations have to be made for persons with disabilities to effectively exercise their rights and areas where their rights have been violated, and where protection of rights must be reinforced.

Optional Protocol to the Convention on the Rights of Persons with Disabilities

The Optional Protocol to the Convention on the rights of Persons with Disabilities is a side-agreement to the convention on the Rights of Persons with Disabilities. It was adopted on 13 December 2006, and entered into force at the same time as its parent Convention, on 3 May 2008.

The Optional Protocol establishes and individual complaints mechanism for the Convention similar to those of the International covenant on Civil and Political Rights, Convention on the Elimination of All Forms of Discrimination against Women and D=Convention on the Elimination of All Forms of racial Discrimination.

Parties agree to recognize the competence of the committee on the Rights of Persons with Disabilities to consider complaints from individuals or groups who claim their rights under the Convention have been violated. The committee can request information from and make recommendations to a party.

In addition, parties may permit the Committee to investigate report on and make recommendations on "grave or systematic violations" of the Convention. Parties may opt out of this obligation on signature or ratification. The Optional Protocol required ten ratifications to come into force.

The Optional Protocol to the Convention allows individuals who are victims of violations of Convention to present complaints before the Committee against a state that has ratified the convention and violates its obligations.

International Convention for the Protection of All Persons from Enforced Disappearance

Enforced disappearance or the arrest, detention or abduction of a person by the state or agents acting n its behalf, who subsequently deny that the person is being held or conceal their whereabouts, placing them outside the protection of the law, has been carried out by regimes all over the world from the Second World war until today.

According to the International Committee of the Red Cross (ICRC), enforced disappearance constitutes a violation of international humanitarian law and human rights, both in international and non-international armed conflict. "It violates, or threatens to violate, a number of fundamental customary rules such as the prohibition of arbitrary deprivation of liberty, the prohibition of torture and other cruel and inhuman treatment, and the prohibition of murder." To prevent the practice of enforced disappearance, which causes unspeakable anguish, fear and sorrow for thousands of families, there was an urgent need for a legally binding universal instrument.In December 2006, the UN adopted the International Convention for the Protection of All Persons from Enforced Disappearance.

The Convention aims to prevent enforced disappearances, uncover the truth when they do occur, punish the perpetrators and provide reparations to the victims and their families. On 23 December 2010, four years after the adoption of the convention by the UN General Assembly, the ICPAPED eventually reached the 20th ratification which was necessary for its entry into force. Iraq was the 20th country that ratified this international treaty.

The Convention is perhaps the first international human rights instrument which recognizes the right of any person not to be subjected to enforced disappearance. It recognizes it as a non-dirigible right which means that no circumstances may be invoked as a justification to carry out enforced disappearances (Article 1 (2)).

Key Provisions

Article 5 of the convention asserts that the widespread practice of enforced disappearance constitutes a crime against humanity and this potentially enables, for instance, the involvement of the Intercalation Criminal Court. Each state party is required to incorporate the provisions of the Convention in its domestic criminal law by making enforced disappearance an offence under its criminal law; holding any person involved, criminally responsible; and making the offence punishable by appropriate penalties.

Article 6 describes who can be held criminally responsible for an enforced disappearance. According to the Article, "Any person who commits, orders, solicits or induces the commission of, attempts to commit, is an accomplice to or participates in an enforced disappearance".

To prevent the occurrence of enforced disappearances, the Convention requires states to adopt stringent safeguards. These preventive measures can be of consequence for national laws, for instance regarding detention. The Convention prohibits secret detention and gives specific rules and regulations with regard to deprivation of liberty including the maintenance of up-to-date official registers of persons deprived of liberty. For all places where people are deprived of their liberty, a register like this should be available. It also requires states to impose sanction on conduct that undermines these safeguards.

Article 21 requires persons to be released from prison in a manner permitting reliable verification that they have actually been released.

Article 24 obliges States to provide training to law enforcement personnel.

The convention contains several provisions on protective measures after a disappearance occurs. The State should for instance enable individual to report an enforced disappearance, protect witnesses and investigate complaints and reports of disappearances.

The convention also establishes several rights for victims. Enforced has been deprived of her/his liberty. Relatives of the disappeared are included in the definition of victim as well as any person who has suffered harm as a direct result of the enforced disappearance.

The right to information is guaranteed under Article 18. It requires every person with a legitimate interest to have access to basic information such as the date, time and place of the deprivation of liberty and the whereabouts of the person. Restrictions of such information are only permitted when a person is under judicial control and the restriction does not lead to an enforced disappearance.

The right to know the truth is guaranteed in Article 24. States should also ensure reparation (including restitution, rehabilitation, guarantees of non-repetition) and prompt and adequate compensation as well as the right to form organizations and associations trying to address the enforced disappearances.

With regard to Children, Article 25 States that States are responsible for the prevention and punishment of the wrongful removal of children who are subjected to enforced disappearance or whose parents are subjected to enforced disappearance. States should search for, identify and return such children to their families.

The Convention also recognizes the importance of International Cooperation (Article 9, 10, 11, 13, 14, 15) to make the convention effective since in many instances, enforced disappearance concern the involvement of more than one State. To this end, it requires State Parties to cooperate in searching for disappeared persons and, in the event of death, exhuming and identifying them and returning the mortal remains.

State parties should submit suspects who are found on their territory to the competent authorities, extradite them to another state, or surrender them to an international criminal court. They should also take care that no person is expelled, returned surrendered or extradited who may be in danger of being subjected to enforced disappearance.

Committee on Enforced Disappearances

The Committee on Enforced Disappearances (CED) is the body of independent experts which monitors implementation of the Convention by the States Parties. All States parties are obliged to submit regular reports to the Committee on how the rights are being implemented. States must report initially within two years of accepting the Convention. The Committee examines each report and makes such suggestions and general recommendations on the report as it may consider appropriate and forwards these to the State Party concerned.

In accordance with Article 31, a State Party may at the time of ratification of this Convention or at any time afterwards declare that it recognizes the competence of the Committee to receive and consider communications from or on behalf of individuals subject to its jurisdiction claiming to be victims of a violation by this State Party of provisions of this Convention.

Unique to the Convention is an urgent humanitarian procedure to search for and find disappeared persons on the request of a relative. This is similar to the task of the existing 'Working Group on Enforced and Involuntary Disappearances'. The Committee has the power to bring "widespread and systematic" practice of enforced disappearance to the attention of the UN General Assembly. The NGOs play an important role before the Committee on Enforced Disappearance. They will be heard before the session of considering the periodic reports of every country and they will be invited to submit written information.

Conclusion

Thus, human rights also called positive rights require active intervention, not abstentions on the part of States. The enjoyment of these rights requires a major commitment of resources and therefore their realization cannot be immediate as in the case of civil and political rights. Economic, social and cultural rights are based fundamentally on the concept of social equality. Realization of these rights, which is generally called the rights of second generation, has been somewhat slow in coming.

In addition to the above rights there is another kind of rights which may be enjoyed by individuals collectively such as right to self-determination or the physical protection of the regroup as such thought the prohibition of genocide. Such rights are referred to collective rights.

Human Rights law obliges a State to refrain from causing harm to its own nationals or other persons within its territorial jurisdiction. Thus, a State is not free to treat its nationals as it pleases despite the fact that it is sovereign. The greatest impact of Human Rights law has been to erode the absolute control which a State had in the classical period. The idea that human rights could be protected by International Law in addition to municipal law developed slowly mainly because State sovereignty-a fundamental principle of international law since its emergence in the seventeenth century, proved a stumbling block in the efforts to impose international legal obligations upon States to protect individuals.

Refrences

[1] Maurice Cranston, What are Human Rights? P. 36

Chapter IV

National Standard

Introduction

The Right to Health has clear links to many other rights. The realization of the Right to Health requires the fulfillment of several interconnected rights of a range of determinates, such as food, education, environment, housing, working conditions, poverty, health care and so on. Unless all these determinants are also addressed, it is not possible to ensure the right to health. The denial or enjoyment of the rights mentioned above can impact a person's ability to achieve the highest attainable standard of health, and conversely, the health status determines the enjoyment of other rights, i.e. a person who is not 'healthy' may not be able to participate fully and actively in economic, social or political activities in society.

Thus, when the State violates one specific right, its interconnectedness to various other rights results in a chain of violations, each of which individually stands as a right, and has its won set of norms and obligations on the state[1]. For example, The Right to Health is interdependent on the Right of Food. In Article 24(2) of the Convention on the Rights of the Child (CRC)[2] and Article 12(2) of Convention on the Elimination of Discrimination against Women (CEDAW)[3] the right to food is considered part of the right to health of both women and children. Therefore, when considering the Right to Health, the above-mentioned Articles should also be taken into account. This is true of all other rights connected to the determinates of health – environment, exclusion, prohibition and basis of sex, caste, class, education, etc.

Similarly Article 21 of the Constitution of India guarantees the Right to life of every citizen, and imposes the duty to protect this right upon the state. The Supreme Court of India has previously stated that the right to life includes the right to live with dignity and all that goes along with it, including the right to food. For example, in response to the writ petition on the 'Right ot Food' by the people's Union for Civil Liberties (PUCL), Rajasthan, in 2001, the Supreme Court judged that the state governments are indeed violation Article 21 of the constitution of India. The Court's judgment in its very essence recognizes the justifiability of the Right to Food, and the protection of this right under the Constitution. The Supreme Court affirmed that where people are unable to feed themselves adequately, governments have an obligation to provide for them, ensuring at the very least that they are not exposed to malnourishment, starvation and other related problems.[4]

The Constitution of India

The Constitution of India does not explicitly recognize health as a Fundamental Right. However, it recognizes the right to life, equality, and freedom of speech, expression and opportunity and to seek judicial redress for enforcement of these rights as fundamental rights. Right to Health is included in

Article 47 of the Directive Principles of State Policy. These constitutional provisions must be interpreted expansively to understand and ensure women's right to health.

The Preamble to the Constitution highlights some of the core values and principles that guide the Constitution of India. Although the preamble is not regarded as a part of the Constitution and is not enforceable in a court of law, the Constitution is interpreted in the light of the preamble and in a majority of decisions the Supreme Court of India has held that the objectives of justice, liberty, equality and fraternity stated in the preamble constitute the basic structure of the Constitution. The preamble directs the state to initiate measures to establish justice, equality, ensure dignity, etc. which have a direct bearing on women's health.

The following Fundamental Rights contained in Part III of the Constitution are related to women's right to health and health care. Right to Equality and Freedom (Article 14-17 and 19) ensure the right to equality before the law and equal protection of the law, prohibition of discrimination on the basis of sex, caste, religion, race or place of birth, equal opportunity in matters of employment and abolition of untouchability. However, the right to equality does not take away the right of the State to initiate affirmative action or provide special provisions for women and marginalized communities (especially women from schedule castes and tribes). In the context of health, any form of discrimination, be it gender or practice of untouchability, has severe implications for health, preventing or limiting access to basic needs and opportunities that impact health and access to health care. For example Women are traditionally responsible for fetching water. Depending on the distance of source of water, the location, the woman's age, caste, health status and various other conditions at home impact her access to water, which in turn affects her health and the health of others in her family.

Right to Protection of Life and Personal Liberty (Article 21) of the Constitution of India ensure that "No person shall be deprived of his / her life or personal liberty, except according to the procedure established by law." While the provision of health services is essential to ensure good health, there are several others factors that influence a person's health. The Supreme Court first recognized this in *Bandhua Mukti Morcha vs. Union of India,* a case concerning the living and working conditions of stone quarry workers in Haryana (near Delhi) and whether these living and working conditions deprived them of their right to life. "The court held that humane working conditions were essential to the pursuit of the Right to Life. It lay down that workers should be provided with medical facilities, clean drinking water and sanitation facilities so that they may live with human dignity".[5] Right against exploitation (Articles 23-24) secures a person or persons against prohibition of traffic in human beings and forced labour, employment of children in factories, mine, or in any other hazardous employment.[6]

Directive Principles of State Policy

As mentioned earlier, the reference to Right to Health in the Indian Constitution is contained in Article 47, which is consigned to the Directive Principle of State Policy

(DPSP) section, with regard to health and health care, article 47 states that it is the Duty of the State to raise the level of nutrition and the standard of living and to improve public health.[7]

Another principle is that the state must strive to secure social order for the promotion of welfare of the people by securing and protecting as effectively, as it may a social order in which justice, social, economic and political, shall inform all the institution of the national life. The state shall, in particular, strive to minimize the inequalities in income, and endeavor to eliminate inequalities in status, facilities and opportunities, not only amongst individuals but also amongst groups of people residing in different areas or engaged in different vocations.[8]

The State must try to ensure that its policies are based on people's (men and women equally) right to an adequate means of livelihood; ensure equitable distribution of wealth and prevent the concentration of wealth and means of production. Equal remuneration regardless of sex; ensure that the existing system of mot abuse the health and strength of men and women, and childrenand that they are not pushed by economic necessity to work in occupations that is deter mental to their age.[9]

Forming networks and coalitions to strengthen campaigns by bringing large numbers of individuals, organizations together on a particular issue/concern. One such example is the Medico Friend Circle, an all-India network of individuals from diverse backgrounds, who have come together to address the health situation in the country.

Gathering information, feedback from community including women to gather first hand information and accurate/true report of the situation. This kind of documentation has been a useful mechanism for campaigns.

Organizing fact finding visits to affected areas and communities. For example a fact finding mission to Gujarat after the carnage, was organized by the Medico Friend Circle (MFC) to assess the functioning of health care services and to examine the extent to which the affected community, particularly women, were able to access these services. Documentation of violations played a critical role in monitoring and highlighting the accountability of the State and other Institution.

Organizing People's Tribunals (Jan Sunwais) to facilitate expression of peoples' grievances and experiences of violations, which they may find difficult to voice in any other forum, this has been a very useful way to create an interface between the people, the State and other relevant actors. For example, several tribunals were organized, in which the survivors of the Bhopal Gas Tragedy presented the reality of their situation – its impact on their health, corruption in disbursement of compensation and several other issues. Prayas, an NGO in Rajasthan, also documented cases of violations of women's right to health care and organized a series of public hearings in collaboration with the National Commission for Women and the State Women's Commission in different districts across the State.

Right against Arbitrary Arrest and Problems of Custodial Violence

The problem of arbitrary arrest and custodial violence are prevalent throughout the country. The manner in which it is committed is horrifying. Generally police arrest a person without warrant in connection with the investigation of an offence and without recording the arrest. The arrested person is subjected to torture by the police in the police lock- up for extracting information for the purposes of further investigation or for the recovery of case property or for extracting confession[10].

Moved by such flagrant violation of human rights and fundamental freedom of the citizens at the hand of law enforcing agencies, the Supreme Court has issued certain directives in *D.K.Basu v.State of*

West Bengal[11] to be followed in all cases of arrest or detention till the legal provisions are made by the Parliament in this respect. These requirements are as follows.

1. "The police personal carrying out the arrest and handling the interrogation of the arrestee should bear accurate, visible and clear identification and name tags with their designations. The particulars of all such police personnel who handle interrogation of the arrestee must be recorded in the register.

2. The police officer carrying out the arrest of the arrestee shall prepare a memo of arrest at the time of arrest and such memo shall be attested by at least one witness, who may either be a member of the family of the arrestee or a respectable person of the locality from where the arrest is made. It shall also be countersigned by the arrestee and shall contain the time and date of arrest.

3. A person who has been arrested or detained and is being held in custody in a police station or interrogation centre or other lock-up, shall be entitled to have one friend or relative or other person known to him or having interest in his welfare being informed, as soon as practicable, that he has been arrested and is being detained at the particular place, unless the attesting witness of the memo of arrest is himself such a friend or a relative of the arrestee.

4. The time, place of arrest and venue of custody of an arrestee must be notified by the police where the next friend or relative of the arrestee lives outside the district or town through the Legal Aid Organisation in the District and the police station of the area concerned telegraphically within a period of 8 to 12 hours after the arrest.

5. The person arrested must be made aware of this right to have someone informed of his arrest or detention as soon as he is put under arrest or is detained.

6. An entry must be made in the diary at the place of detention regarding the arrest of the person which shall also disclose the name of the next friend of the person who has been informed of the arrest and the names and particulars of the police officials in whose custody the arrestee is.

7. The arrestee should, where he so requests, be also examined at the time of his arrest and major and minor injuries, if any present on his/her body must be recorded at that time. The 'Inspection Memo' must be signed both by the arrestee and the police officer effecting the arrest and its copy provided to the arrestee.

8. The arrestee should be subjected to medical examination by a trained doctor every 48 hours during his detention in custody by a doctor on the panel of approved doctors appointed by Director, Health Services of the State or Union Territory concerned. Director, Health Services should prepare such a panel for all tehsils and districts as well.

9. Copies of all the documents including the memo of arrest, referred to above, should be sent to the Area Magistrate for his/her record.

10. The arrestee may be permitted to meet his/her lawyer during interrogation, though not throughout the interrogation.

11. A police control room should be provided at all District and State head quarters, where the information regarding the arrest and the place of custody of the arrestee shall be communicated by

the officer causing the arrest, within 12 hours of effecting the arrest and at the police control room it should be displayed on a conspicuous notice board".

Right to Work, Right to Education and Right to Public Assistance

Article 41 of the Indian Constitution requires that " the State, shall within the limits of its economic capacity and development, make effective provision, for securing the right to work, to education and to public assistance in cases of unemployment, old age ,sickness and disablement, and in other cases of undeserved want .''

Right to Just and Humane Conditions of Work

Article 42 of the Constitution of India requires that " the State shall make provisions for securing just and humane conditions of work and for maternity relief ."

This Article exhibits the concern of the framers of the Constitution for the welfare of the workers.

Right to Living Wages for Workers

Article 43 of the Indian Constitution provides : " The State shall endeavour to secure, by suitable legislation or economic organisation or in any other way, to all workers, agricultural, industrial or otherwise , a living wage ,conditions of work ensuring a decent standard of life and full enjoyment of leisure and social and cultural opportunities and ,in particular, the State shall endeavour to promote cottage industries on an individual or cooperative basis in rural areas ."

Article 43 sets out the ideals to which our Social Welfare State has to approximate in an attempt to ameliorate the living conditions of the workers.

In *Bijay Cotton Mill Ltd. v. State of Ajmer*[12], the Court held that the fixation of minimum wages of labourers under the *Minimum Wages Act 1948,* was in the interest of the general public and ,therefore , not violative of the freedom of trade , secured to the citizens under Article 19(1)(g).

The compulsory closure of the industrial concerns on National and Festival holidays has been justified under Article 43 so as to enable the workers to fully enjoy their leisure and participate in social and cultural activities[13].

The 'living wage' is to be distinguished from 'minimum' and 'fair wage'. While 'living wage' is such wage as enables the male earner to provide for himself and his family not merely the bare necessities but a measure of frugal comfort[14].

Right against Exploitation

Articles 23 and 24 of Indian Constitution guarantee "the fundamental right against exploitation". This right is secured to every person, whether citizen, non-citizen or an alien. The protection contained therein, is available not only against the State but also against private individuals[15]. These provisions are to be read with Articles 39(e) and 39 (f) which impose obligation on the State for protection of children and youth against exploitation and against moral and material abandonment .

Article 23(1) provides "Traffic in human beings and beggar and other similar forms of forced labour are prohibited and any contravention of this provision shall be an offence punishable in accordance with law"

It prohibits "traffic in human beings", "beggar" and other similar forms of forced labour . It further declares that any contravention of this prohibition shall be an offence punishable by law . Article 23(1) , thus , envisages legislation for the enforcement of the prohibition contained therein .

To enforce the constitutional prohibition against *"traffic in human beings"*, Parliament , in the exercise of powers under Article 35 , enacted the *Suppression of Immoral Traffic in Women and Girls Act , 1956* . The law is renamed as the *Immoral Traffic (Prevention) Act , 1956* .

In *Gaurav Jain v. Union of India*[16], a three- Judge Bench of the Supreme Court held that the problem of *prostitution* had become one of serious nature and required considerable and effective attention. The Court issued directions for the constitution of a Committee to examine the problem and for the segregation of the children of prostitutes from their mothers living in the prostitute homes and to allow them to mingle with others and become part of the society .

Employment of Children

Article 24 of the Indian Constitution provides*:" No child below the age of fourteen years shall be employed to work in any factory or mine or engaged in any other hazardous employment"*.

The Supreme Court in *Labourers Working on Salal Hydro Project v. State of J & K*[17], held that building construction work was such hazardous employment where children below 14 years should not be employed .

Right to Education (Article 21-A)

Article 21A of Indian Constitution provides:" The State shall provide free and compulsory education to all children of the age of 6 to 14 years in such manner as the State may , by law, determine".

Article 21A added by the Constitution (86th Amendment) Act , 2002 makes education from 6 to 14 years old ,an independent fundamental right , within the meaning of Part III of the Constitution. It is popularly known as ''*primary education.*"

Right of a Citizen to admission to Educational Institutions (Article 29 (2))

Article 29(2) provides :" *No citizen shall be denied admission into any educational institution maintained by the State or receiving aid out of State funds on grounds only of religion , race , caste , language or any of them*".

In *State of Bombay v. Bombay Education Society*[18], the Government's Order banning admission of all those whose language was not English into schools having English as medium of instruction was struck down as violative of Article 29 (2) .

Compulsory Early Childhood Care & Education for Children (Article 45)

Article 45 of Indian Constitution provides : " The State shall endeavour to provide early childhood care and education for all children until they complete the age of six years".

Promotion of Educational and Economic Interest of Weaker Sections (Article 46)

Article 46 of Indian Constitution enjoins :" The State Shall promote with special care the educational and economic interests of the weaker sections of the people , and , in particular , of the Scheduled Castes and the Scheduled Tribes , and shall protect them from social injustice and all forms of exploitation".

The expression "weaker sections of the people" is not defined in the Constitution . It includes all sections of the society , who were rendered weaker due to various causes including poverty and natural and physical handicaps[19].

Article 21 of Indian Constitution and Prisoners Rights

Above all the Human Rights Enforcement Agencies of India the Supreme Court of India has supreme inherent powers to get the human rights properly enforced in Indian territory.

In *Maneka Gandhi v. Union of India*[20], the Supreme Court has interpreted Article 21 so as to have widest possible amplitude . Protection of Article 21 is well extended to under-trials , prisoners and even to the convicts . It has been ruled that a prisoner , be he a convict , under-trial or a detenu , does not cease to be a human being . His conviction does not reduce him into a non - person whose rights are subject to the whims of the prison administration , the Court said. Even when lodged in the jail , continued to enjoy all his fundamental rights including the right to life . On being convicted of crime and deprived of their liberty in accordance with the procedure established by law , prisoners still retain the residue of Constitutional Rights . In this context , it may, therefore , be stated that the Supreme Court while interpreting Article 21 , has laid down a new constitutional and prison jurisprudence . Out of several important rights recognized by the Human Rights Enforcement Agencies of India some rights or protections for the prisoners are as below .

Right to Free Legal Aid -Right to Appeal

The right to first appeal from the Sessions Court to High Court , as provided in the *Criminal Procedure Code* , has been held in *M.H. Hoscot v. State of Maharashtra*[21], to be a component of fair procedure and basic to civilized jurisprudence .

While holding the right to appeal as integral to fair procedure , the Court explained that " the two important ingredients of the right to appeal *: (a) service of a copy of a judgment to the prisoner in time to enable him to file an appeal, and (b) provision of free legal service to a prisoner who is indigent or otherwise disabled from securing legal assistance*".

The Court further laid down that right to free legal aid at the cost of the State to an accused, who could not afford legal services for reasons of poverty , indigence or incommunicado situation , was part of fair, just and reasonable procedure implicit in Article 21. *Free legal aid* to the indigent has been declared to be" a State's duty and not government charity".

Right to Speedy Trial

*A procedure cannot be reasonable, fair or just unless it ensures a **speedy trial** for determination of the guilt of the person deprived of his liberty[22].*

In *Hussainara Khatoon (No I) v. Home Secretary, State of Bihar*[23], it was brought to the notice of the Supreme Court that an alarming large number of men, women, children including, were kept in prisons for years awaiting trial in Courts of law. The Court took a serious note of the situation and observed that it was a *crying shame on the judicial system which permitted incarceration of men and women for such long periods of time without trials*.

Though, the right to speedy trial has not been specifically enumerated as a fundamental right in our Constitution, but the Court held that" it is implicit in the broad sweep and content of Article 21 as interpreted by the Court in *Maneka Gandhi v. Union of India*[24]. The Court thus observed:

No procedure which does not ensure a reasonably quick trial can be regarded as reasonable, fair or just and it would fall foul of Article 21.

Reiterating the above view with approval in *Hussainara Khatoon (No II) v. Home Secretary, State of Bihar*[25], the Court held that detention of under-trial prisoners, in jail for period longer than what they would have been sentenced if convicted, was illegal as being in violation of Article 21.The Court, thus, *ordered the release from jail of all those under-trial prisoners, who had been in jail for longer period than what for which they could have been sentenced had they been convicted*.

Having noticed that people in India were simply disgusted with the State of affairs and were fast losing faith in the Judiciary because of the inordinate delay in disposal of the cases, the Apex Court in *Pradeep Kumar Verma v. State of Bihar*[26], required the authorities to do the needful in the matter urgently to ensure speedy disposal of cases, "before the situation goes totally out of control"[27].

In *A .R.Antulay v. R.S.Nayak*[28], a Constitution Bench of five learned Judges of the Supreme Court dealt with the question and laid down certain guidelines for ensuring speedy trial of offences[29].

A Constitutional Bench of seven learned Judges of the Apex Court in *P. Ramchandra Rao v. State of Karnataka*[30], reiterated with approval the propositions expounding the right to speedy trial, laid down as guidelines in *A.R.Antulay's case*[31].

Right against Inhuman Treatment –Third Degree Methods

The incidents of torture, assault, injury and deaths in police custody, have been said to be the worst form of human rights violation[32].

In *Kishore Singh v. State of Rajasthan*[33], the Court held that the use of " third degree " methods by the police was violative of Article 21.

Right against Custodial Violence

In *Sheela Barse v. State of Maharashtra*[34] the Supreme Court condemned violence committed on women prisoners confined in the police lock-up in the city of Bombay.

Later in *D. K. Basu v. State of W.B.*[35], the Supreme Court held that torture by police struck a blow at the rule of law. *Custodial Violence* has been held to be a calculated assault on human dignity, perhaps one of the worst crimes in a civilized society governed by *Rule of Law*. Any form of torture or cruel, inhuman or degrading treatment, would fall within the inhibition of Article 21, whether it occurred during investigation, interrogation or otherwise.

Right to a fair trial /fair investigation

Free and fair trial has been said to be the sine qua non of Article 21. It is said that justice should not be done but it should be seen to have been done. So said, the Supreme Court in *K.Anbazhagan v. Supdt. of Police*[36], transferred, the trial of cases pending against the C.M. of Tamil Nadu from the Court of Addl. Sessions Judge, Chennai to the State of Karnataka with the direction to the latter to appoint special judge for the trial of the cases.

Fair investigation has been held included in *fair trial*. The Supreme Court in *Nirmal Singh Kahlon v. State of Punjab*[37] observed: "fair investigation and fair trial are concomitant to preservation of fundamental right of an accused under Article 21 of the Constitution of India". Holding that the State had a larger obligation, i.e. to maintain law and order, public order and preservation of peace and harmony in the society, the Court said that a victim of a crime was equally entitled to a fair investigation.

The Apex Court in *Zahira Habibullah Sheikh v. State of Gujrat*[38], said that *right to fair trial* be available not only to the accused but also to the victims, their family members and relatives, as also, the society at large. The right has been held to be a part of *rule of law* which is an important facet of Articles 21 and 14.

Right to Bail

In *Babu Singh v. State of U.P.*[39], the appellants, six in number, were acquitted by the Sessions Judge in a murder case. In appeal by the State, the High Court convicted them and sentenced them to life imprisonment. The appellants applied for bail during pendency of their appeal before the Supreme Court.

The appellants were the entire male members of their family and all of them were in jail. For that reason, their defence was likely to be jeopardized. During appeal before the High Court, the State did not press for their custody. During that period of five years, there was nothing to indicate that there had been any conduct on their part suggestive of disturbing the peace of the locality, threatening anyone in the village or otherwise thwarting the life of the community or the course of justice.

Keeping in view the above circumstances, the Supreme Court held the appellants eligible to be enlarged on bail.

Having regard to the above consideration, the Supreme Court held that "right to bail" was included in the "personal liberty" under Article 21 and its refusal would be deprivation of that liberty which could be authorized in accordance with the procedure established by law.

However, recently in *Rajesh Ranjan Yadav v. C.B.I.*[40], the Apex Court has ruled that there is no absolute rule that a long period of incarceration, by itself, would entitle the accused to obtain bail. It depends on facts and circumstances of each case.

Right against handcuffing

Handcuffing has been held to be prima facie inhuman and therefore unreasonable, over-harsh and at the first flush arbitrary". It has been held to be unwarranted and violative of Article 21.

In *Prem Shankar v. Delhi Administration*[41], the Supreme Court, by majority, struck down Para 26.22 of the *Punjab Police Rules*, 1934, as violative of Articles 14,19 and

21. Para 26.22 of the Rules provided that every under-trial who was accused of a non-bailable offence punishable with more than three years prison term would be routinely handcuffed. The Court ruled that *handcuffing should be resorted to only when there was " clear and present danger of escape " of the accused under-trial, breaking out of police control*.

Right against Bar Fetters

In *Sunil Batra v. Delhi Administration*[42], the Supreme Court laid down that the treatment of a human being which offended human dignity, imposed avoidable torture and reduced the man to the level of a beast, would certainly be arbitrary and could be questioned under Articles 21 and 14.

Therefore, putting bar fetters for an unusually long period without due regard for the safety of the prisoner and the security of the prison would certainly be not justified.

In the writ petition, the facts were that Charles Sobhraj, French National, was arrested on 6th July, 1976 and was detained under Section 3 of the Maintenance of Internal Security Act, 1971. Sobhraj alleged that ever since he was lodged in Tihar Central Jail, he was put in bar fetters and the fetters were retained continuously for 24 hours a day.

Right against Solitary Confinement

In *Sunil Batra v. Delhi Administration*[43], the petitioner, Sunil Batra was sentenced to death by the Delhi Sessions Court and his appeal against the decision was pending before the High Court. He was detained in Tihar Jail during the pendency of the appeal. He complained that since the date of his conviction by the Sessions Court, he was kept in solitary confinement. Batra contended that Section 30 of the Prison Act ,1894, did not authorize the jail authorities to impose the punishment of solitary confinement

,which by itself was a substantive punishment under Sections 73 and 74 of the Indian Panel Code ,1860 and could be imposed by a Court of Law. That, it could not be left to the whim and caprice of the prison authorities.

The Supreme Court accepted the argument of the petitioner and held that imposition of solitary confinement on the petitioner was violative of Article 21.

Right to Personal Liberty

For enforcing human rights namely *right to personal liberty* at national level, Supreme Court has defined this right in different ways in different cases from Gopalan to Maneka Gandhi in the following way.

The Supreme Court in *A. K. Gopalan v. State of Madras*[44], the first case in this regard, wherein the petitioner, a leader of the Communist Party was detained under the Preventive Detention Act, 1950, took a literal view of the expression "personal Liberty", and held that since the word "liberty" was qualified by the word "personal" which was a narrower concept, the expression "personal liberty" did not include all that was implied in the term "liberty".

So interpreted, the expression" personal liberty" meant nothing more than the liberty of the physical body, i.e. *freedom from arrest and detention from false imprisonment or wrongful confinement*.

Later, in *Kharak Singh v. State of U.P.*[45], the Court did not follow the above restrictive interpretation of the term, and held that "personal liberty" was not only limited to bodily restraint or confinement of person only. The Court held:

"Personal liberty" is used in Article 21 as a compendious term to include within itself all the varieties of rights which go to make up the 'personal liberty' of a man other than those dealt with in the several Clauses of Article 19(1). While Article 19(1) deals with particular species or attributes of that freedom, 'personal liberty' in Article 21 takes in and comprises the residue.

In this case, the petitioner, Kharak Singh was charged in a dacoity case but was released as there was no evidence against him. However, being suspicious of his designs, the police under the *U.P. Police Regulation*, opened a history-sheet for him and imposed on him surveillance which included secret picketing of his house by the police and domiciliary visits at night and verification of his movements and activities

.He was, thus, visited by the police in the night, time and again, for the purpose of making sure that, he was staying home or whether he had gone out.

The Court laid down that an unauthorized intrusion into a person's home and the disturbance caused to him thereby violated his right to "personal liberty" enshrined in Article 21.

In *Maneka Gandhi v. Union of India*[46], the Supreme Court expanded the horizons of the expression "personal liberty" and gave it the widest possible meaning. The Court held:

The expression 'personal liberty' in Article 21 is of the widest amplitude and it covers a variety of rights which go to constitute the personal liberty of a man and some of them have been raised to the status of distinct fundamental rights and given additional protection under Article 19.

It may be noticed that While in *Kharak Singh case*[47] the freedoms of Article 19(1) were excluded from the scope of "personal liberty" of Article 21, according to *Maneka Gandhi decision*[48], they are within it and form part of " personal liberty". It thus follows that *a law depriving a person of ' personal liberty ' has not only to stand the test of Article 21 but it must also stand the test of Article 19*

A New Dynamic Dimension-Facets of Personal Liberty

Thus, in *Maneka Gandhi*[49] case, the Supreme Court gave a new dimension to Article 21 and it was with this decision that the Court started laying down a new constitutional jurisprudence. By taking recourse to creative interpretation by Courts, expensive meaning of constitutional and human rights has all along been given, which has led to creation of new rights[50]. One of the most important aspect of the right to personal liberty is right to privacy.

Right to Privacy

" Privacy" is defined as "the state of being free from intrusion or disturbance in one's private life or affairs"[51]. It is " the rightful claim of an individual to determine to which he wishes to share himself with others and control over the time, place and circumstances to communicate with others"[52]

In *R. Rajagopal v. State of Tamil Nadu*[53], the Supreme Court held that the "right to privacy " meant a " right to be let alone". Explaining the scope of the "right to privacy" which was held to be implicit in the right to life and personal liberty guaranteed under Article 21 the Court observed :

A citizen has a right to safeguard the privacy of his own , his family, marriage , procreation , motherhood, child bearing and education among other matters. None can publish anything concerning the above matters without his consent-whether truthful or otherwise and whether laudatory or critical.

A Division Bench of the Supreme Court in *People's Union for Civil Liberties v. Union of India*[54], explained that the right to hold a telephone conversation in the privacy of one's home or office , without interference could certainly be claimed as right to privacy , a part of the right to life and personal liberty. Except in cases , when the *Indian Telegraph Act* , 1885 empowers the State to intercept messages , telephone tapping would be violative of the right to privacy, the Court held.

The right to privacy forming part of the right to personal liberty is , however , not absolute and may be lawfully restricted for the prevention of crime , disorder or protection of health or morals or protection of rights and freedoms of others.

Right to Health of Women

Right to life is considered one of the fundamental rights, and health is one of the vital indicators reflecting quality of human life. In this context, it becomes one of the primary responsibilities of the state to provide health care services to all its citizens. India, despite being a signatory to the Aima Ata Declaration of 1978, which promised 'health for all' by 2000, is far from realizing this objective. On paper, India has an excellent health care structure that has the potential to reach a large section of the population. Yet, despite this elaborate structure and the rapid advancement of medical sciences, the reality is deplorable. The percentage of population actually covered by the public health care services is reportedly a mere 30 per cent. Although programmes are being constantly reviewed and revised, the problems persist and continue to worsen.

Evolution of Health Care System in India

The health policies, plans, and programmes n India mostly evolved during the national movement against colonial rule. The British authorities set up a Health Survey and Development Committee, commonly known as the Bhore Committee (1946)[55] that was also greatly inspired by the aspirations of the national movement.

Some of the key recommendations of the Bhore Committee were:

- Integration of preventive and curative health services all administrative levels;
- Development of primary health centres in two stages;
- Major change in medical education;
- Formation of district health board for each district;
- Inter- sectoral approach to health service development.

It also recommended a comprehensive proposal for development of a national programme of health service for the country[56]. Subsequently in 1948, the Sokhey Committee[57] recommended that manpower and services be developed from the bottom upwards. The Committee represented 'a people centred and pluralistic' model of development[58]. However, in the post Independence era, i.e., in the 1950s and 60s, advanced research institutes, medical colleges with tertiary hospitals and primary health centres emerged, while the sub-centres at village level lagged behind. India experienced a crisis in the late 60s, when it went through widespread drought that raised concerns about the 'development model', adopted so far. The international community put the onus of this crisis on the rising population growth, which was seen to be a hindrance to India's growth and development.

Changes in the global arena

Meanwhile, countries world over were witnessing a major transition in their political and economic climates. The post second world war period was marked by liberation of many countries from hundreds of years of colonial rule, rapid industrialization, particularly in East and South East Asia, and emergence of the USA as a strong industrial power.

However, this economic growth faced a severe setback in the 70s resulting from the oil price hike in 1973. This crisis signaled the end of this era and led to two simultaneous development. First, a worldwide economic recession and inflation which the West tried to overcome in every possible way[59]. Secondly, massive profits were made by the Oil and Petroleum Exporting Countries (OPEC), which was invested in the international banks and monetary institutions giving these institutions the power of re-defining the economic world order.

As the slump in the economy swept the globe, the developed countries sought to expand their markets across national boundaries, with obvious targets being third world countries like India. Countries, that were themselves hit hard by the oil crisis, faced further problems as a result of unfair trade practices e.g., export of raw materials to the developed countries (the prices of which were sharply declining in the world market) and import of manufactured goods at a substantially higher price. In the face of growing crisis, the only option left to the third world countries was to take loans from the West through international financial institutions like the International Monetary Fund (IMF) and World Bank (WB), who imposed stringent conditions to safeguard their interests. This gave rise to Structural Adjustment Programmes (SAPs) – a powerful tool for economic restructuring that affected the livelihoods and health of millions of people, especially in the marginalized communities of the world.

The unfair trade agreements in the name of liberalization, coupled with the SAPs of the 1980s, had a severe impact on the economies of the developing countries. The resulting economic recession and growing dependence on loans from international financial institutions forced the governments to withdraw their support to some of the crucial entitlements and benefits that their citizens rightfully enjoyed. Health was one area that was severely affected. The public health system in the developing world deteriorated because of cuts in heath budgets and reforms in health system which were tied as conditionality to loans from the financial institutions, introduction of service charges in public institutions, and the simultaneous drive for privatization.

The years following the economic reforms in the late eighties saw a sharp decline in the quality of health service in the country. Some of the major developments in this phase were:

- A growing aggression on the part of agencies like the World Bank and IMF in shaping social, economic and political priorities of the country and their consistent thrust for privatization;

- Under various states Health Systems Development Projects, the World Bank was seen to play a significant role in re-organizing the health sector in the whole country in the name of alleviating poverty. India was compelled by the international financial institutions to reduce public expenditure in health through increasing privatization. In accordance with the conditions laid down by the WB/IMF, there was a 20 per cent reduction in the allocation for health services in the union budget. This led to the marginalization of the public sector and the expansion of private sector. "The World Bank promotes health care as a commercial activity with no money on treatment dictate, resulting in denial of right to health and undermining state responsibility in providing basic health care to its citizens," to the poor, especially women, who are the poorest of the poor[60].

- There was an imposition of the so-called "international initiatives in health", through a combination of development aid agencies and international organizations. The health budgets of the nation experienced huge cuts in the name of health sector reforms in the 1990s. the already under financed health services of the public sector was denounced as inefficient and too costly to be revived and concepts of private-public partnerships, user fees, etc. were introduced in primary and tertiary health care.

Comprehensive healthcare incorporates the concept of Primary Health Care (PHC) that stresses prevention rather than cure. It believes that health is an outcome of socio- economic, political and technological advancements, and health care of socio-economic, political and technological advancements, and health care should involve community participation and use of technology that is acceptable, affordable by the people and appropriate to meet their needs. The Comprehensive Health Care was replaced by the idea of 'Selective Health Care' at the interest of the donor agencies. Very soon, World Health Organization (WHO) considered it impractical and too costly to handle the compels systems involved in comprehensive care as compared to specific medical and technological interventions, and health care became restricted to cost-effective interventions.

Selective Health Care was translated into a series of vertical programmes that compromised the provisions for the comprehensive health services. However, the vertical programmes were not only technocratic and imposed on the masses, they also made India dependent on the North for funds, supply of vaccines and other logistic support. Hence, despite the weaknesses of these programmes, in terms of their economic, administrative and epidemiological sustainability, they were pushed through for political reasons rather than out of consideration for reat needs of such programmes in the country.[61]

Increase in drug prices and effect of TRIPS

Along with budget cuts, infrastructural decline, privatization and introduction of user charges, another significant factor responsible for the increase in health costs was the repaid liberalization of the pharmaceutical industry resulting in sharp increase in drug prices and the issue of patents. These spiraling costs have had a significant impact on access.

Price regulation in the pharmaceutical sector is an important instrument of public policy for promoting equity in access to health care. At present about 65 per cent of the Indian population lack access to essential life saving medicines despite India being recognized as a global drug manufacturer[62]. The Pharmaceutical Policy (PP) 2002 of the Government of India (GOI) wants to dilute drug price control by suggesting criteria for price control that will reduce the basket of price control to a bunch of irrelevant 30 or so drugs. The kinds of drugs that would be left under price control are mostly irrelevant to public health. Even the Drug Price Control Order of 1995 conspicuously omitted drugs for anemia, diarrhea, the majority of drugs for tuberculosis, hypertension and diabetes, and all drugs for cancer.

The Trade Related Intellectual Property Rights (TRIPs) agreement has influenced the drug pricing and policy in a negative way for India. The issue of drugs has shifted from the realm of health to the realm of trade – a situation made worse by the rise of multinational pharmaceuticals that are trying to control and own knowledge in the name of intellectual property rights[63]. In reality, the provisions under the TRIPS agreement undermine some of the every process that helped India become one of the leading countries in drug manufacturing with some of the lowest prices in the world. The effect is exemplified in the attempts of the government to reformulate the pharmaceutical policy and amendment of the Indian Drug and Cosmetics Act (1948) to reduce the number of drugs under price control, and make space for clinical trials respectively in the name of liberalization. For India it would mean wiping out of the Indian public sector, small scale sector and overpricing of a large number of essential and life saving drugs and the already vulnerable population be exposed to the unethical experimentation by the drug companies. In short, we have reached a state of 'poor health at high costs'.

Health Policies and Programmes in India

A brief review of the government policies and programmes over the last 55 years is a reflection of how the healthcare system responds to health and particularly women's health. India has never had an explicit policy for women's health, but a range of policy decisions and measures has directly influenced women's health. This section mentions some of the policies and programmes under the National health programmes that, to our mind, have been crucial in determining the health situation of women in India.

Since independence, several policies and programmatic interventions have been formulated to meet the health needs of people in the country. Besides, the specific policies that were initiated, the five-year plans, are a statement of the sectoral policies and programmes introduced by the Government of India. The progress of the five year plans, from the first introduced in 1951-56 to the tenth five year plan (2002-07) are indicative of the shifts in the government's priorities and commitment vis-à-vis specific health issues.

The Ministry of Health and Family Welfare (MOFHW) comprises of the Department of Health, Department of Family Welfare and the Department of Indian System of Medicine and Homeopathy. In addition to general health services provided by MOHFW, specific health and nutritional needs of women are provided through the Integrated Child Development Services (ICDS) Programme under the Ministry of Human Resources Development and newly formed Ministry of Women and Child Development, that was only a department under the MOHFW till 2005.

Under the provision of the Constitution of India, Public health is primarily a state subject. National Health Programmes have been designed with flexibility to permit the state public health administration to create their own programmes according to their needs and depending on the epidemiological profile of the population. The implementation of the national health programmes carried out through the state government has decentralized public health machinery. The centre will play a coordinating role and provide technical and financial support, wherever it is felt necessary.

Below, we discuss some of the policies and programme briefly to critically examine their effects on the health status of women.

National Health Policy (NHP)

India committed itself to universal health care in the Bhore Committee report developed way back in 1946. Subsequent to the Alma Ata commitment, the GOI passed the National Health Policy (NHP) in 1983. The NHP talked about comprehensive primary health care services linked to extension and health education; large scale transfer to knowledge, skills and requisite technologies to 'health volunteers'; intersectoral cooperation and better utilization and strengthening of traditional systems of medicine[64].

Since then, there have been marked changes in the larger climate and determinant factors relating to the health sector. The NHP 2002 is a continuation of the earlier indicated trends. The new policy deliberates on the need to improve access to health services among all social groups and in all areas, and proposes to do so by establishing new facilities in deficient areas and improving those existing. Recognizing that women and other underprivileged groups are most affected by poor access to health care, it aims at improving such groups;' access to basic services. Most importantly, the central government is to give top funding priority to programmes prompting women's health. The policy sets forth several time bound objectives including reduction of MMR. IMR, mortality due to TB and malaria by 2010, and zero growth of HIV/AIDS by 2007.

The new policy indentifies many of the deficiencies plaguing the health care system and proposes a substantial increment in government expenditure on health care. However, in terms of its prescriptions, it represents a retreat from the fundamental concept of the NHP 1983 that was committed to the 'Health for All by 2000' through the universal provision of comprehensive primary health care services. In contrast, NHP 2002 conveniently omits the concept of comprehensive and universal health care, thus reducing primary health care to primary level care. The silence maintained on village health worker (first contact in the primary health care) and strengthening public referral services exemplify the trend[65].

The policy, while on one hand is totally silent and ambiguous on the need for essential drugs, price control and standardized regimens of treatment, regulation of private medical colleges/institutions and medical research, on the other, many of its formulations pave way for greater privatization of the system. Employing user fee in public hospitals, promoting 'health tourism' by making provisions for patients from other countries to avail domestic facilities for treatment in India, encouraging 'setting up of private insurance for expanding the scope of covering secondary and tertiary sector under private health insurance packages', etc. mark the government's intention of legitimizing further privatization and departing from providing comprehensive, secondary and tertiary care. [66] last but not the least, health issues of women and children have been reduced to a section of rhetoric and passing references without specific prescriptions. Neither does it consider the steady decline of the female-male sex ratio over the few decades as a cause concern[67], nor does it highlight any measures to prohibit sex selective abortions such as licensing and regulation of prenatal diagnostic centers. It also fails to acknowledge the problem of malnutrition, or suggest strategies and interventions to tackle the issues.

National Population Policy (NPP) 2000

In 1951, the draft outlined for the First Five-year Plan, recognized 'Population Policy' as 'essential to planning' and 'family planning' as a step towards improving the health of the mothers and children. Women's health concerns received less attention than fertility control, and family planning became the focus. The first Family Planning Programme (FPP) was formulated in 1952. The methods propagated then were rhythm and barrier methods, like diaphragms, jellies and foam tablets. In the year 1966, Department of Family Planning was established in the Ministry of health. The sixties saw a shift to Intra Uterine Devices (IUDs) and the introduction of cash incentives for doctors, motivators and the targets. The promotion of barrier methods was then stopped. In the seventies, the stress shifted to sterilizations, where men were targeted for vasectomies. With the declaration of Emergency in 1975, the government declared a virtual war against ht poor by way of coercive mass sterilizations. Forced sterilization was one of the main reasons for the fall of the government. Interestingly, all subsequent government avoided the propagation of vasectomies, and shifted their focus on women.

A statement of NPP was drafted and, in 1991, a Committee of Population was appointed which strongly recommended NPP. In the year 1993, a Committee on Population, set up by the National Development Council. Proposed the formulation of a National Population Policy. In 1999 the draft NPP was made available and on February 2000, the cabinet adopted the NPP[68].

The National Population Policy (NPP), adopted in 2000, lays out several objectives and goals to realize the long-term objective of 'stabilizing population but 2045 at a sustainable level'.

- The immediate objective is to meet the unmet need for contraception and health infrastructure;
- The medium term objective is to bring the Total fertility Rate (TFR) to replacement levels by 2010 through intersectoral action;
- The long-term objective is to achieve a stable population, consistent with sustainable development by 2045.

The policy also states Socio-Demographic Goals to be achieved by 2010, some of which are:

- Reducing IMR, MMR;
- Achieving universal immunization, access to information/ counseling;
- Containing spread of infectious diseases;
- Promoting vigorously small family norm;
- Delaying age at marriage

Women's activists, health activists criticized the policy on many crucial the policy on many crucial grounds. First and foremost, the macro issues of income, employment, food basic health and livelihood issues don not find a mention in the NPP. Secondly, the NPP articulates stabilization of population as the precondition for economic development. The quality of health care services including preventive and primary don not find a place in the NPP document.

Though NPP 2000 emphasizes on delayed marriage, it is silent about vocational training and occupational opportunities for empowerment, which reflects that its goals are still very much limited to fertility reduction[69]. Violence against women, men's involvement in family planning and strengthening MCH services do not get any attention in the entire policy.

Though India is a signatory with the International Conference on Population and Development (ICPD), which promotes target free approach, it continues to use disincentives as an implementation tool to achieve targets. Contravening the NPP, most states in India have formulated their own population policies, which focus on population control through neither two-child nor, the two-child norm has shifted the entire burden of birth control on women and further victimized women.

National Nutrition Policy (NNP), 1993

The National Nutrition Policy (1993) advocates a comprehensive inter-sectoral strategy for alleviating all the multi-faceted problems related to nutritional deficiencies, so as to achieve an optimal state of nutrition for all sections of society, but with emphasis on women and children. The strategies adopted include – screening of all pregnant women and lactating mothers for chronic Energy Deficiency (CED); identifying women with weight below 40 kg and providing adequate ante-natural, intra-partum and neo- natural care under the RCH programme, and ensuring they receive food supplementation through the Integrated Child Development Services (ICDS) Scheme. The ICDS, launched in 1975, provides supplementary feeding to bridge the nutritional gaps that exist in respect of children below 6 years and expectant and nursing mothers. However the ICDS programme has not been able to reach the nutritional need of children below three years.

The policy however, has failed in many ways to meet the nutritional requirements of the population. Though there has been a rise in the Country's food production, an ineffective distribution system has failed to benefit the masses. At the implementation level, there is a lack of co-ordination between the different departments that are supposed to provide supportive services- like safe drinking water, sanitation, day care services – and programmes that are related to women's empowerment, nor-formal education and adult literacy.

Moreover, the policy thrust has been towards micronutrient supplementation rather than addressing the root causes of malnutrition. According to studies, the dismal nutritional scenario is reflected in the persistence of under nutrition in the last few decades, with a marginal reduction (only 20%) in under nutrition. Today, India with less than 20% of the world's children, accounts for over 40% of under nourished children. Under-nutrition in pregnant women and low birth weight rate has not shown any decline.

The National Nutrition Bureau (NNB) has also been ineffective in screening nutritional disorders like CED among pregnant and lactating women, and identifying their needs. Very often, the nutritional education that is imparted is far removed from the reality of these women's lives and they fail to relate or articulate their nutritional requirements.

National Mental Health Programme

A National Mental Health Programme was launched in 1982, keeping in view the heavy burden of mental illness in the country and the inadequacy of the health system to meet the specific mental health needs. This programme aimed to shift the basis of practice from the traditional (psychiatric) services to community care.

However, in reality, the NHMP is only a footnote to the national health policy, and does not offer any (fiscal or technical) support for building community initiatives. In practice, the treatment of mental health problems is still heavily relying on the bio- medical model and is limited to the dispensing of drugs. Mental healthcare services are limited to those diagnosed with severe illness, where the patient is treated as a 'societal burden'. The pattern of institutional care, especially for women, reeks of neglect and paternalism and requires gender sensitive cross-referral system[70].

The GOI also launched the District Mental Health Programme (DMHP) in 1996-1997 under the recommendation of the Central Council of Health and Family Welfare. The programme, initially launched in 4 states, was extended to 22 districts in 20 states by the year 2000 with a grant assistance of Rs. 22.5 lakhs each[71]. The goal was to develop a community-based approach that has been neglected despite the programme commitment towards it. The other objectives were to impart public education in mental health to increase awareness and reduce stigma, early detection and treatment through both OPD and indoor services, and providing data from the community to the state and central levels for future planning of mental health programmes.

The programme has been criticized as giving more importance to curative services rather than preventive measures. There is also a shortage of professional manpower, and the training programmes are not adequate. Moreover, the medical care provided is still custodial in nature and requires a therapeutic approach[72].

Reproductive and Child Health

The mother and Child Health (MCH), nutrition and immunization programmes were brought under the umbrella of the Family Welfare Programme and was finally transformed into the Reproductive Child Health (RCH) programme[73]. The national RCH programme was launched in 1997 to provide integrated health and family welfare services for women and children. The programme aimed at improving the quality, distribution and accessibility of services and to meet the health care needs of women in the reproductive ages and children more effectively.

The components included:

- Prevention and management of unwanted pregnancy;
- Services to promote safe motherhood and child survival;
- Nutritional services for vulnerable groups;
- Prevention and treatment of reproductive tract infections (RTIs) and sexually transmitted infections (STIs);
- Reproductive health services for adolescents;
- Health, sexuality and gender information, education and counseling;
- Establishment of effective referral systems;

The second phase of the programme, RCH II sought to address the inaccessibility problem of the population by re-looking at the location of sub-centers, PHCs and CHCs, working in convergence with other departments such as ICDS, Water and Sanitation, etc. it also aims at upgrading the RCH facilities at the PHC by providing for obstetric care, MTP and IUD insertion. Hiring of private anesthetics, where none exist and referral transport facilities for poor families are some of the components of the programme.

While the RCH programme entered its second phase, a five-state social assessment of RCH I (1997-2002) revealed[74]:

- Health services were not available at suitable timings for women;
- Unresponsiveness of the health system to problems concerning mobile population;
- Complete neglect of adolescent health needs;
- Low priority accorded to treatment of gynecological morbidities among women, even as the untreated side effects of contraceptives and post delivery complications continued to burden women;
- Failure to involve men in the programme, thus rendering the RCH programme as 'women centric'.

Despite the guidelines of the RCH programme and the existing reproductive health care services, there are certain issues that have been completely neglected and ignored by the experts. Women are unable to seek care for problems, which are not related to pregnancy and other gynecological complications. For instance, there are no services for occupational health problems, domestic violence or abuse and mental health problems. In addition to this, the programmes deny a commitment to respond to women's health needs throughout the life cycle and to go beyond the constricted conceptualization of their reproductive roles as concerned only with child bearing.[75]

National Rural Health Mission

The National Rural Health Mission (NRHM 2005) – launched in 18 states that were identified as having poor health indicators- emphasizes on comprehensive primary health care for the rural poor. The main goal of the mission is to provide for effective health care facilities and universal access to rural population. The principle thrust areas as identified in the document are:

- Strengthening the three levels of rural health care- sub-centre, PHC and the CHC. It also states that all 'assured services' including routine and emergency care in Surgery. Medicine, Obstetrics and Gynecology and Pediatrics in addition to all the National Health programmes; and all support services to fulfill these should be available and strengthened at the CHC level[76].

- New health financing mechanisms for additional resource allocation and up gradation of facilities.

- Appointing ASHA (Accredited Social Health Activist) at the village level as the link worker for the rest of the rural public health system.

- Private public partnerships and regulation of private sector.

The programme document identifies all these as attempts to establish the horizontal linkages of various health programmes and provide comprehensive primary health care rather than promoting the vertical programmes, which has till now failed to provide health for all.

However, NRHM 2005 has been criticized by health activists and women's groups alike as being 'old wine in a new bottle'. Only a marginal proportion of the increased health budget has gone into the rural health system improvements under NRHM and in reality the budgets for all Family Welfare activates including the RCH II package has been clubbed together as the budget for NRHM[77]. A consequence of such reallocation is the danger of NRHM activities being usurped by RCH programme.

The performance indicators of the ASHA and her compensation are related to RCH and there is a high possibility that this disproportionate emphasis on family planning and RCH will undermine the effectiveness of other primary health care components[78].

Hence, though the NRHM document reflects the renewed commitment of the government to provide comprehensive health care, it has inbuilt problems of becoming selective and abdicating the government's responsibility for healthcare provisioning.

Other Programmes

In the process of planning, a series of vertical programmes evolved towards control and eradication of communicable diseases such as TB, malaria, leprosy, etc. however, despite the vertical programmes, India is experiencing a resurgence of various communicable diseases. About 5 lakh people die from TB every year and malaria has remained at a high level of around two million cases annually.

The vertical programmes are not based on establishing a wide network of permanent health services to cater to the needs of masses in the country. Most of the programmes seem to offer simple, less effort and resource demanding option, which in no way raise concerns over the larger structural issues of poverty and inequity. The vertical programmes run through a fragmented approach, as they do not locate certain diseases within its specific context, and moreover, they are very expensive and unsustainable in the long run. The trend towards fragmentation of health programmes to vertical programmes should be reversed.

The national health programmes should be integrated in the primary health care system with decentralized planning, decision-making and implementing with the active participation of the community. Focus should be shifted from bio-medical and individual based measures to social, iconological and community based measures.[79] Hence, the existing policies and programmes need to be reviewed in the context of changing socio economic situation in the country.

Women's access to health services is much less in comparison to men. The underlying reason being their lower status in the family and lack of decision-making power regarding ill health, expenditure on health care and non-availability of health care facilities prevent them from seeking medical help. Women's lack of time due to existing unequal division of labour and the socially sanctioned 'feminine' quality of 'sacrifice'. Besides, the perceptions of acceptable levels of discomfort for women and men lead to gender differences in willingness to accept that they are sick and seek care. Women wait longer than men to seek medical care for illness. This is partly due to their unwillingness to disrupt household functioning unless they become incapacitated.

Relatively high mortality rates of women are a reflection of unequal gender relations, inequalities in resource distribution, lack of access and availability of drugs and health services in our country. A look at the female to make death ration (i.e. 0.84, for the period 1992-93) at the neo-natal stage shows that mortality rates are higher in case of males. There is a significant reversal in the picture in the post-neonatal and subsequently the 1-4 age groups, where the female to male death ratios are 1.13 and 1.43 respectively. These differentials highlight the consistent gender bias inherent in seeking health care for the girl child. Many studies have clearly shown that girl children below the age of four years displaying symptoms of pneumonia were not taken to a health provider of given any treatment at home as compared to similarly affected male children of this age group.[80]

In India, pneumonia and anemia constitute the major causes of death in the 0-4 age group, tuberculosis of the lungs pose a risk in the 15-50 age groups. The other causes of mortality include bronchitis and asthma, gastroenteritis, diseases of the nervous system and maternal mortality.[81] Poor nutritional status, coupled with lack of poor health care for girls and women underlie causes of high mortality and morbidity in India. "In India 1 out of 3 women in the age group 15-49 is undernourished as per the BMI"[82] (NFHS II 98- 99). Studies show that access to nutrition and healthcare is skewed in favour of boys and men, which in turn, affect gender differentials in mortality. There is a definite bias in feeding nutritious food to boys and male members of the family. In northern states, it is usual for girls and women to eat less tham male members. For instance, the dietary pattern indicates that in comparison to adult men, women consume approximately 1,000 fewer calories per day, far below the Recommended Dietary Allowance Nutritional deprivation not only hinders women from reaching their full growth potential, but also results in severe and chronic anemia lack of appropriate care during pregnancy and childbirth, and the inadequacy of services for detecting and managing complications, explains most of the maternal deaths. According to a study, 37 per cent of all pregnant women in India receive no prenatal care during their pregnancies. Moreover, women in rural areas are much less likely to receive prenatal care than women in urban areas (18 per cent and 42 per cent, respectively)[83]. This is a cause of great concern as these deaths are preventable with improved attention to access to health care, emergency obstetric care, and proper ante-natal and postpartum care. Apart from maternal mortality, early marriage, frequent and repeated childbearing and discrimination faced throughout the life cycle results in adverse health outcomes like RTI/STIs, uterine prolapsed, and etc. a district study in Maharashtra showed that reproductive problems, urinary tract infections, aches and pains and weakness made up 47% of all reported morbidity[84]. Despite the Medical Termination of Pregnancy (MTP) Act in place since 1971, an estimated 4-6 million illegal abortions occur every year. While, 6-9% of these occur in adolescent girls, 16% are women between 20-34 years[85]. These unsafe abortions also have negative consequences for women's health.

Women and Communicable Diseases

In addition to the poor nutritional status, heavy work burden and maternal and primal ill-health, communicable diseases including Malaria, Tuberculosis. Encephalitis, Kala Azar, Dengue, Leprosy, etc. contribute significantly to the heavy burden of disease faced by women.

Communicable disease remain the most common cause of death in India. Despite the arsenal of diagnostics, drugs and vaccines that have been developed during this century, medical researchers and practitioners contuse to struggle against an ever-growing number of emerging infectious diseases such as HIV and hepatitis etc.[86] Structural inequalities of gender and economic resources enhances the risk of communicable disease among poor. Although both men and women are equally exposed to communicable diseases, there are concrete evidences to show that women suffer far more than men in terms of decision making and approximately 70% of the poor, and then the interaction between poverty and gender may represent the most important risk factor to be addressed in efforts to arrest communicable diseases[87]. There exist crucial linkages of communicable disease- particularly TB and Malaria, perhaps they are so common – with issues related poverty, the environmental degradation and the change of lifestyles and food habits, etc.

Malaria –that staged resurgence in the 1980's before stabilizing at a high annual prevalence of nearly 2 million cases[88] - affects women in various ways. Repeated attacks of malaria, especially falciparum malaria in already anemic women results in worsening of anemia. Pregnant women with malaria are known to have a high incidence of abortion, still birth and low birth weight babies. These women have a higher risk of death. Like Malaria, **Tuberculosis** is one of the biggest killers of women in general and of women in the reproductive age group in particular. The transition from infection to the disease and its implication is rooted not merely in the biology but in the environmental, social and material conditions of living. When women get infected, they are either sent back to their parental home for treatment of deserted. On one hand, women find it difficult to travel to distant health centers or hospitals for the diagnosis and treatment of TB, as the treatment requires regular visits to the health centers and, on the other, there is the absence of support system at home and financial help to meet the high costs of medicines.

The non-pulmonary TB, like genital TB is difficult to diagnose and after being diagnosed, remains untreated. Many times, this can cause infertility that has severe implication on women. The ill, treatment and ostracism meted out to a childless woman are nearly universal. 58% of **Leprosy** cases recorded in the world comes from India[89]. Leprosy presents itself not only as a medical disease, but is associated with immense psychological trauma and social stigma. Women inflicted with leprosy most of the time face desertion. Ironically, infliction of leprosy has been accepted as a ground for obtaining divorce that intensifies women's vulnerability.

The issue of **HIV/AIDS** presents a complex picture and has emerged as a major right issue over the years for those infected with it. The first evidence of HIV infection in India was discovered in a female sex worker in Chennai in 1986. Since then, studies conducted all over India have shown that the infection is prevalent in a number of population groups all over the world. The NACO estimates the number of people with HIV/AIDS in India as 5.1 million in 2004.

Hysterectomies of Mentally Challenged Women

The roots of many mental ailments lie in social structures and practices. Any attempt to deal with mental health holistically would automatically take into account the root causes and raise fundamental questions about social practices and norms.

The stress of work, both domestic and occupational, leaves a woman little time and space for herself. Living in hostile environments, women have no one to express or share their feelings with. Often suppressed feelings and frustrations find their own escape routes. However, the society's response to such conditions is hardly rational or sensitive.

Women going through such phases are either beaten to remove the 'evil spirit' that is believed to have 'occupied the body' or, in some rare occasions, worshipped deities. People therefore resort to spiritual healing and black magic to treat mental illnesses.

In situations, where women lack autonomy, decisions-making power and opportunities, they have very little control over the determinants of mental health and mental health care. In many cases they are sent to asylums by labeling women as schizophrenic patents, especially in order to discard unwanted spouse, extraction of more dowry, usurping the property of the widowed woman, etc. many times their own parents do not want to take them back home after the treatment. Two thirds of women in mental asylums are normal women, who may be suffering from slight depression due to various emotional and physical causes.

Rights of women, who have been diagnosed with mental problems, are violated, based on medical opinion and they are certified and forcibly detained. They are denied various social, political rights including the right to vote, right to enter into any kind of contract, custody of child.

Women and Occupational Health

To understand the occupational aspects of health, it is necessary to have a detailed examination of women's work in terms of the actual activity undertaken, the hours of work entailed, the remuneration, if any, and the effects of all these on their nutritional status and physical as well as mental health. The working environment for women, both at home and at work place, affects her physical conditions. These include inadequate lighting, insanitary conditions, absence of any toilet facilities, poor airflow and ventilation, to name a few. Sexual exploitation, harassment at work place are regularly experienced by almost all sections of women in both formal and informal sectors. The most common occupational hazard for women is over-work. Over working has further grave implications on the health of women.

In rural areas, where women work as agricultural labourers, they are exposed to pesticides and chemical fertilizers that can cause diseases of the liver and nervous system, cancer, blindness or deformities. The tasks performed by women are usually those that require them to be in one position for long periods of time, which can adversely affect their reproductive health. A study in a rice-growing belt of coastal Maharashtra found that 40 per cent of all infant deaths occurred in the months of July to October. The study also found that a majority of births were either premature or stillbirths. The study attributed this to the swatting position that had to be assumed during July to August, the rice transplanting months.

In urban areas, where 80% of the women workforce are in unorganized sector like household industries, building construction and other petty trades, the hazardous work environment and absence of security and welfare mechanisms make women prone to serious health consequences, rape and other forms of sexual harassment.

Carrying and lifting heavy loads often have serious health consequences for women, like menstrual disorders, prolapsed of the uterus, miscarriage, and back problems, especially spinal problems.

Women who are involved in collection of industrial, hospital and household wastes suffer from intestinal and skin infections, poisoning from contact with empty chemical containers, bacterial and viral infections, hepatitis B, etc. the following chart illustrates some of the occupations and their related health implications on women.

'The women's movement has no beginning or origin' and, that apart, one cannot compartmentalize the movement into isolated divisions and phases. But to have a comprehensive understanding, we have tried to identify some of the most significant struggles that have either been initiated by the women's movement or have found active participation and support from the women's movement, as these have had serious implications on the lives of women in one way or another, in this chapter, we have first tried to briefly trace the historical roots of the women's movement. Following this, we have pieced together certain struggles/ campaigns that have had direct implication on the health and rights of women. We have then looked at a few of those initiatives that were related to the larger context of health. Finally, we have highlighted some initiatives that in the process of critiquing and challenging the prevailing approach and policies have also tried to explore alternatives.

Right to Health and the Women's Movement

According to the fact-finding team, members of which included women's groups, not only the legal system, but the medical system too was unresponsive towards the needs of the victims of sexual violence. Survivors had little access to counseling, no attention was paid to issues relating to consequences of the sexual violence like pregnancy, abortions and Sexually Transmitted Infections (STI) – all of which accumulated to a violation of their sexual and reproductive health and rights.

When some of these victims approached the justice system, the investigative and legal procedures furthermore victimized the women. In many cases, the police were the instigators and perpetrators of sexual violence, and in instances where rape was accompanied by murder, there was a tendency to priorities murder. This reflected the inefficacy of the criminal justice system in dealing with incidences of communal violence involving sexual violence. The choices of the women who have been victims of sexual violence were silenced not only by the police, medical and legal system but also by the families and communities who sought to hide their 'shame'.[90]

These long sustained movements drew a large number of women activists form the middle classes together with women from different segments of the society. With the experience of questioning rape, dowry and sati, it was felt important also to expand the discourse, look at women's relationship, and control over their own bodies. It is in this context that women's health, as the overall wellbeing became a central issue, which led to the emergence of women's health movement. A vivid instance is the issue of rape, and sexual violence, which brought up the nature of women's relationship with their bodies.

Women's general health and reproductive health rights were brought to the forefront through several campaigns against the introduction of hazardous contraceptives like EP drugs, Net En, Norplant, Depo-Provera, Sex selective abortions and coercive population control policies of the State. Women's groups raised questions on the safety of hormonal contraceptive technologies, of the way in which clinical trials were carried out, on notions of informed consent way and on general issues of women's health in the context of India's Family Welfare Programme. Furthermore, women's health activists interminably criticized the fact that women were only addressed by the Health care system as reproductive beings, and their other health needs were largely ignored.

Below, is an attempt to document the major campaigns encompassing women's health issues.

HDEP Drug issue

The campaign against High Dose Estrogen-Progesterone (HDEP) occupies a significant place in the history of women's health activism, HDEP drugs were brought into the market in the 1950s for the treatment of missed menstrual periods. By the1970s, the use of the drug became popular not only in a variety of gynecological problems, such as menstrual irregularities, dysfunctional uterine bleeding, and dysmenorrheal and in others, but also for pregnancy testing. EP drugs were also used for pregnancy testing, as the woman whose periods did not start after taking EP drugs, was presumed to be pregnant. The drug was increasingly misused ot induce abortion. Although no pharmaceutical company has ever claimed that these drugs will induce abortion, there was enough evidence in India that these drugs were prescribed by doctors for this purpose, and were sold over the counter[91]. Evidence showed that the drug resulted in harmful side effects that included abortions, still births and abnormalities in birth. Studies also claimed that EP drugs could lead to congenital heart disease in the foetus, appearing years after birth, and they were unreliable as pregnancy tests and ineffective as treatment for missed periods. In 1982, it was estimated that about 1,80,000 women were using the drug.

A nationwide campaign was led by the All India Drug Action Network (AIDAN) along with non-governmental organizations working on health, consumer and women's rights issues. Lawyers, autonomous women's groups and individuals including doctors were also involved in the campaign.

Campaign Process in Brief

Following the campaign, the Drug Control Authority issued a ban on the drug. Then, however it was challenged by the drug companies in the court. The women's movement, along with the drug consumer movement further strengthened the issue. When the Supreme Court, two years later, ordered the Drug

Control Authority to set up a public inquiry to take the decision on the banning of the drug, women's groups and drug consumer groups were ready with the evidence of abuse and misuse of the drug in several contexts.

Although the Supreme Court directed the government to conduct a public hearing on the drug issue, the hearing was poorly organized. Announcements for the hearing were published as a routine public notice in the three cities of Delhi, Kolkata and Mumbai, where the hearing would be conducted. The government's apathetic attitude became clear when public notices were put surreptitiously and there was no attempt to contact concern persons. For instance, notices were published on the back pages of daily newspapers along with routine advertisements and tender notices. Moreover, women who had suffered adversely were hardly in a position to undertake the burden of the technical and official formalities.

The women's movement in association with the drug consumer movement put in a commendable effort to mobilize the women who were adversely affected by the drug. It was a long battle and after five years of continuous campaign, in 1988, the Indian Government banned the manufacture and sale of the high dose combination of EP drugs.

The urgency of addressing reproductive health issues in the women's movement was increasingly realized. Women's activists became aware of the political dynamics of the drug companies that targeted women for testing their products, without proper information and consent.

Campaign against Long-acting hormonal Contraceptives

In the bid to meet unrealistic population control targets and as part of the liberalization policies, the Indian authorities have in the past few years realized drug regulations in order to expedite the introduction of long acting, invasive, hazardous hormonal contraceptives, such as the injectables (Net-en and Depo-Provera) and sub-dermal implants (Norplant) into India, that is likely to cause irreversible damage to their own and their progeny's health. Women's groups, health groups and human rights groups throughout the country have initiated a consistent campaign to oppose the introduction of these injectables and implants given the potential for abuse, non-completion of mandatory trials and the lack of accountability of pharmaceutical agencies.

Injectables	Commonly Known as	Dosage	Manufacturing Company
Depot medroxyprogesterone Acetate (DMPA)	Depo-Provera	150 mg every 3 months	Upjohn Co.USA (former), Presently Pfizer
Norethisterone	Net-en	200 mg every 2 months	Schering AG, Germany

Hazardous Effects of Depo-Provera and Depo-Provera

Severe side effects of Net-en and Depo-Provera are well documented, which include menstrual disorders, cessation of the monthly cycle or irregular bleeding general weakness, migraine headaches, and severe abdominal cramps. Depo can also lead to cancer of the breast and uterus, weight loss, loss of libido, heavy and prolonged menstrual bleedings and at times complete amenorrhea. Moreover, studies have shown that injectable contraceptives like Depo-Provera can also lead to osteoporosis. This is again fraught with grave consequences for poor women who have low bone density due to poor nutritional status.

Clinical trials of these inject able contraceptives were being conducted by Indian Council of Medical Research (ICMR) since the mid seventies. The United States Food and Drug Agency (USFDA) banned the use of Depo for contraception. In 1975, ICMR discontinued the Depo-Provera trials, but the drug itself was not banned. There was no licensing policy and hence the drug could not be imported from other countries. A renowned gynecologist and former Chairperson of Indian Association of fertility and sterility, Dr. C. L. Jhaveri filed a case against the Drug Controller of India and the Union of India for being refused a license to import the drug. A women's organization (Women's Centre, Mumbai), a health network (Medico Friend Circle) in coalition with the government filed a petition against Dr. Jhaveri in 1985. They argued that the use of the drug in India's Family Planning Programme could be disastrous for women's health. Following this, Dr. Jhaveri was prohibited form importing the drug or using it on women.[92]

In order to assess the acceptability of Depo-Provera with a view to introduce indictable contraceptives in the National family Welfare Programme, ICMR initiated the Phase IV (Programme Introduction) trial in 1983-84, in both urban and rural centres. A rural health centre in Patancheru, a village close to Hyderabad in Andhra Pradesh, was one of the centres where this study was conducted.

In April, 1985, some members of the Stree Shakti Sanghatana (SSS), a women's group in Hyderabad, learnt of net-en trials taking place in Patancheru Women from the poorest class were recruited for the trials. They were not informed of either its side effects or contraindications. When SSS intervened and explained the side effects and long-term implications of the drug to the women, only 5 out of 50 women remained for the trials.

Subsequently, women's groups such as SSS, Saheli, Chingari filed a writ petition in the Supreme court against the Union of India, ICMR, Drug Controller of India (DCI) and others, asking for a stay order on the Net-En clinical trials in India. However, the government's admission at the close of the case in 2000, that mass use of Depo-Provera in the FP programme was not advisable, was a clear indication that there were potential risks associated with the injectable and that there was a need for closer monitoring and follow up. Following the public attention on unethical trials n Patancheru, Depo-Provera was placed at the backstage while clinical trials on Norplant, a hormonal implant, was set in motion.

A brief study of the women who have undergone Norploant trials in Baroda, conducted by the Forum for women's Helath, revealed the unethical and unscientific way the trials were conducted. The issue of informed consent, checking women for contraindications, follow up care and counseling was completely ignored[93]. The counseling or information that is given to her about this new method is just the following: 'These rods are of Norplant. It is a new method whose trial is going on. With a small operation, these rods will be inserted under the skin in your arm. It will work for five years and give you contraceptive protection. After five years, you have to get it removed. Come to us, we will do it whenever your want...."[94] The hospitals were mainly concerned with the number of acceptors, continuation and drop were mainly concerned with the number of acceptors, continuation and drop our rates. Women's complaint related to heavy bleeding, amenorrhea, etc. were not taken into consideration.

Women's groups in Delhi, Mumbai and other cities took the initiative and protested against the introduction of Norplant. All these groups took an active role in the campaign and met regularly to discuss strategies of the campaign, compile information on these contraceptive methods and send information to other groups to involve them in the campaign. They submitted a memorandum to the Health Minister demanding the exclusion of Norplant from the National Family Welfare Programme. They also made a joint representation to the Ministry of Health concerning their opposition to the government's plan to introduce injectables and implants.

At this juncture, women's groups realized that the contentious issue of hormonal contraceptives needs to be addressed comprehensively, as USFDA finally approved the use of Depo as a contraceptive method in 1992 after repeated requests by the manufacturing company Upjohn, and the DCGI approved its use by private practitioners in 1993 in India. Subsequently the Indian Government had also planned to approve the entry of Depo-Provera in the Family Welfare Programme without conducting the mandatory Phase 3 trials. Upjohn, the American multinational company, thus gained access to one of the largest markets for contraceptives without following the mandatory requirements.

Women's groups, health groups and human rights groups throughout the country have opposed the introduction of this injectable given the potential for abuse, non-completion of mandatory trials and the lack of accountability of pharmaceutical agencies. Conclusion from analysis of major studies from all over the world have compelled a call for a complete ban on injectable contraceptives, and particularly its introduction in the public (National Family Welfare Programme) sphere, because fo the health hazards it poses. They also strongly protested against the government's approval of a Post Marketing Surveillance to be carried out simultaneously by the pharmaceutical company Upjohn.

In 1994, Jagori AIDS Awareness Group and other individuals along with some women's group filed a case in the Supreme Court against Depo-Provera, asking to include it as a bannable drug. In the course of preparing the petition, substantial data and medical research work was studied with help from doctors who were supportive of the campaign, after much lobbying and pressure from Sama, Saheli, AIDWA, Jagori, MFC and many other women's and health groups, the Drug Technical Advisory Board (DTAB)_, on the direction of the Supreme Court, passed a recommendation stating that Depo-Provera is not recommended for inclusion in the Family Welfare Programme. Right from the experience in Patancheru in Andhra Pradesh in 1985, women's groups have monitored the violation of 'informed consent' while administering contraceptives during clinical trials and research. "Unveiled reality – A Study on Women's Experiences with Depo-Provera, an injectable contraceptive conducted by Sama (2000) reveal that women in Delhi were administered injectable contraceptives in a Public hospital without informed consent. Vital adverse effects of the contraceptive were withheld from women, thereby depriving them of the right to make an informed choice.

More recently in 2004, in a series of state-wise public hearings on the Right to Health initiated jointly by the National human Rights Commission (NGRC) and Jan Swasthya Abhiyan (JSA), testimonies of women's experience with Depo-Provera were collected and presented by Sama before the NHRC and health officials from different states. The NHRC panel was surprised that a public health establishment was administering Depo- Provera and subsequently has demanded an explanation from the officials for the same.

In 2004, a workshop in Manesar (27-29 Oct 04), was organized and co-ordinated by parivar Seva Sanstha (a National level NGO), in collaboration with Government of India, UNFPA and Packard Foundation through Population Foundation of India to "expand choices of contraception" by the introduction of injectables. Sama, AIDWA, Saheli and Delhi Science Forum strongly opposed the move. They mobilized many health and women's groups across the country and submitted a Memorandum to the Health Minister.

Subsequently, the Minister of Health and Family Welfare responded as follows: "in this connection I am to inform you that Injectable Contraceptive which was accorded marketing permission is being used in the country on the prescription of a physician since early 90s. however Government of India is not contemplating to introduce the same in the National Family Welfare program, till the study on the effects of injectable contraceptive on Indian women's health is completed by ICMR and the NIRRH, Mumbai and the findings are favourable. Based on the results of these studies, the Department will take a decision on the introduction of injectables under the National Family Welfare Program". (Letter to Saheli from Dr (Mrs) MS Jayalakshmi, Deputy Commissioner (RSS), MOHFW, No. N. 14013/22/2000/TO, dated 19.4.2005.

There were several predicaments, which the movement encountered on its way. The paramount concern was whether to go for a blanket rejection of all hormonal contraceptives or only those, which don not grant user control to women. The concern was also regarding provision of safe and effective contraceptives to those demanding contraceptives. Even women's groups cannot be perceived as a homogenous entity with a similar stand on issues related to contraception. One strand of thought within the movement defends the use of such injectables and implants is the only way poor and powerless women can have control over their lives (the contraceptive is an injectable, so neither husbands nor in laws would come to know of the contraceptive method and they can escape pregnancy). So, where does the movement head of rand how does it arrive at a consensus? Contrary to the above view, the widespread availability of Depo can dilute efforts to challenge the basic social and economic conditions that produce women's powerlessness. Moreover, the drug's side effects can never justify its use.[95]

The Battle against Sex-selection and Selective Abortion of Female Foetuses

Female infanticide has been an age-old practice in India. Female babies were killed by feeding them poisonous berry extracts, opium or suffocating them. A few decades back science has added a new dimension of sophistication to this practice.[96]

In 1974, amniocentesis was being clinically tested in India as a technique for detecting foetal abnormalities. The survey outcome of 11,000 couples who has volunteered for the test at All India Institute of Medical Science (AIIMS), new Delhi, revealed that the basic motivation for this enthusiastic response had been the possibility to know the sex of the child during pregnancy. By 1975, it was quite evident that the tests were being followed by the abortion of female fetuses.[97]

The tests carried out at AIIMS were stopped by 1979. There were reports from some North Indian states where medical practitioners were blatantly advertising their services. An advertisement for the amniocentesis test claimed "Better Rs 500 now than Rs 5 lakh later."[98] There were some others, which referred to daughters as "liability to the family and a 'threat' to the nation's population."

In the year 1982, a three-point position was arrived at a meeting convened in New Delhi, wherein: firstly, an appeal was made to the government to restrict the use of amniocentesis to only teaching and medical research establishments. Secondly, the Indian Medical Council was requested to take stringent action against members involved in the practice. Thirdly, women's organizations were to keep a vigil against the exponential growth and spread of the practice.[99]

Although, the government had taken steps to restrict the practice of the test, the efforts were futile. The sex determination business had spread its roots in various pockets of India. This was the phase when the campaign against sex determination consolidated itself. In the early 1980s, the Forum against Sex, Determination and Sex-Pre-selection (FASDSP) and later on, the Doctors against Sex-Determination and Sex-Pre-Selection 9DASDSP), was formed. These groups in alliance addressed various issues in relation to the new reproductive technologies, undertook surveys and public awareness drives. This phase was a landmark in women's activism. Women's groups identified and exposed doctors who were performing these tests, addressed the public through speeches and posters, organized marches and rallies and wrote articles in the media.

In 1986, a women's group filed a petition in the Bombay High Court following the death of a woman who underwent the test in the same year. The FASDSP brought together a number of women's groups and social action groups to create public awareness on the issue. A special task force was set up to look into the issue of sex-determination and to suggest a law to ban the test in the state of Maharashtra. At the end of the eighties, the Maharashtra government finally banned the use of amniocentesis and the other pre- natal diagnostic techniques. However, this was not the end of the campaign. The campaign then demanded for a national legislation, as the sex-determination tests continued unabated in other states in India.

The centre banned all sex-determination tests in 1994, under the Pre-Natal Sex- Determination Technologies (PNDT) Act. Enforced in 1996, the Act aimed to check sex selective abortion and maintain a balance in the sex ratio. The act prohibits ultrasound tests on pregnant women without valid reasons. It was mandatory for doctors running ultrasound clinics to obtain written consent of the concerned women as well as permission of the competent authority before performing ultrasonography. Tests only to detect genetic, sex-linked or metabolic disorders, chromosomal abnormalities or certain congenital malformations by registered clinics or laboratories are permitted. According to the PNDT Act, determining the sex of the foetus is a punishable crime and doctors/relatives who encourage such a test – or even the woman herself – could be fined up to Rs 50,000 along with serving jail terms from three to five years.

Unfortunately, the Act was not free from lacunae, as it did not ban the emerging sex- pre-selection tests. Moreover, the Act had some inherent contradictions. It did not seek to criminalize the doctor under the Indian Penal Code, but let the Medical Council of India deal with violations of the Act. As a result, not a single doctor had been booked or tried under the PNDT Act of 1994. At this point, two organizations CEHAT and MASUM along with Sabu George filed a Public Interest litigation (PIL) in February 2000 against the Union of India in the Supreme Court.[100]

The PIL precipitated a massive response, mainly because in 2001 the Census revealed that the sex ratio, categorically in the 0-6 age group was dangerously skewed. In Maharashtra, which had appreciable human development indicators, the sex ratio of children below six years fell from 946 girls per 1000 boys in the 2001 census.[101]

Following the PIL, the Supreme Court directed the Government of India and the states to ensure strict enforcement of the Act to stringently monitor the activities of ultrasound diagnostic clinics to prevent illegal sex selective abortion and strengthen implementation. In 2003, PNDT Act of 1994 was revised to become the PC & PNDT (Pre-Conception and Pre-Natal Diagnostic Techniques) Act of 2003.

Quinacrine is an anti-malarial drug, used in the form of oral tablets and occasionally as an injection to treat the malarial fevers. Jaime Zipper, a Chilean scientist, first published reports in the late 1960s and early 70s about the potential use of quinacrine slurry (later developed as pellets) for chemical sterilization on women. It has gradually gained ground and promoted as an effective mode of female sterilization over the last three decades, despite the opposition by women's health activists. There are several contraindications of the method, both short and long term and reliable data is still not available. The efficacy is yet to achieve a satisfactory rate and chances of ectopic pregnancies are quite high.

The short-term complications of quinacrine sterilization may range from pain in the lower abdomen, itching of the vagina, headaches and dizziness, infection of the pelvic cavity, effects on central nervous system. There are issues relating to its effects on the uterus in case of failure of the method. Chances of ectopic pregnancies (pregnancy occurring outside the uterus) are also higher in the event of quinacrine administration. Several issues regarding the long-term complications of the method remain unresolved. The reversibility of the method is not yet established.

In India, quinacrine sterilizations have never received any official approval and DCGI did not grant either approval or license for clinical trials, mass use, distribution, import or manufacture of Quinacrine except for oral use as an anti-malarial drug. In fact, though ICMR was permitted to conduct a limited trial for 50 women. It has initiated and abandoned the trials due to high failure rate. However, a significant section of the NGO sector and private practitioners all over the country have been carrying out illegal quinacrine sterilizations for the last twenty years, subjecting women to unethical trials and exposing them to several health risks. The women's groups and health activists in India launched a campaign against quinacrine sterilization. They argued that it is unacceptable by any standard, and all unethical trials and use of quinacrine be immediately stopped.

Ganatantrik Mahila Samiti, a women's organization in Kolkata protested against the use of quinacrine and was supported by a large number of women's groups. There were protests in Delhi by women's groups and other health groups. In July 1997, a Public Interest Litigation (PIL) to ban Quinacrine was filed by All India Democratic Women's Association (AIDWA) and Centre for Social Medicine and Community health of Jawaharlal Nehru University, Delhi. In March 1998, the Supreme Court of India delivered a judgment for the banning of Quinacrine pellets for female sterilization.

Despite the ban by the Supreme Court, a study report of 2003 revealed that quinancrine non-surgical sterilizations were being carried out in some parts of West Bengal without informing the women of possible side effects and they were not asked to sign any consent form or release form. Such findings necessitate that the campaign be strengthened and punitive measures be taken up against those who have violated the restriction, so that such malpractices could be stopped in future.

Challenging Population Control policies and Two-child Norm

During the last 15 years, population control in India has moved away from a tightly connected system of policies imposed by the central government. Instead individual states have devised population policies of their own and have relied on targets and coercion as the mechanism to achieve 'population control'. About ten states, namely Madhya Pradesh, Rajasthan, Uttar Pradesh, Haryana, Himachal Pradesh, Orissa, Chhattisgarh, Gujarat, Maharashtra and Andhra Pradesh came up with state Population Policies, which deter parents of two children from having a third. These policies employ disturbing new incentives and disincentives and tread on the rights and health of the people, especially those having a marginal existence in the society – poor, Dalits, tribals, and women. The State population policies (SPP) of the referred states comprised features such as:

- Disentitlement of the third child to ration under public distribution system'

- Parent to be penalized in their jobs, if they hold a government job;

- Withdrawal of a range of welfare programs;

- Bar people from contesting elections and also removing them from existing posts in the Panchayat Raj Institution after the birth of the third child

- Introduce long acting hormonal contraceptives in the Family Welfare Programmes.

Women's organizations in Delhi played a critical role in initiating a public debate on the whole issue of population control from 1993 onwards. But with the SPP coming in place in 10 states, they argued that these coercive policies are both anti-women and anti- poor and are against the Cairo Declaration[102] and NPP principles. A consistent campaign against population control policies and two child norm was taken up by Sama, AIDWA, CWDS, Sheli, Delhi Science Forum, Medico friend Circle, Jan Swasthy Abhiyan, CSSM- JNU, Health watch up-Bihar, forum for women's health and many other women and health groups along with individual researchers and academicians. The movement gained momentum through debates, studies seminars, press conferences and public tribunals.

A memorandum to the National Human Rights Commission (NHRC) was submitted on 2002, as the campaign group felt that the measures mentioned in SPP or these States violate human rights of people and should not be included in the population policy. The memorandum requested the NHRC to direct the states to comply with the directives and not to use population policies to deny basic rights.

After receiving the memorandum, the NHRC issued notices to the state governments. The states were asked to explain the questionable provisions in their population control policies.

A study on the implications of state population policy on the local self-governance (panchayat raj institutions (PRIs) by Sama and MP BGVS showed that the two child norm disproportionately impacts adivasis, dalits, especially women and in general the poor. Nearly 50% of the 128 respondents were dalits and adivasis (SCs and STs) of which almost 40% were women, most being non-literate, landless and from the lowest category of average monthly household income.

A large number of younger men and women in the reproductive age group are adversely affected by this norm. the study highlighted, for example, an emerging trend whereby older women/mothers/mothers-in-law replaced vacated posts of daughters/daughter-in-law.

The study also revealed that the norm has far reaching implications for women. Forced abortions, giving up a child for adoption, desertion and abandonment of women and children were used as strategies to prevent disqualification and continue as representatives.

Another study of the implications of the two child norm by Mahila Chetna Manch in Orissa, Haryana, Madhya Pradesh and Rajasthan highlighted that implementation of the norm had led to an increase in the number of pre-natal sex determination tests that resulted in the abortion of female fetuses. A study by the organization SUTRA in Himachal Pradesh shows that the districts with the highest juvenile sex ration have the highest disqualification, while those with the lowest sex ratio show no or very few disqualifications.

A People's Tribunal organized by HRLN, Sama, JSA, Health watch UP Bihar and Hunger Project held at Delhi, nearly 70 women from 15 states such as Uttar Pradesh, Rajasthan, Himachal Pradesh, Madhya Pradesh, Haryana, Tamil Nadu, Gujarat and Bihar assembled in Delhi to depose before a Public Tribunal. On the pretext of promoting small family, as many as 4000 men and women from the states of Rajasthan, Madhya Pradesh, Chhattisgarh and Haryana have been disqualified from various panchayat positions on the grounds of infringement of the two-child norm.

After a long campaign, publication of reports and findings[103] on the ill effect of such policies especially on women and advocacy with the parliamentarians, the states of Himachal Pradesh and Madhya Pradesh have finally revoked the two child norm in May and November 2005, respectively.

The women's movement thus had played a crucial role in systematically campaigning against hazardous contraceptives, coercive population policies and sex selective abortion. However, there had not been systematic engagement of the movement with Assisted Reproductive Technologies[104] making our understanding of these technologies and their implication on women inadequate. It is important to understand the context in which these technologies are used, uses/abuse to which they are put to and the implications that these have on women's health and lives. This is because, where at one level there is unavailability of necessary medical technologies, at the other level there is over medicalization. What becomes fundamental for the women's movement is to question the social stigma associated with infertility. But simultaneously also to deglamorise these technologies by bringing in the real picture of low also to deglamorise these technologies by bringing in the real picture of low success rate, side effects of the hormonal drugs that are used in the treatment and anguish of women undergoing treatment. Given the pace at which these technologies are invading lives of women, these issues cannot be left unattended by the ongoing women's movement of the country.

Campaigning for a Rational Drug Policy

Both health groups and consumer groups have been campaigning for a Rational Drug Policy based on the principle of essential drugs. In the absence of rational drug use by the prescribers and the consumer, it is obvious that a rational drug policy alone would not be able to benefit the public. The major demands of the rational drug campaigners have been withdrawal of hazardous and irrational drugs. Control of drug prices, proper screening of therapeutic efficacy of a particular combination of medicine, and protection of the population against potential misuse.[105]

Looking for new markets and higher profits, multinational pharmaceutical companies were pressurizing third world governments to liberalize their drug policies that were otherwise protective of the interests of the national pharma companies as well as those of the consumers. In reaction to the Indian government's drug policy that was solely interested in creating and maintaining a stronghold of the international pharmaceutical sector, a network called the All India Drug Action Network (AIDAN) was established in 1982. AIDAN argued that the exorbitant drug prices were leading to further inaccessibility of essential and rational drugs for the marginalized sections. It also critiqued the irrational drug use by doctors and the increasing drug dumping the phenomena by which drugs banned in Western/developed countries are marketed in poor countries like India (For instance, Novalgin, a common pain killer manufactured by hoecht, was banned in West Germany, but freely available – even without prescription – and indiscriminately used in India).

The campaign for a Rational Drug Policy has also been fighting for the availability of essential drugs at affordable prices and for the withdrawal of irrational and dangerous drug combinations. It is also lobbying for the use of generic names of drugs, since the manufactures sell the same drug under different brand names and charge exceptionally high rates to make profits. For example, Paracetamol is sold by different companies under different brand names like Crocin, Calpol, etc. thse tablets are priced as 80-90 paise per tablet, whereas the actual manufacturing cost of paracetamol is about 15 paisa per tablet.

In 1983, LOCOST was established by a majority of the activists who were a part of the larger rational drug campaign. LOCOST has been successful n demystifying the production process and demonstrated that drugs can be manufactured and sold well below current market prices. In retaliation to the prices charged by national and international pharmaceuticals that are generally beyond this citizen's reach the project has evolved about 80 law cost generic drugs.

In 1986, an all-India seminar on National Drug Policy was organized in Delhi by the Delhi Science Forum and Federation of Medical Representatives Associations of India (FMRAI), among many other organizations. The seminar addressed issues of inadequate supply of essential drugs, proliferation of non-essential drugs and irrational pharmaceutical products, hazardous implications of drugs, issues related to pharmaceutical industries, pricing and profitability, and the question of self-reliance in developing countries. This dialogue between several national organizations, scientific institutions, international organizations significant tone to forward the national policy on drugs in India.

The rational drug campaign is currently pressing the government for a price regime. It ahs critiqued the Pharmaceutical Policy 2004 for withdrawal of price regulatory mechanisms. Under the new policy, the number of drugs under price control has been reduced to 74 drugs as compared to the earlier 347 drugs that enjoyed protection under the Pharmaceutical Policy of 1979. It argued that this would lead to further inaccessibility and impoverishment of the masses.

LOCOST, Jan Swasthya Sahyog (JSS), AIDAN and the Medico Friend Circle (MFC) have filed a series of supportive affidavits in the Supreme Court in 2003. These groups have questioned the rationale behind the criteria for drug price control in the Pharmaceutical Policy 2002. (PP 02): "It is our submission that the policy will increase the price of medicines and therefore have a long-term effect, for the worse, on the health of people, especially poor people".

The Bhopal Gas Tragedy – A Sustained Campaign

The Bhopal disaster (December 3rd, 1984) was caused by the accidental release of 40 tones of Methyl Isocyanate (MIC), a dangerous and toxic gase, from a pesticide plant of the Union Carbide India Ltd. the factory was located in the heart of Bhopal and the gas leak ended up killing almost 20,000 was instantly poisoned by the gas leak. The effects of the contamination are felt and seen even today, after almost two decades.

While certain health consequences were common to both women and men, women additionally suffered from health problems that were specific to them. The gas will continue to affect generations of women. Among women who were pregnant at the time of the disaster, 43% suffered spontaneous abortion. In the years that followed, the spontaneous abortion rate remained four to ten times worse than the national Indian average. Only 50% of pre-adolescent girls, who were exposed to the gas, had normal menstrual cycles. It is now coming to light that even girls who were exposed in infancy and were in their mother's wombs are experiencing 'menstrual chaos'.

MFC was the first to carry out an epidemiological study of the Bhopal gas tragedy and did a pregnancy outcome study in Bhopal nine months after exposure to the toxic gas. The study found that women who were pregnant at that time of gas exposure suffered from spontaneous abortions, still births, diminished fetal movements, and menstrual disorders. Another study by MFC uncovered large differences between more and less exposed neighborhoods in their frequencies of menstrual problems, such as shortening of cycle, excess bleeding during menstruation, vaginal discharges, etc.

A study report, 'Surviving Bhopal: Toxic Present, Toxic Future', in 2001, by Srishti, a Delhi-based environmental NGO highlights the fact that "not only the soil, but also the groundwater, vegetables and even beast mild is contaminated to various degrees by heavy metals like nickel, chromium, mercury and lead, Volatile Organic Compounds (VOCs) like dichlorobenzene and halo-organics like dichloromethane and chloroform cause as serious health threat not only to those currently exposed but also to future generation".[106]

National Campaign for Health care as a Fundamental Right

In an effort to establish the right to basic healthcare as fundamental (Constitutional) rights, JSA aimed to build a national social consensus on the issue. As a part of the process to establish health rights, a series of Regional public hearings on Right to Health Care were organized by JSA in collaboration with the NHRC in various parts of country.

To ensure that the State takes the public hearings seriously, JSA groups in various states started a process of documenting cases of denial of healthcare.

Information was collected with the help of a specific protocol, and cases where denial of health services has led to the loss of life, physical damage or severe financial loss to patients were brought into the forefront. These case studies depicted the real status of the primary health care services in the country.

A series of Regional Public hearings were organized in different pockets of the country, where the documented case studies on denial of health care were presented.

Western	Southern	Northern	Eastern	North-eastern
Bhopal in july 2004	Chennai in August 2004	Lucknow in September 2004	Ranch in October 2004	Guwahati in November 2004

These major regional hearing, each attended by hundreds of delegates was followed by a culminating event, i.e., the National Public Hearing on Right to Health Care organized by JSA and NHRC on 16-17 December 2004 at New Delhi. Subsequently, a National Action Plan was released by the NHRC with inputs from JSA towards operationalising the right to health care within the Indian context. The state units of JSA demanded implementation of the NHRC 'National Action Plan'[107] on Right to Health Care on World health Day, 2005.

One of JSA's main tasks now is to pressurize government not only to implement the NHRC Action Plan, but also to work towards a comprehensive legislation that will guarantee the right to health care to all citizens of India.

Monitoring NRHM: A People's Rural Health Watch

Several members of JSA were involved in the Task Groups of the National Rural Health Mission in an attempt to make the NRHM more effective and sensitive to the needs of the disadvantaged people and communities. There have been some concrete recommendations from the JSA to this end. However, the Mission is fraught with limitations. JSA raised a large number of concerns relating to the conceptualization, design and implementation of the Mission. In this context, JSA has planned to take up an ongoing activity to monitor and influence the Mission in a pro-people direction through the formation of a 'People's Rural health Watch'.

This process was initiated in May 2005 and is expected to do the following:

- Monitoring of the actual implementation at state level, through surveys of health facilities, systems and reviews;
- Analysis of available documents regarding NRHM including task group recommendations, funding sources and financial allocations, etc.;
- Distribution of a NRHM Action Alert Kit that would put reflect JSA's position on the NRHM, and guide local groups and organizations on how they can possibly engage with and monitor the implementation of the NRHM.

Decentralization of Health – An effort by Mine Workers of dalli rajhara

The Chhatisgarh Mines Shramik Sangh (CMSS), an independent trade union of iron mine workers of Drug district of Chattisgarh. The workers demanded for fair wages and safe working conditions with basic facilities. The struggle subsequently expanded to include primary education and health. The mine workers initiated a health programme after the death of a woman worker during childbirth. A need was felt for an appropriate health care facility that was accessible to the workers and the Shaheed Hospital began taking shape. The hospital was built from the contributions of the mine workers. A small group of the doctors sympathetic to the movement engaged full time with the hospital. Some of the mine workers volunteered to be the health workers who, while continuing to work in the mines, devoted time to the hospital. Some of the workers were not educated and some had very little formal education. Initially they were apprehensive about their capabilities, but with time, they became highly skilled at nursing, operation theatre work, and management functions of the hospital. Today the hospital has 80 beds, with a lab and an X-ray machine. The mine workers with the support of CMSS made the project a success.[108]

Low cost Standard Therapeutics – LOCOST

LOCOST was founded in 1983 as an important alternative source of medicines for the poor to access drugs at affordable price3s. it is a public, non-profit charitable trust registered in Baroda in Gujarat that has demonstrated that standard rational drugs can be manufactured and sold at a much affordable price, thereby dispelling the myth of high priced drugs as the only effective ones. In retaliation to the prices charged by national and international pharmaceuticals that are generally beyond this citizen's reach, the project has evolved about 80 low cost generic drugs. LOCOST has been supplying drugs to over 100 civil society organizations, NGOs and social action groups for the past 23 years, who in turn make them available to the poor. This has helped groups and individuals to circumvent the virtual monopoly of drug manufactures. Currently functioning in Gujarat, Maharashtra and Karnataka, it has also been involved in advocacy for a people oriented drug policy and rational therapeutics, envisaging further threat to poor consumers in the central government's plan to decontrol the prices of the current list of schedule drugs as part of the overall liberalization programme.

Federation of Medical and States Representatives' Association of India (FMRAI)

This National Federation of Medical and Sales representatives has 47,000 members, most of which are from pharmaceutical industry. The federation has nearly 300 centres covering all important cities in all the states. The federation deals with service and working conditions of the members with nearly 200 pharmaceutical companies.

The federation, apart from trade union issues, deals with the issues related to medicines and health rights of the people. FMRAI since 1978 has campaigned for a rational pharmaceutical policy. FMRAI vigorously campaigned against super 301 imposed by USA and later took up a campaign of popularization of patent issues among the public. It is the only federation, which initiated a country wide, strike against the Patents Amendment Bill of 1998. FMRAI has formed separate cells in the states for redressal of the problems of the women medical representatives. Nearly 10% of the member is women.

Search for Alternatives – a Shodhini Experience

The women's movement has played a crucial role in critiquing the hegemony of western medical science. It initiated a self-help approach and demanded for non- discriminatory, women friendly health care services irrespective of caste class and religion. Dissatisfied with modern health are services, some women's groups held a national consultation in October 1987 in SRED, Tamil Nadu where 50 women's health activists from both rural and urban areas gathered to discuss the state of women's health. A member of the Geneva Women's Health Collective that had begun to explore non- allopathic alternatives was also present at this meeting.

In the course of the discussion, it was obvious that while there were a number of similar remedies and cures being used in different parts of the country, much was dying out with the passing on of older women. There was an urgent need to document and recorded this knowledge, which has been passed down form woman to woman over generations. A small group, action Research on Alternative medicines and Women's health was formed that brought together a number of field based organizations to collect, collate, test and document information on traditional medicine under 'Shodhini'. It attempted to discover meaningful alternatives in health that would respond to women's health needs in India, especially the needs of socio-economically marginalized women. A woman-oriented approach aimed at evolving a simple, natural and cost-effective health care system, it also aimed at increasing women's control over their own bodies by understanding its rhythms and power, and looking after their own health needs by training local women in simple gynecology through self help. Another objective was also to empower women healers by reclaiming and validating their traditional knowledge and enhancing status.

The research finding was compiled into a book 'Touch Me, Touch-me-not' in 1997 and was translated into many Indian languages.

Appropriate Technologies for Health – Jan Swasthy Sahayog (JSS)

There has been rapid development of technology in the last few years but it has eluded the public health system, specifically women's health. Among the health workers in the village level there is no or poor access to technology who has to deal with common women's health problem on a daily basis. To make some of these technologies available and accessible, Jan Swasthya Sahayog (JSS) a voluntary, non-profit, registered society founded by a group of health professionals in Bilaspur district of Chattisgarh, JSS in involved in research activities to develop and validate low-cost health care and diagnostic technology, including appropriate solutions to common health problems, and also making them available for all marginalized groups. JSS has evolved simple but accurate technologies that are acceptable and cheap and hence can be used in low resource settings. Other than developing simple tools like thermometers and Bold Pressure instruments, patient friendly teaching stethoscope, in regard women's reproductive health there is a reproductive health test battery for diagnosis of urinary and baginal infections, pregnancy, pre-esclampsia; safe delivery kits, tests for anemia and also developed herbal remedies. The efforts are an answer to the high technology driven private health care sector and rapid withdrawal of the public health system that is increasingly undermining the health of the poor.

Sadaphuli – barefoot Gynecologists of MASUM

The health activists explored alternative avenues of readdressing women's health needs through the formation of self-help groups. One such successful experiment is Sadaphuli, a Self-help group for Women's Health by Mahila Sarvangin Uttakarsh Mandal (MASUM), a community based women's organization in Pune district of Maharashtra. It was recognized that socio-cultural barriers and taboos inhibited women form expressing any problem even remotely associated with reproduction and sexuality. These problems were often neglected or left untreated. Most women were shy and afraid to talk to or be examined by male doctors present at the local primary health centers or the rural hospitals.

In response, MASUM initiated the Feminist Health Centre (FHC) and village based health centers known as the Sadaphuli Kendras (Sadaphuli literally meaning ever blossoming flower – vinca rosea) in 1994 & 1995 respectively. The women's health programme here is built on the self help principle, which aims to empower women with knowledge of their own bodies and addresses unequal relationship between the provider and receiver because of the possession of knowledge and skills with the provider, by sharing information. It recognizes the emotional, social and environmental factors that affect health and works towards addressing these issues.

The community based health workers (called the Sadaphulis) have been trained to conduct breast examinations as well as speculum and bi-manual examinations for detection of reproductive tract infection and other gynecological problems. In addition to this, at the Feminist Health Centre, pap smear test are conducted to detect cervical cancer. High-risk pregnancies are identified and necessary precautions are suggested. Reproductive tract complications and infections are also identified and women are encouraged to initiate a dialogue with their partners about sexual health.[109]

Counseling of Women Victims of Violence in a Public Hospital: the DILAASA project

With an aim to sensitize the public health system to gender and violence issues and to develop a health-based response to domestic violence. CEHAT and the Public Health Department of the Brihanmumbai Municipal Corporation (BMC) have established Dilaasa at K.B. Bhabha Hospital, Bandra (West), Mumbai. Dilaasa means 'Reassurance' and seeks to provide social and psychological support to women survivors of domestic violence. Dillaasa believes that every woman has a right to a safe home, right to a life without violence;' there is no excuse for domestic violence. Through collaboration with Majlis and Lawyers Collective legal aid is provided to women. There is provision for temporary shelter for a short period at two shelters in the city. The hospital also provides 24-hours shelter under medical observation.

Training is one of the ongoing activities of the centre. The hospital staff is being sensitized to gender issues so that they are able to screen women survivors of domestic violence and refer them to the centre.[110]

Jan Swasthya Abhiyan (JSA)

JSA emerged as the campaign platform from the People's health Assembly process in India n December 2000. Jan Swasthya Abhiyan is a coalition of 20 National networks and move than 1000 organizations from all over the country working in the field of health, science, women's issues and development. Since early 2000, the activities of JSA in India are being carried out a the local, state and national levels. Some of JSA's key areas of activities are:

- Initiating 'Watch Groups' to monitor and advocate health situations, implementation of programmes and policies;
- Analysis and critique of health and related policies;
- Campaigning for right to health care as fundamental right;
- Organizing public dialoguers, conventions, seminars, workshops and peoples tribunals on right to health and health determinants;
- Development of information sheets, alerts booklets on health issues, policies, programmes on health issues;
- Advocacy for strengthening the public health system;
- Advocating regulation of the private health sector;
- Critiquing the National Health Policy and advocating pro-people changes in the health sector.[111]

In the *Paschim Banga Khet Samity vs. State of West Bengal,* 1996, the petitioner(s) aggrieved by the indifferent and callous attitude on the part of the medical authorities at the various State run hospitals in Kolkata in providing treatment for the serious injuries sustained by the petitioner following a train accident, filed this writ petition.

The Supreme Court held that the Article 21 imposes an obligation on the state to safeguard the right to life of every person. Preservation of human life is thus of paramount importance. The government hospitals run by the State and the medical officers employed therein are duty-bound to extend medical assistance for preserving human life. Failure on the part of a government hospital to provide for timely medical treatment to a person in need of such treatment results in violation of his right to life guaranteed under Article 21. Therefore, the failure of a government run health centre to provide timely treatment is violative of a person's right to life. Further, the court ordered that Primary health care centres be equipped to deal with medical emergencies. It has also been held in this judgment that the lack of financial resources cannot be a reason for the state to shy away from its constitutional obligation.[112]

"The Constitution envisages the establishment of a welfare state... providing adequate medical facilities for the people is an essential part of the obligations undertaken by the government in this respect and discharges this obligation by running hospitals and health centres."

In line with its general approach of frequently offering comprehensive remedies that go beyond merely providing redress for the victim and also laying down the necessary policy and administrative steps to be taken by the state in the wider public interest, the court not only ordered compensation but also directed by the type of facilities that the state government had to provide. This included hospitals and emergency provision (ambulances and communication) by formulating a blueprint for primary health care with particular reference to treatment of patients under an emergency as part of the state's public health obligation under Article 47. Furthermore, the Court ruled that its orders should apply to other states, together with the national government, and that they should be sent a copy of the judgment.[113]

In *Paramanand Katara vs. Union of India, 1989*, a Division Bench of the Supreme Court admitted an application filed under Article 32 by a practicing advocate along with a new item entitle: "Law Helps the Injured to Die" published in The Hindustan Times, New Delhi, as a public interest litigation. The petitioner, through this public interest litigation, had highlighted the difficulties faced by the injured persons in getting medical treatment urgently required to save their lives, in view of the refusal by many doctors and hospitals on the ground that such cases are medico-legal cases. In that case, the petition narrated the unfortunate incident of a person dying due to the non-availability of immediate medical treatment. "The Court extensively death with the professional ethics of the medical profession and issued a number of directions to ensure that an injured person is instantaneously given medical aid, notwithstanding the formalities to be followed under the procedural criminal law. The court declared that the right to medical treatment is a Fundamental Right of the people under Article 21 of the Constitution. The court issued directions to the Union of India, Medical Council of India, and Indian Medical Association etc. to give wide publicity to the Court's directions in this regard[114]. "The Supreme Court regarding obligation of state to provide emergency medical treatment, said that whether the patient was innocent of criminal, it was the obligation of those in charge of community health to preserve the life of the patient"[115].

Care and Treatment in Mental Health Institutions

Since mental health takes a back seal and is largely ignored, public litigation and media exposure plays a role in highlighting gross violations of human rights Judiciary therefore, plays a specific role in addressing some of the critical mental health care needs of the country. Supreme Court and state high court decisions have tried to address the issues pertaining to denial of right to mentally ill people.

The courts in India have held in a number of cases that mental health is an integral and inseparable part of health and have repeatedly extended that there lies a positive duty on the part of the Government to promote health and rights to live with human dignity which are fundamental rights enshrined in Article 21 of the constitution of India. The guiding principles enunciated by the Apex Court in some of these judgments are referred as under:-

- In *Hussainara Khatoon (No.1) vs. Home Secretary, Bihar,* it was held by the Apex Court that "right to a speedy trial, a fundamental right, is implicit in the guarantee of life and personal liberty enshrined in Article 21 of the Constitution". Speedy trial is the essence of criminal justice. These principles were reiterated in Abdul Rehman Antuley vs. R. S. Nayak in which detailed guidelines for speedy trial of an accused were laid down even though not time limit was fixed for trial of offences.

- In a public interest litigation (PIL), involving *Veena Sethi vs. State of Bihar* case in 1982, the court was informed through a letter that some prisoners who had been insane at the time of trial but had subsequently been declared sane had not been released due to inaction of the state authorities and had remained in jail for 20 to 30 years. The court directed them to be released forthwith, considering the requirement of protection of right to life and liberty of the citizen against the lawlessness of the state.

- In a public interest petition *Dr. Upendra Baxi vs. State of Uttar Pradesh & others* was filed before the Hon'ble Court (1981) to enforce human rights of protective home inmates at Agra, UP, who were kept in abject dehumanized living conditions, the Hon'ble court issued various appropriate directions from time to time in order to ensure that the inmates of the Protective home at Agra do not continue to live in inhumane and degrading conditions and that the right to life with dignity enshrined in Article 21 of the Constitution is made real and meaningful for them.

- In a set of Public Interest Petitions *B. R. Kapoor & others vs. Union of India* and others (1983) and PUCL & Others vs union of India & others (1983), filed before the Hon'ble Court regarding Shahdara Mental hospital, Delhi, Hon'ble court observed that the Mental hospital located at the capital of the country should be run by the Union of India and not by Delhi Administration. The Hon'ble court directed that the Mental hospital located at Shahdara should be modeled on the lines of similar psychiatric specialty obtaining at the institution run by NIMHAS at Bangalore, and also directed to examine as to whether the hospital could be attached to a teaching institution which has post graduation specialization in Psychiatry, neurology and neuron Psychiatry. This led to the formation of the Institute of human Behaviour and Allied Sciences, IHBAS.

In the case of *Chandan Kumar Bhanik vs. State of West Bengal* (1988) the apex Court observed: "Management of an institution like the mental hospital requires flow of human love and affection, understanding and consideration for mentally ill persons these aspects are far more important than a reutilized, stereotyped and bureaucratic approach to mental health issues".

- In the case of *Sheela Barse vs. Union of Indian and others* (1993) the apex Court observed that admission of non-criminal mentally ill persons in jails is illegal and unconstitutional; All mentally ill persons kept in various central, district and sub jails must be medically examined immediately after admission; Specialized psychiatric help must be made available to all inmates who have been lodged in various jails/subs jails; Each and every patient must receive review or revaluation of developing mental problems; a mental health team comprising clinical psychologists, psychiatric nurses and psychiatric social workers must be in place in every mental health hospital.

- The apex Court in its judgment in *Rakesh Chandra Narayan vs. State of Bihar* (1986) had laid down certain cardinal principles. These are: Right of a mentally ill person to food, water, personal hygiene, sanitation and recreation is an extension of the right to life as in Article 21 of the Constitution: Quality norms and standards in mental Health are non- negotiable; Treatment, teaching training and research must be integrated to produce the desired results; Obligation of the State in providing undiluted care and attention to mentally ill persons is fundamental to the recognition of their human right and is irreversible.

The apex Court in *Rakesh Chandra Narayan vs. State of Bihar* case requested the National Human Rights Commission (NHRC) to be involved in the supervision of mental health hospitals at Agra, Ranchi and Gwalior w.e.f. 11.11.1997 it stated as under:

"Having death with this matter for some time, we have formed the opinion that a better method for supervision of the functioning of Agra Protective Home is necessary. Now that the benefit of the National Human Rights Commission (NHRC) with statutory powers under the Protection of Human Rights Act, 1993 is available and since most of the problems associated with the functioning of Agra Protective Home are such that they can be better dealt with by NHRC we consider it expedient to make this order to involve the NHRC in the exercise. It is likely that the pendency of this matter and the directions made by this court may have to some extent inhibited the NHRC in exercise of its ordinary functions relating to Agra Protective Home so far. The order we make herein will also have the effect of removing any such impression or inhibition. We have today made an order in WP (Criminal) No. 1900/81 (Dr. Upendra Baxi vs. State of U.P. and Others) requesting the "we now request the NHRC to be involved in the supervision of the functioning of Agra Protective home to ensure that it functions in the manner as is expected for achieving the object for which it has been set up"

The Hon'ble court further observed "This matter pertains to the functioning of the Agra, Gwalior and Ranchi mental Asylums. We have today November 11th 1997 in *Dr. Upendra Baxi v State of Uttar Pradesh & Others* requested the NHRC to be involved in the supervision of the functioning of Agra Protective home in the manner indicated in the order. We are of the opinion that the same kind of order needs to be made in this matter also relating to Agra, Ranchi and Gwalior asylums. Accordingly, we request the NHRC to perform this exercise in the same manner".

The Hon'ble court vide order dated 12.5.2000 disposed of the Writ Petition (Dr. Upendra Baxi, observing "Now that the National human Rights Commission is seized of the matter it will not be appropriate for this court to proceed any further in this writ petition. The petition is accordingly consigned to the records if and when the Commission requires any help or assistance from the court it is at liberty to make an appropriate application. The writ petitions are disposed of".

Conclusion

The National Health Policy (NHP) 2017, proposes an ambitious health agenda, especially with regard to the enhancement of public spending on health from the current level of 1.15% of GDP to 2.5 %. However, the policy does not address many issues pointed out in the draft NHP 2015.[116] This commentary analyses the negation of the right to health in the policy.

The policy explicitly rejects the idea of legislation on the right to healthcare, thus also negating the rights-based approach to health care. The policy states: "The policy while supporting the need for moving in the direction of a rights based approach to healthcare is conscious of the fact that threshold levels of finances and infrastructure as a precondition for an enabling environment, to ensure that the poorest of the poor stand to gain the maximum and are not embroiled in legalities. The policy, therefore advocates a progressively incremental assurance based approach, with assured funding to create an enabling environment for realizing health care as a right in the future".

Further, it also states: "Right to health cannot be perceived unless the basic health infrastructure like doctor-patient ratio, patient -bed ratio, nurses-patient ratio, etc. are near or above threshold levels and uniformly spread -out across the geographical frontiers of the country".

The policy cites the following reasons for the rejection of separate legislation on the right to health. First, India's economic and health system development is not up to the level to make the right to health justifiable i.e. legally enforceable by the courts. Second, since health falls within the state list there is a lack of clarity with regard to the utility of a central legislation while the state government is responsible for health.

Third, the lack of clarity with regard to the scope of the legislation: whether the focus of the legislation should be on the enforcement of public health standards or the obligation of the government to ensure entitlements on public health.

It elaborates on the operational challenges to make the right to health a legally enforceable right and states: "Excellent health care system needs to be in place to ensure effective implementation of the health rights at the grassroots level. Right to health cannot be perceived unless the basic health infrastructure like doctor-patient ratio, patient

-bed ratio, nurses-patient ratio, etc. are near or above threshold levels and uniformly spread -out across the geographical frontiers of the of the country". This tantamounts to a rejection of the legal obligation on the right to health, especially since the right to healthcare is a critical entitlement of right to health guaranteed under various international legal instruments and the Indian Constitution.

From a legal perspective, the government of India is under a legal obligation to protect the right to health including the right to healthcare even in the absence of dedicated legislation. This legal obligation emanates from the following facts. First, India has undertaken an international obligation to protect the right to health through the ratification of various human rights treaties. Second, both the Supreme Court of India and High Courts recognised the right to health as a fundamental right that falls within the scope of Article 21 of the Constitution.[117]

Refrences

[1] Sama-Women's Group for Gender and Health (2005) Advancing Right to Health: The Indian Context, Beyond the Circle.

[2] Children's Convention (adopted 1989; entered into force 1990): convention setting forth a full spectrum of civil, cultural, economic, social, and political rights for children, http:..wwww1.umn.edu/humanrts

[3] Women's Convention (adopted 1979; entered into force 1981): The first legally binding international document prohibiting discrimination against women and obligating governments to take affirmative steps to advance the equality of women, http://www1.umn.edu/humanrts

[4] www.hrschool.org

[5] www.cehat.org/rthc

[6] This information is downloaded from the website of Ministry of Law and Justice (Legislative Departments)

[7] This information is downloaded from the website of Ministry of Law and Justice (Legislative Departments)

[8] Article 38, i & ii

[9] Article 19

[10] See: D.K. Basu v. State of West Bengal ,(1997) 1 SCC 416;1997 AIR SCW 233.

[11] (1997) 1 SCC 416; 1997 AIR SCW 233.

[12] AIR 1955 SC 33 .

[13] M.R.F.Ltd .v Inspector, Kerala Government ,AIR 1999 SC 188.

[14] See Express Newspapers Ltd. v. Union of India, AIR 1958 SC 578 .

[15] People's Union for Democratic Rights v. Union of India , AIR 1982 SC 1473 .

[17] AIR 1934 SC 177 . See also M C Mehta v. State of T .N., AIR 1997SC 699 , wherein the Apex Court directed the Central Government to convene a meeting of the concerned Ministers

[18] Principal Secretaries of the respective State Governments to evolve the principles/policies for progressive elimination of employment of children below 14 years of age , in Sivakashi Match Industries and other named notorious industries . Like directions were issued in B.M.M. v. Union of India , AIR 1997 SC 2218 in respect of carpet industries in the State of Uttar Pradesh .

[19] Indira Sawhney v. Union of India , AIR 1993 SC 477 .

[20] AIR 1978 SC 597.

[21] AIR 1978 SC 1548

[22] See Moses Wilson v. Kasturiba , AIR 2008 SC 379

[23] AIR 1979 SC 1360.

[24] AIR 1978 SC 597.

[25] AIR 1979 SC 1369. The same view was expressed in Hussainara Khatoon (No III) v. Home Secretary, Bihar, AIR 1979 SC 1377; M. V. Chauhan v. State, AIR 1997 SC 3400.

[26] AIR 2007 SC 3057.

[27] Moses Wilson v. Kasturiba, AIR 2008 SC 379.

[28] AIR 1992 SC 1701.

[29] For guidelines see Prof.Narendra Kumar, Constitutional Law of India, 2008, 331-32. See also Pankaj Kumar v. State of Maharashtra, AIR 2008 SC 3077.

[30] AIR 2002 SC 1856

[31] A.R. Antulay v. R. S. Nayak, AIR 1992 SC 1701.

[32] Justice A. S. Anand, former CJI, "Third-degree methods, Criminal Act", The Tribune, 11-12-2000. See also Rama Murthy v. State of Karnataka, AIR 1997 SC 1739.

[33] AIR 1981 SC 625.

[34] AIR 1983 SC 378.

[35] AIR 1997 SC 610.

[36] AIR 2004 SC 524.

[37] AIR 2009 SC 985.

[38] AIR 2006 SC 1367.

[39] AIR 1978 SC 527.

[40] AIR 2007 SC 451. See also Akhtari Bai v. State of M. P., AIR 2001 SC 1528.

[41] AIR 1960 SC 1535.

[45] AIR 1963 SC 1295.

[46] AIR 1978 SC 597.

[47] Kharak Singh v. State of U.P., AIR 1963 SC 1295.

[48] Maneka Gandhi v. Union of India, AIR 1978 SC 597.

[49] Ibid

[50] Bombay Dyeing and Manufacturing Co.Ltd. v. Bombay Environmental Action Group, (2006) 3 SCC 434.

[51] District Registrar & Collector v. Canara Bank, 2005 (1) SCC 496.

[52] See R. Sukanya v. R. Sridhar, air 2008 Mad.244, wherein the Madras High Court held publication of telecast of matrimonial proceedings, meant to be conducted in camera, as invasion of right of privacy

[53] AIR 1995 SC 264. See also Govind v. State of M.P., AIR 1975 SC 1378.

[54] AIR 1997 SC 568. In this case, the PUCL filed a petition, by way of P I L, in the wake of the report on "Tapping of politicians' phones" by the CBI, published in an issue of "Main Stream".

[55] The Bhore Committee was constituted by the government in 1940 to prepare a comprehensive proposal for the development of national programme of health services. They submitted the same in 1946. Several National Programmes were developed based on their recommendations.

[56] Gopalan Dr. Sarala & Shiva Dr. Mira (2000) National Profile on Women, health and Development, VHAI, New Delhi.

[57] National health (Sokhey) Sub-Committee (called the Sokhey Committee) and was a part of the National planning Committee constituted by the National Congress in 1940. Its report was presented in 1948.

[58] Ritu Priya, 2005, Public Health Services in India: a historical Perspective in Leena V. Gantgolli, Ravi Duggal and Abhay Shukla (ed) Review of health Care in India

[59] This is the period when economic restricting happened and MNCs emerged. It started with the industrial giants diversifying production in order to capture the world market and revive the economy. While factories in the West were closing down, lots of mergers happened as the big industrialists bought in the smaller ones and expanded their base in third world countries where labour was cheap and the economy that was suffering from inflation did not have much option but to accept and invite these giants to tide over the flux.

[60] 'World Bank Funded Health Care – A Death Certificate for Poor' by Dr Vineeta Gupta

[61] Banerji, Debabar (2001) 'Landmarks in the Development of Health Services in India' in Imrana Qadeer, Kasturi Sen, K. R. nayar (ed) Public Health and the Poverty of Reforms, pg 46

[62] Dabade, Gopal (2006) In Perspective 'Can the poor buy life-saving drugs?' Deccan Herald, April 2006

[63] Srinivasan and Shiva (2002) 'Medicines and Health Care: Women's Perpective' in Renu Khanna, Mira Shiva & Sarala Gopalan (ed) Towards Comprehensive Women's Health Programme and Policy. SAHAJ for women & Health (WAH!)

[64] See NHP 2002, 1.2 www.nic.in

[65] Jan Swasthya Abhiyan 'Policies affecting health care and violation of health rights'. Paper presented at the National Public Hearing on Right Care 2004.

[66] Ibid

[67] Das, Abhijit (2002) 'The Current Policy Scenario in India' in Renu Khanna, Mira Shiva & Sarala Gopalan (ed) Towards Comprehensive Women's Health Programme and Policy. SAHAJ for Women & Health (WAH!)

[68] Seminar 511, March 2002, pg 25.

[69] Qadeer, Imrana (2002) 'Women's Health Policies and Programmes: A Critical Review' in Khanna & Gopalan (ed) Towards Comprehensive Women's Health Programmes and Policy, pg 243

[70] Davar, Bhargavi (2002) 'Dilemmas of Women's Activism in Mental Health' in Khanna, Shiva and Gopalan (ed) pp 472

[71] http://www.mohfw.nic.in/kk/95

[72] National Institute of Health and Family Welfare http://www.ndcnihfw.org/html/Programmes/NationalMentalHealth.htm

[73] Qadeer, Imrana (1999) 'Policy on Women's Health' for National Consultation towards Comprehensive Women's Health Policy and Programmes Feb 18-19.

[74] Sama Team (2005) 'Reproductive Health services: The tran

[75] Ibid

[76] Dasgupta, Rajib (2006) 'Quality Assurance in the National Rural Health Mission (NRHM): Provisions and Debates' in Background Papers for MFC Annual Meet.

[77] People's Rural Health Watch of JSA (2005) Action Alert on National Rural Health Mission.

[78] Ibid

[79] PHA Charter

[80] NFHS 1995

[81] Gopalan, Sarala and Mira Shiva (2000) National Profile on Women, Health and Development: Country Profile India, WHO

[82] BMI – Body Mass Index is a reliable index of adult chronic energy deficiency

[83] IIPS, 1995 in Sarala Gopalan and Mira Shiva National Profile on Women, Health and Development 2000 VHAI, Delhi.

[84] Gopalan and Shiva (2000) National Profile on Women, Health and Development.

[85] Kapilasthrami, Anuj (2005) Women's health: A decade of skewed priorities, NGO Country Report.

[86] Hartigan Pamela, 1999, Communicacble Diseases, Gender, and Equity in Health.

[87] Ibid.

[88] Annual prevalence rate in 2003 as given in http://www.globalhealthreporting.org/countries/India.asp

[89] Ibid

[90] From report of International Initiative for Justice in Gujarat addressing Sexual violence against Women Committed by State and Non-State Actors organized by Citizen's Initiative (Ahmedabad), PUCL Shanti Abhiyan (Vadodara), FAOW, Communalism Combat, Awaaz-E-Niswaan, Stree Sangam (Mumbai), Saheli Jagori, Sama and Nirantar (Delhi), Organised Lesbian Alliance for Visibility and Action (OLAVA), Pune) and other women's organizations in India.

[91] http://www.locostindia.com

[92] Gandhi, Nandita and Nandita Shah (1992): The Issues at Stake: Theory and Practice in the Contemporary Women's Movement in India, Kali for women, New Delhi, pp 15. Prakash, Padma (2005): Women's Health Movement in India: A Historical Perspective.

[93] Lakshmi lingam, Ed. (1998) Understanding Women's Issues: A Reader, Kali for Women, New Delhi.

[94] Contraceptives: Our choices, their choices, Forum for Women's Health, 1995.

[95] Hartmann, Betsy (1987): Reproductive Rights and Wrongs: The Global Politics of Population Control.

[96] Gandhi, Nandita and Nandita Shah (1992): The Issues at stake: Theory and Practice in the Contemporary Women's Movement in India, Kali for Women, New Delhi.

[97] Indu Agnihotri and Vina Majumdar (1995): Changing terms of Political Discourse: Women's Movement India, 1970s-1990s, Ecconomic and Political Weekly, Vol…no… pp 1869-1878.

[98] Gandhi, Nandita and Nandita Shah (1992): The issue of Stake: Theory and Practice in the Contemporary Women's Movement in India, Kali for Women, New Delhi.

[99] Indu Agnihotri and Vina Majumdar (1995): Changing terms of Political Discourse: Women's Movement India, 1970s-1990s, Ecconomic and Political Weekly, Vol…no… pp 1869-1878.

[100] Gupte, Manisha (2003): A walk down a memory lane: an insiders reflections on the campaign against sex-selective abortions, MASUM

[101] Ibid

[102] The International Conference on Population and Development was held in Cairo in the year 1994. The declaration condemned coercive population policies and favoured a population policy based on reproductive health and rights of women. India was one of the signatories among 179 countries that ratified the declaration.

[103] Studies by SUTRA in Himachal Pradesh and Sama-Resource Group for Women and health in Madhya Pradesh on impact of Two Child Norm

[104] Assisted Reproductive Technologies is a group of reproductive technologies, which assist conception and pregnancy. The category of technologies used for assisting reproduction range from simple methods like artificial insemination to method such as in-vitro fertilization (IVF).

[105] Shiva, Mira (1986) 'Essential Drugs – Concept, need and implementation' in Amit Sen Gupta (ed) Drug Industry and the Indian People, DSF & FMRAI

[106] Lakshmi Murthy, Bhopal: Tragedy Without End

[107] Fro details on National Action plan refer annexure II.

[108] People's health Care. Initiative in Chattisgarh district Binayak Sen

[109] Bandewar Sunita paramedics in mr practice: a feasibility evaluation & www.masum.org

[110] Efforts that Worked – A few Case studies, advancing Right to Health: The Indian Context by Sama-Resource Group for Women and Health.

[111] Expect from Report of the National Workshop on Right to Health Care: September 5, 2003 & National Public Consultation on Health Care as Human Right: September 6, 2003

[112] www.cehat.org/rthc

[113] Byrne, Iain (2005) Making the Right to Health a reality: Legal Strategies for Effective Implementations, Commonwealth Law Officer, Inter rights Visiting Fellow, Human Rights Centre, Essex University

[114] Justice A. S. Anand, in M.C. Bhandari Memorial Lecture Public Interest Litigation as Aid to Protection of Human Rights, www.ebc-india.com

[115] Justice Anand (2003) Inaugural Address, National Consultation on Health Care as a Human Right, Jan Swasthya Abhiyan and NHRC

[116] See Phadke, Anant (2015), "Slippery Slope for Public Health Services", EPW Vo.50 (9) 10-32; Chowdhury, Javid (2015) : National Health Policy 2015: A Narrow Focus Needed", EPW, Vol.50 (9), 25-30; Rao Mohan et all, " Draft National health Policy 2015 : A Public Health Analysis", EPW Vol50(17) 94-101.

[117] http://www.livelaw.in/national-health-policy-2017-right-health-negation-reality/

Chapter V

Role Of Human Rights Enforcement Agencies Of India

Introduction

The United Nations Charter is the first international document having an objective of promotion of Human Rights and Fundamental Freedoms. In its early days, the UNO, its Economic and Social Council, and the Human Rights Commission, worked on the notion that the International Bill of Rights should have a declaration of general principles, having moral force and separate Covenant having legally binding force on those states which ratified it, and the mode of their implementation. Thus came into existence the Declaration of Human Rights adopted by the General Assembly, December 10, 1948. The Declaration has influenced many states drafting their Constitutions having these right as part of their Constitution, and therefore enforceable by municipal courts. However, the Declaration does not have the force of law, through its moral influence is substantial.

Implementation of Human Rights under Covenants and First Optional Protocol

A State which has ratified the Covenant on Civil and Political Rights has obligation to secure these rights to its people. Each State Party to the present Covenant undertakes to respect and to ensure to all individuals within its territory and subject to respect and to its jurisdiction the right recognized in the present Covenant, without distinction of any kind , such as race , colour, sex language , religion , political or other opinion , national or social origin, property, birth or other status.

Where not already provided for by existing legislative or other measures, each State Party to the present Covenant undertakes to take the necessary steps, in accordance with its constitutional processes and with the provisions of the present Covenant, to adopt such legislative or other measures as may be necessary to give effect to the rights recognized in the present Covenant. Each State Party to the present Covenant undertakes:

(a) To ensure that any person whose rights or freedoms as herein recognized are violated shall have an effective remedy , notwithstanding that the violation has been committed by person acting in an official capacity:

(b) To ensure that any person claiming such a remedy shall have his right thereto determined by competent judicial ,administrative or legislative authorities, or by any other competent authority provided for by the legal system of the State, and to develop the possibilities of judicial remedy:

(c) To ensure that the competent authorities shall enforce such remedies when granted.

On the other hand, a State ratifying the Covenant on Economic, Social and Cultural Rights merely acknowledge its responsibility to promote better living conditions to its people and other rights under the Covenant, Article [2] of the Covenant runs:

Each State Party to the present Covenant undertakes to take steps, individually and through international assistance and co-operation, especially economic and technical to the maximum of its available resources, with a view to achieving progressively the full realization of the rights recognized in the present Covenant by all appropriate means, including particularly the adoption of legislative measures. The State Parties to the present Covenant undertake to guarantee that the rights enunciated in the present Covenant will be exercised without discrimination of any kind as to race, colour, sex, language, religion, political or other opinion, national or social origin, poverty, birth or other status.

Developing countries, with due regard to Human Rights and their national economy, may determine to what extent they would guarantee the economic rights recognized in the present Covenant to non-nationals.

The instrumentalities for the implementation of the implementation of the Covenant provisions are:

(a) Human Right Committee,

(b) Periodic Reports, and

(c) Conciliation Commission.

The purpose of the Covenant is to persuade the States so far as possible to enact suitable legislation so that human rights could be enforced by the municipal courts of each state – party to the Covenants. Mostly human rights are violated by the States. The objective of Covenants is to protect the individual from such excesses.

Implementation Provisions under the Covenants

For the implementation of the provisions of the Covenant Civil and Political Rights, the main instrumentality envisaged is the Human Rights Committee. The procedure for constituting Human Rights Committee is that each State Party nominates its two nationals who are persons of high moral character and recognized competence is the field of human rights. Consideration should also be given to the usefulness of his having some legal competence.[1] Out of the persons so nominated by the State parties, eighteen members are elected by secret ballot.[2] The human rights committee consists of eighteen members.[3]

A member of the Committee is eligible for re-nomination. At least four months before the date of each election of the Committee (other than an election to fill vacancy) the Secretary –General of United Nations is required to address a written invitation to the State –parties to the Covenant to submit their nominations for membership of the Committee within three months. Thereafter a list was prepared in alphabetical order of all the persons so nominated with an indication of the State parties not later than one month before the date of election. The Secretary –General is required to convene a meeting of the State parties to elect members to the Human Rights Committee.[4] At Such meeting two-thirds of the State parties will constitute a quorum. Those persons who obtain largest number of votes and an absolute majority of the votes of the representatives of the States- parties present and voting will be declared elected.[5] The Committee should not include more than one national of the same State. At the same time consideration has to be given to equitable geographical distribution of membership and to the representation of the different forms of civilization and of the principle legal systems.[6] The initial election should take place not later than six months after date of into force of the Covenant [Article 30 (1)].

The term of the Human Rights Committee is four years. The members are eligible for re-election provides they are nominated by State-parties to the Covenant.[7] However, the term of half of the members of the first Committee would expire at the end of two years after the first election. The retiring nine members will be chosen by lot by the Chairman of the Committee.[8]

The elections for the new Committee will be held in the same manner as of the first Committee.[9]

In the event of a state falling vacant on account of the death or resignation of a member of the Committee or on account of his removal by the unanimous opinion of other members,[10] the Chairman is required to inform the Secretary –General will declare the seat vacant, and the process for the election to the vacant seat will be started provided the term of the member to be replaced does not expire within six months for the declaration of the vacancy.[11] The member of the Committee so elected will hold office only for the remainder of the term of the member who had vacated the office.

The member of the Committee will be entitled to such remuneration from the United Nations on such terms and conditions as the General – Assembly may decide.[12]

The meeting of the Committee are to be held at the headquarters of the United Nations or its office at Geneva.[13]

Necessary staff and facilities for the effective functioning of the Committee will be provided by the Secretary – General of the United Nations.[14] The Committee elects its own officers for a term of two years. They may be re-elected.

Twelve members constitute the quorum of the Committee[15] and all decisions of the Committee, are taken a majority vote of the members present.[16]

The Committee will formulate its own rules of procedure.[17]

Before entering upon his office, each member will make a solemn declaration in open Committee that he will perform his functions impartially and conscientiously.[18]

The members of the Committee are entitled to all facilities, privileges and immunities of experts on mission for the United Nations as laid down in the Convention on Privileges and Immunities of the United Nation.[19]

Reporting Procedure

Under the Covenant the State parties have an obligation to submit reports on the measures they have adopted to give effect to the human rights envisaged under the Covenant, and progress made in the enjoyment of these rights. Such reports are to be made within one year of the entry into force of the present Covenant, and thereafter whenever the Human Right Committee requests a state-party to submit its report. All reports are to be initially submitted to the Secretary- General of the United Nations who is required to transmit them to the Committee for consideration. Such Report should indicate the facts and difficulties, if any relating to implementation of the Covenant provision.[20]

The Human Rights Committee considers such reports and transmits its comments and observations to the State –parties concerned. The Committee may also transmit to the Economic and Social Council these comments along with copies of the repot it has received.[21] The State-parties to the Covenant may also submit to the Committee observations or any comments of the committee.[22] The Secretary- General of the United Nations may, after consultations with the Committee, transmit to their specialized agencies concerned copies of such part of the reports as may fall within their field of competence.

Optional Protocol to the International Covenant on Civil and Political Rights

Under the Covenant on Civil and Political Rights it is only the State who has *locus standi* to file complaint or communication, as the complaints are designated. The individual has been conferred such a right under the first Optional Protocol to the Covenant on Civil and Political Rights. An individual may now lodge a complaint against a state violating human rights under the Covenant. However, such a Complaint can be lodged only against a State party to the Covenant. Article 2 of the Protocol runs:

A State Party to the Covenant that becomes a party to the present protocol recognizes the competence of the Committee to receive and consider communications from individuals subject to its jurisdiction who claim to be victims of violation by that State Party of any of the rights set forth in the Covenant. No Communication shall be received by the Committee if it concerns a State Party to the Covenant which is not a party to the present protocol.

An individual who claims that any of his rights enunciated in the Covenant has been violated and he had exhausted all available domestic remedies may submit a written communication to the Human Rights Committee for consideration.[23] No anonymous communication will be entertained. The same would be fate of a complaint which is incompatible with the previsions of the Covenant.[24]

Once a communication against a state is entertained, the Human Rights Committee would bring it to the attention of the alleged delinquent State. Such a State would submit to the Committee its explanation clarifying the matter and the remedy, if any, within six months.[25]

Thereafter the Human Rights Committee would proceed to consider communications in the light of all written information made available to it by both the parties. The Committee will consider such communication only after ascertaining that the same matter has not been examined under another procedure of international investigation or settlement and after ascertaining that the individual complaint has exhausted all domestic remedies available to him. The Committee will consider the entire matter in closed door meetings and thereafter will communicate its views to the individual complaint and the State concerned.[26]

In its annual Report, the Human Rights Committee will include a report of its activities under the protocol.[27]

It should be noticed that the Protocol all along used the expression "communication "and not complaint. Though, virtually communication is nothing but a complaint. It should also be noticed that the Committee does not render "decision". Even the word "recommendation" has not been used. The expression used is "views".

One may say what the value of mere "views" is when Committee is not competent even to make its recommendation much less to render a decision. Its views are not binding on the state concerned. The Human Rights Committee includes these "views" in its annual report. This means that the activities of the alleged delinquent state will come before the international community. It will certainly gather public opinion. The delinquency of the State will come under the gaze of everybody. All states will know that the delinquent state is not adhering to the provision of the Covenant.

In our submission, the greatest relevance of this provision is that an individual can expose the delinquent state before the international community and people. In our submission even if no direct benefit accrues to the individual addressing a communication to the human rights committee about abuse of human rights, the greatest gain is that individual has got *locus standi* to come before international forum.[28]

Implementation of the Human Rights under the Covenant on Economic, Social and Culture Rights

We have seen earlier that there is the marked difference in the process of implementation of human rights under the two Covenants. While Article 2 of the Covenant on Civil and political Rights lays down that "each state part to the Covenant undertakes to respect and ensure to all individuals human rights under the Covenant, the Covenant on the Economic, Social and Cultural Right merely lays down that each state party to the Covenant undertakes to take steps progressingly to achieve the implementation of human rights under the Covenant.[29]

Reports

The mode of implementation of the Covenant provision is, what may be called "Reporting Method". This has been indicated in Articles 16 to 23. The Parties to the Covenant, the Human Rights Commission and the Economic and Social Council have to submit reports.

Firstly, the State – Parties to the present covenant have to submit report on the measures adopted and progress made by them in achieving the observance of the Human Rights to the Secretary-General of the United Nations. The Secretary – General will then transmit these reports to the Economic and Social Council for consideration in accordance with the provision of the Covenant. Copies of the report or part thereof will also be send to the specialized agencies by the Secretary-General so far as relating to any matter falling within their area of responsibility.[30]

The State- Parties are to submit their reports in stages, in accordance with a programme to be established by the Economic and Social Council. Such programmes are to be chalked out by the Council within one year of the coming into force of the Covenant. The Reports of the States should indicate factors and difficulties, affecting the degree of fulfillment of obligations under the Covenant.

Article 18 stipulates that the Economic and Social Council may make arrangements with the specialized agencies in respect of their reporting to it on the progress made in achieving the observance of the provisions of the present Covenant falling within the scope of their activities. These reports may include particulars of decisions and recommendations on such implementation adopted by their competent organs.[31]

The Economic and Social Council may also transmit to the Human Rights Commission for study and general recommendation or for information the report, concerning human rights submitted by the State- parties to the Covenant.[32]

On the recommendations of the Commission on Human Rights the State and the specialized agencies may submit their comments to the Economic and Social Council.[33]

The Economic and Social Council is empowered to submit its report to the General Assembly with recommendations of general nature and a summary of the information received from states and specialized agencies on the measures taken and the progress made in achieving general observance of the human rights recognized by the Covenant.[34] The Council may also bring to the attention of other organs of the United Nations ,their subsidiary organs and specialized agencies concerned for furnishing technical assistance on any matter arising out of the reports made by the State and others which may assist such bodies in deciding on the advisability of international measures likely to contribute to the effective implementation of the Covenant provision.[35]

One may tend to be sceptical on the enforcement of human rights by the reporting method. However, one should not forget that implementation of economic , social and cultural rights very much depends upon the economic progress of a state . The reporting method tends to promote the observance of the obligations undertaken under the Covenants at least in some measures. It certainly does strengthen international co- operation among the states. No one will deny the limitation of the reporting method. The method itself suffers from infirmities .There is lack of co-ordination among the States and various organs and agencies of the United Nations .But the Covenant does recognize and tend to promote international responsibility for providing assistance in the promotion of human rights.

Remedial Fundamental Right under the Constitution of Indian

The enumerated and guaranteed fundamental rights would be no more than paper tigers, if the right to enforce fundamental rights is not made a fundamental right itself. It is the remedial fundamental right which gives teeth to all fundamental rights. Article 32 , which enshrines the remedial fundamental right, has been described as "the cornerstone of the democratic edifice,"[36] as "the protector and guarantor of fundamental rights,"[37] or as the qui vive".[38] It has been said repeatedly that it is the duty of the courts to guard the remedial fundamental right and to protect it 'zealously and vigilantly'.[39] Article 32 guarantees the right to move the Supreme court by appropriate proceeding for the enforcement of the fundamental rights guarantee by part III of the Constitution.[40] Clauses (1) and (2) of Article 32 run as under:

1. The right to move the Supreme Court by appropriate proceedings for the enforcement of the rights conferred by this part is guaranteed.

2. The Supreme Court shall have power to issue directions or orders or writs , including writs in the nature of habeas corpus, mandamus, prohibition and certiorari which may be appropriate for the enforcement of any of the rights conferred by this part.

Article 32 (4) lays down that this fundamental right cannot be suspended except as otherwise provided by the Constitution. Articles 358 and 359 provide for the suspension of certain fundamental rights during the period of promulgation of Emergency. Under Article 226 also the fundamental rights can be enforced by moving the High Courts. Other rights can also be enforced under Article 226.

We would proceed to discuss (i) enforcement of the fundamental rights in part tow, (ii) various writs in part three, and (iii) suspension of the fundamental rights during a proclamation of Emergency in part four of this part of the Chapter.

ENFORCEMNT OF FUNDAMENTAL RIGHTS: ARTICLE 32 CLAUSES (1) & (2)

Who can invoke the Jurisdiction?

The general rule is that any person, natural or artificial, whose fundamental right is violated can invoke the jurisdiction of the Supreme Court under Article 32. The infraction of the fundamental right of the petitioner is the condition precedent for moving the court under Article 32.[41] A person who is not interested in the subject – matter of the order has no *locus standi* to invoke the jurisdiction of the court.[42]

However, actual infringement of the fundamental right need not be proved: a petition would lie even if there is an imminent danger of the infraction of a fundamental right.[43] A shareholder has no right to enforce the fundamental right of the company since the company possesses a distinct personality than that of a shareholder,[44] unless the infraction of the right of a company also involves the infringement of the fight of the petitioner.[45] *In Maganbhai Ishwarbhai Patel v. Union of India,*[46] the petitioner challenged the Indo- Pakistan Agreement under which a part of Rann of Kutch was agreed to be transferred to Pakistan.

He challenged the agreement on the ground that once that area was ceded to Pakistan his fundamental right of going or residing there would be violated in future. The Supreme Court observed that a petition would not lie merely on the basis of mere apprehension of infringement of a fundamental right but the Supreme Court nonetheless agree to hear this petition as the court found that the right of the petitioners who claimed infraction of fundamental right had some temporary and almost ephemeral connection.

It is in the case of a writ of *habeas corpus* that a petition can be filed by person who fundamental right is infringed on by any other person on behalf of an imprisoned or defained person.

Public Interest Litigation

The rule of *locus standi* has undergone a fundamental change. In Public Interest Litigation any person or organization may move the Supreme Court if a breach of fundamental right of any person or organization may move the Supreme Court if a breach of fundamental right of any person or group of persons is alleged .In the words of Bhagwati, J:

"The narrow confines within which the rule of standing was imprisoned for long years as a result of inheritance from the Anglo-Saxon system of jurisprudence have been broken and a new dimension has been given to the doctrine of locus standi which has revolutionized the whole concept of access to justice in a way not known before it.[47]"

The Learned judge added that having regard to the peculiar socio-economic condition prevailing in India where there is considerable poverty, illiteracy and ignorance, obstructing and impeding accessibility to the judicial process, it would result in closing the doors of justice to the poor and deprived sections of the community if the traditional rule of standing evolved by Anglo-Saxon jurisprudence that only a person wronged can sue for judicial redress were to be blindly adhered to and followed , and it is therefore, necessary to evolve a new strategy by relaxing this traditional rule of standing in order that justice may become easily accessible to the lowly and the lost. Thus the present position is that wherever a person to whom legal injury is caused or legal wrong is done who, by reason of poverty, disability or social and economically disadvantageous position, is not able to approach the court for judicial redress, any member of the public or any public organization may move the court on his or their behalf for judicial redress. But it is necessary that the individual or organization who moves the court for judicial redress is acting bona fide with a view to vindicating the cause of justice and not for personal gain or private profit or out of political motivation or some other oblique consideration.[48]

It may now be taken to be established that wherever a person or class of persons to whom legal injury is caused or legal wrong is done and who, by reason of poverty, disability or socially or economically disadvantageous position, is not able to approach the court for judicial redress, any member of the public, any public organization, may move the court on his or their behalf for judicial redress. In such cases the court may be moved by any member of the public by addressing a letter drawing the attention of the court to such legal injury or legal wrong, and the court would set aside all technical rules of procedure and entertain the letter as a writ petition on he judicial side and taken action upon it. In *S.P Gupta v. Union of India,*[49] Bhagwati, J., observed :

"The Court has to innovate new methods and devise new strategies for the purpose of providing access to justice to large messes of people who are denied their basic human rights and to whom freedom and liberty have no meaning."

The law seems to have crystallized in this : whenever there is a public injury caused by an act or omission of the State or public authority which is contrary to the Constitution or the law , any member of the public acting *bona fide* and having sufficient interest can maintain an action for redressal of such public wrong or public injury .The strict rule of standing which insist that only a person who has suffered a specific legal injury , can maintain action for judicial redress us relaxed and replaced by a broad rule which gives standing to any member of the public who is not a mere busybody or a meddlesome interloper but one who has sufficient interest in the proceedings. In the absence of a machinery to effectively represent the public interest generally in courts, it is necessary to liberalise the rule of standing in order to provide judicial redress for public injury arising from breach of public duty or from other violation of the constitution or the law by allowing public spirited persons and organizations to move the court and act a general or group interest , even though , they may not be directly injured in their own rights. It is only by liberalizing the rule of *locus standi* that it is possible to effectively police the corridors of power and prevent violations of law. The oppression might be financial, commercial, corporate or governmental.[50]

Bangalore Medical Trust v. B. S. Muddappa,[51] provides an apt illustration. The question was : whether a private nursing home with modern facilities and sophisticated instruments is more conducive to the public interest than a park as it was stressed that even if the conversion of the site suffered from any infirmity procedural or substantive the High Court should have refrained from exercising its extraordinary jurisdiction and that also in favour of those residents may of whom did not have their houses around the park and thus could not be placed in the category of persons aggrieved. It was also empasised that the hospital with research centre and even free service being more important from social angle, the inhabitants of the locality could not be said to suffer any injury much less substantial injury. The Supreme Court said that a private nursing home could neither be considered to be an amenity nor it could be considered improvement over necessity like a public park. The exercise of power in conversion of public park into private nursing home therefore was contrary to the purpose for which it is conferred under the statute.[52]

Thus the public interest litigation is essential for maintaining the rule of law, furthering the cause of justice and for acceleration the pace of realization of the constitutional objectives.

Of course, what is sufficient public interest to give standing to a member of the public would have to be determined by the court in each individual case. It has, of necessary, to be the discretion of the court. The limitation of the doctrine of public interest litigation has been spelled out in *Judges' Transfer case*. These are:

(a) If the individual or organization moving the court for judicial redress is not acting *bona fide* with a view to vindicating the cause of justice but for personal gain of private profit or out of political motivation or some other oblique consideration, the court should not allow itself to be activised at the instance of such person and must reject his application. In the words of Tulzapurkar, J: Those who move the Court should not be wayfarers, interlopers, officious interveners, or busy-bodies without any interest or concern of their own in the subject –matter.[53]

(b) Ordinarily, this jurisdiction may be confined to cases where legal wrong or legal injury is caused to a determinate class or group of persons or the constitutional or legal rights of such determinate class or group of persons or the constitutional or legal rights of such determinate class or group of persons is violated, and the court should not, as far as possible, entertain cases of individual wrong or injury at the instance of a third party, where there is an effective legal aid organization which can take care of such cases.

(c) The distinction between locus standi and justifiability should be kept in view, and thus it is not even default on the part of the state or public authority that is justifiable. Mr. Justice Bhagwati cautions that the court must take care that it does not over-step the limits of its judicial function and trespass into the areas which are reserved to the executive and the legislature by the Constitution.[54] Mr. Justice Venkataramiah cited two instances in which court will not interfere, viz., questions of international relations, and national security.[55]

(d) Where there is a public injury by the act or omission of the state or a public authority but such act or omission also causes a specific injury to an individual or to a specific class or group or individuals, and if the latter, who are primarily injured, do not maintain any action, the member of the public who complains of a secondary public injury cannot maintain the action, since granting of relief in such cases could mean foisting a relief on the person or specific class or group of persons primarily injured, which they do not want.

Breach of Fundamental Rights

The question whether public interest litigation can be initiated in the Supreme Court where no breach of fundamental right is involved came before the court in *People's Union of Democratic Rights v. Union of India.*[56] The Supreme Court answered the question in the negative. But, then, what is breach of fundamental rights has to be looked at in a broader perspective. In the construction of Asiad Game complex, the Union of India, Delhi Development Authority, and Delhi Administration were involved These authorities had given construction work to several contractors who had hired contract labor. The contract labor was hired through agents known as *Jamadras*. Through these *Jamadars,* workers were brought to construction site from different part of the country .The Union for Democratic Rights alleged:

(a) That workers were not paid the minimum wage (the minimum wage was fixed at Rs 9.25 per day and out of it the Jamadars deducted Re. 1 as their commission), which was clearly a violation of the Minimum wage Act.

(b) That in the payment of wages discrimination was made between man and woman, and women workers were paid only Rs 7.00 per day and the balance of Rs 2.25 was retained by the *Jamadars, this was clearly a violation of Equal Remuneration Act , 1976.*

(c) The children below the age of 14 were employed which was a violation of the

Employment of Children Act , 1938 as well as Article 24 of the Constitution .

(d) That amenities and facilities as laid down in the *Contract Labour (Regulation and abolition) Act 1970* were not provided and thus it was a clear violation of the several provisions of the Act.

(e) That amenities and facilities as laid down in the *Inter -State Migrant Workers (Regulation of Employment and Conditions of Service) Act 1979* were not provided which was a clear violation of the provision of the Act.

The Union of India and other authorities in their reply denied the violation of any of the aforesaid provisions by the contractors. However, the Union of India did admit that the Jamadars were probably making some deductions out of the wages paid to the workers. As to the employment of children below the age of 14, it was asserted by the Union of India and other authorities that the Children Act, 1938 was not applicable to construction workers. The court observed that it was unfortunate that the Union and the State Government have not made applicable the Act to the construction works, clearly a hazardous occupation, despite the fact that India is a party to Covenant No 59 , adopted by the ILO which prohibits child labour. However, Article 24 of the Constitution lays down that no child below the age of 14 employed to work in any factory or mine or engaged in any other hazardous employment. This was clearly a violation of Article 24. As to the violation of the provisions of the Inter-State Migrant Workmen (Regulation of Employment and Conditions of Service) Act , 1979 was concerned the Union of India averred that since the Rules under the Act were not finalize , the Act was not enforceable in Delhi . The court observed that it was unfortunate that rules have not been finalized but, nonetheless, those provisions of the Act whose enforcement did not require framing of the Rules were certainly enforceable. Bhagwati, J.,observed:

So far as the rights and benefits conferred upon migrant workmen under the provision of sections 13 to 16 the Act are concerned, the responsibility for ensuring such rights and benefits vests not only on the contractors but also on the Union of India, the Delhi Administration, and DDA who is the principal employed in relation to the construction work entrusted by it to the contractors.

The court observed that allegation relating to violation of the provision of the Equal Remuneration Act ,1946 is in effect and substance a complaint of breach of the principal of equality before the law enshrined in Article 14. Similarly, allegation regarding non observance of the provision of the Contract Labour (Regulation and Abolition) Act ,1970 and the Inter-State Migrant Workers (Regulation and Employment and Conditions of Service) Act , 1979 was in effect and substance a complaint relating to violation of Article 21. It is now the established view that Article 21's guarantee of the right to life is not confined to physical existence but also included within its scope and ambit the right to live with basic human dignity, and the state could not deprive any one of this right because no procedure by which such deprivation might be effected could ever be regarded as reasonable, fair and just. Since these status are nothing but the recognition of this aspect of the fundamental right to life, any violation of any of the provisions of the Acts is in effect a violation of this fundamental right.

Relating to breach of Minimum Wage Act 1948, the court observed that the statute was nothing but an effort to implement the fundamental right relating to "prohibition of traffic in human beings and forced labour". The words used in Article 32(1) are: "beggar and other similar from of forced labour." The Bhagwati , J., very cogently argued that payment of wages less than the minimum wages is nothing but another form of forced labour . The learned Judge observed:

"It may therefore be legitimately presumed that when a person provides labour or service to another against receipt of remuneration which is less than the minimum wage, he is acting under some force or some compulsion which deprives him to work through he is paid less than what he is entitled to receive."

Thus it would appear that a public interest petition will lie in the Supreme Court wherever there is a breach of any social legislation, since social legislations are passed to ensure fundamental rights for the weaker section of society, the right which are usually denied to them. It is submitted that a writ petition will also lie whenever there a breach of any law which is passed in pursuance to any Directive Principle of State Policy, since the Directive Principles are as much fundamental part of the Constitution as are fundamental rights.

Over –burdening of the Court

The over –burdening of the already over-burdened court by the public interest litigation is a spacious argument and should not deserve attention. This argument has been put forth repeatedly as if this is only causes for mounting areas in the Supreme Court. This is far from being true. The public interest litigation in the Supreme Court is only a fraction of total number of cases filed in the Supreme Court. It is not even one per cent of the total number of case filed in the Supreme Court .Further , should the doors of the highest court be closed to the poor because this adds up to the arrears of pending cases? Are the doors of the court open only to those who can afford the file regular petition? When the rights of the rich to exploit the poor is upheld by the Supreme Court, it is praised, applauded and acclaimed for its boldness and courage and independence and fearlessness, but in the worlds of Bhagawati., J..:

"If the fundamental right of the poor and helpless victims of injustice is sought to be enforced by public interest litigation, the so – called champions of human rights frown upon it as waste of time of the highest court of the land, which , according to them , should not engage itself in such small and trifling matters."

The Province of PIL: Some Illustrative Cases

The public interest litigation's province has become very wide. By virtue of Article 32, the Supreme Court has been able to widen the horizons and intervene whenever injustice is caused or being caused by state action or by lack of it and has tried to help the poor, helpless and helpless people who have no means to approach the Supreme Court or who do not know whom to approach. Thus , whether it is blinding of under – trial prisoners or flesh – trade or languishing children in jails or poor homes , pitiable situation in so –called women's home which have become virtual brothels , protection of pavement and slum dwellers, payment of minimum wages , or equal pay for equal work , freeing of bonded labour, protection of environment and ecology and the like have found a sympathetic judicial forum in the Supreme Court , and the Supreme Court have not hesitated in talking appropriate action. Here we would take two illustrative cases.

Rural Litigation and Entitlement Kendra v. State U.P .,[57] led to the closure of a certain lime stone quarries on the ground that these quarries were a great hazard and were affecting the ecology of the area adversely . *M.C.Mehta v. UOI ,*[58] resulted in the closure of tanneries which were polluting Ganga.

Mukti Sangrsh Movement v. State of Mach .,[59] sought to prevent reckless exploitation of river running through some parts of Maharashtra which was adversely affecting its bed due to reckless quarrying of its sand , while *F. K. Hussain v. Union of India ,*[60] sought to prevent lowering of underground water level on account of its reckless withdrawal by electric pumps.[61]

Judicial Predicament and Public Interest Activism

Today , the province of public interest litigation has widened so much that the every injury, every grievance , is sought to be brought under it , so much so that executive is finding it difficult to copy it and finding ways to evade direction of the courts. Judiciary too is trying to restrain its activism .It is declining to issue directions in policy matters. Thus judiciary is in a predicament: how far it could go and where it should not .This has been so well expressed by Prof. Parmanand Singh that we cannot resist the temptation of quoting him extensive.[62] He says:

"Public Interest Litigation (PIL) has to day become a byword for judicial involvement in social , political and economic affairs of the Indian society and state . Through legal activism, the judges are seeking to take a leading part in prescribing the goals of just social and new patterns of behaviours so that critical ills are remedied, the inadequacies in the body politics are rectified and the hopes and aspirations of the masses are satisfied. Over the years PIL activism is fast moving into new arenas, arousing heightened expectations from the judges that they are available to provide relief from all kinds of miseries, oppressions and misfortunes. Atrocities on the scheduled caste, criminalization of politics,

corruption in public life, custodial violence, forced prostitution and child-abuse, environment pollution and horde of other issues are attracting remedial attention of the courts. The judges are asked not only vindicate the governmental commitment to the welfare of the poor and the repressed but also to maintain communal harmony , social control and social peace, preserve rule of law prevent the decline in public morality. In addition to this, everything we are witnessing that anything and everything can be a subject matter of PIL. Thus the right to work, shelter, low cost housing, pure drinking water, minimum income, food, pollution free environment and a horde of other basic human needs are claimed as guaranteed legal rights."

At the same time it is painfully apparent that the political economy emerging in India ever since Independence has only resulted in the formation of new social classes of land owning prosperous farmers , traders , money-lenders, wealthy politicians, bureaucrats and other dominant classes who are controlling the social and economic institutions and cultural networks and are promoting the capitalists path of development .The contemporary social economy is encouraging the barbarity of "primitive accumulation" of early capitalism , by legal proliferation of contract mafias, education mafias , religious mafias and other dominant groups who are powerful enough to manipulate political power for accumulation of economic power . In other words, the structure of political economy has provided enormous resources as well as legal and normative value system favorable to these new social classes. The logic hectic-profit chase by the emerging new prosperous economic classes has accelerated the process of pauperization, loss of purchasing power, and mass unemployment.

Territorial jurisdiction

Under Article 32 the Supreme Court has very wide jurisdiction. Any order, direction or writ issued by the Supreme Court Article 32 can be issued not merely anywhere in India but beyond the territorial limits of India to all those authorities who are functioning inside or outside India under the control of Union Government. Article 142 lays down that the decree and order of the Supreme Court are enforceable throughout the territory of India. But it is Submitted this limitation does not apply to orders, directions and writs issued under Article 32: if an authority abroad is under the control of the Government of India , an order , etc can be enforced by passing suitable order against the Government of India.[63]

Against Whom a Writ, etc., Lies

An order, direction or writ issued under Article 32 lies against the Government of India or State Government or against authority under the power or control of the Government of India or any State Government. Since fundament rights are enforceable against the State . Article 12 defines "State" as "the Government and Parliament of India and the Government and the legislature of each of the States and all local or other authorities within the territory of India or under the control of the Government of India." In *Electricity Board, Raj , v. Mohan Lal,*[64] the Supreme Court held that "other authorities will include all authorities created by the Constitution or statute and on whom powers are conferred by law, and it is not necessary that the statutory authority should be engaged in performing the governmental functions. Thus bodies created for promotion of education or economic interest of the people would be such authorities. The Rajasthan Electricity Board was held on be such an authority. *Indian Airlines Corporation v. Sukhdeo Singh,*[65] and *U.P State Warehousing Corporation v. C.K.Tyagi,*[66] took the view that a corporation set up by a statute is not an "authority," since only those come under "authority" which exercise governmental or quasi-governmental function. These decisions have been overruled by the Supreme Court in *Sukhdeo Singh v. Bhahat Ram.*[67]. The majority by the four to one, held that the term "other authorities" under Article 12 was wide enough to included every authority created by statute and functioning within the territory of India or under the control of the Government of India. It was held that the Oil and Natural Gas Commission, Life Insurance Corporation , and Industrial Finance Corporation are such authorities and , therefore, orders, direction and writs can issued against them.

In *Ujjain Singh v. State of U.P.*[68], the Supreme Court held that a writ, etc., could not be issued against a quasi-judicial authority on the sole ground that provision of the Act or the term of notification issued there under had been violated. But in the following cases writ, order , etc .., are maintainable against the quasi- judicial authorities, (a) when statute or rules framed there under are *ultra vires* and any action taken there under is violative of a fundamental right, (b) when such authority acts without jurisdiction or assumes jurisdiction wrongly and an action of such authority is volatile of any fundamental right, and (c) if the action of the authority is procedurally *ultra vires*, such as when there is a violation of principles of natural justice. Hidayatullah, C.J ., summed up the rule thus : a person has right to move the Supreme Court under Article 32 when an action is taken under an *ultra vires* statute or when the action is without jurisdiction through the statute is *intra vires* or when principles of natural justice are , violated, But no action would lie where error of law of fact is committed in exercising jurisdiction founded on a valid law.[69] In case coming before the 44th Amendment, it was held that whenever an illegal tax affected the fundamental right to property under Article 31 (1) an action under Article 32 would lie.[70] After the abrogation Article 31 by the 44th Amendment this would not be so.

No Writ can be Issued against High Courts

The Supreme Court has expressed the view that judicial adjudications, order and decrees by themselves do not violate fundamental rights. In *Sridhar v. State of Maharastra,*[71] the Supreme Court was called upon to determine whether an order of the High Court prohibiting the publication of the testimony of a witness in newspaper violated the fundamental right under Article 19 (1)(a) ? It was held that no writ could be issued against a High Court .Whether or not an adjudication by a High Court suffers from any infirmity can be considered only in an appeal.

Petitions

Whenever a breach of fundamental rights is alleged by the legislature or the executive, the jurisdiction of the Supreme Court can be invoked. But if the enforcement of a fundamental right is not involved Article 32 is not available.[72] Thus the breach of the right of freedom of trade and commerce guaranteed under Article 301,[73] or of any other right, or legality or illegality of an action or *ultra viresness* of a statute,[74] cannot be questioned under Article 32 if breach of a fundamental right is not involved. For these matters, the jurisdiction is conferred on the High Court under Article 226. But the validity of a law can be challenged under Article 32 if it involves a question of enforcement of any fundamental right.[75]

For the enforcement of the fundamental rights , the procedure under Article 32 is by "appropriate proceedings" which means that a petition has to be original side of the Supreme Court. This is sometimes called "the extraordinary original jurisdiction" of the Supreme Court. The appropriateness of the proceeding would depend upon the particular writ or order which a petitioner claims and it is in that sense that the right has been conferred on the citizen to move the Supreme Court by appropriate proceedings."[76] Since the jurisdiction Under Article 32 is extraordinary, the Supreme Court has very wide discretion in matter of providing remedy for the enforcement of fundamental rights. The right under Article 32 is itself a fundamental right. No fetters can be placed on this right. It was no this reasoning which led the Supreme Court to strike down its own rule providing for security from the petitioner.[77] But this does not mean that the Supreme Court cannot regulate the procedure. It has the power to make rules which will govern the procedure and practice for the filing of petitions under Article 32.

In early cases the Supreme Court expressed the view that if a petitioner made out a case under Article 32, the Supreme Court had no discretion. It must grant an appropriate writ or order in favour of the petitioner;[78] it was the duty of the Supreme Court to do so.[79]

Article 32(2) specifically mention five types of directions, orders, writs viz., *habeas corpus*, *mandamus, prohibition , quo warranto* and *certiorari*. The Supreme Court has power to issue any one of these as well as to frame any writ or order or direction which it may consider appropriate in a given case.[80] In the words of Mukherjea, J.,: "We can make an order or issue a writ in the nature of *certiorari* (or any order, or direction or writ) in all appropriate case all appropriate cases and in appropriate manner, so long as we keep in view the board and fundamental principles of the exercise of jurisdiction in the matter of granting such writs in English law.[81] However, it would be correct to say that once the breach of fundamental right is established, the Supreme Court has no discretion in the matter and much award appropriate relief. The following propositions may be taken as well established:[82]

A. The writ, order or direction under Article 32 is issued as a matter of course once a violation of a fundamental rights is established and technical applicable to suits like the provision of section 80, Civil Procedure Code are not applicable to proceedings under Article 32.

B. But this general rule does not imply that the Supreme Court is required to ignore and trample under foot all laws of procedure, evidence, limitation, *res judicata* and the like. The court is not bound to grant relief :

   (i) When petition contains misleading and inaccurate statements, or it would be against public policy to accept such a petition.

   (ii) When petition is barred by *res judicata*,[83]

   (iii) When petition is barred by laches.

C. The existence of an alternative remedy does not bar the jurisdiction of the Supreme Court under Article 32 .

D. The existence of the concurrent jurisdiction of the High Court under Article 226 does not bar a person who alleges violation of a fundamental right to approach the Supreme Court directly.

Jurisdiction of the High Court under Article 226

Under Article 226 the High Court has concurrent jurisdiction with the Supreme Court in the matter of granting relief in cases of infraction of fundamental rights , through the High Court exercise jurisdiction incase of any other right too . This does not imply a person who alleges violation of a fundamental right must first approach the High Court. One can approach the Supreme Court directly. That is so has been very cogently stated in *Romesh Thapar v. State of Madras,*[84] thus: " that Article 32 does not merely confer power on this court , as Article 226 does on the High Court , to issue certain writs for the enforcement of the right conferred by Part III or for any other purposes as part of this general jurisdiction. In that case, it would have been more appropriately placed among Articles 131 to 139 which define that jurisdiction. Article 32 provides a guaranteed remedy for the enforcement of those rights and this remedial right is itself made a fundamental right by being included in Part III. This court is thus constituted as the protector and guarantor of fundamental rights and it cannot, consistently with the responsibility so laid upon it, to refuse to entertain applications seeking protection against infringement of such rights".

The High Court under Article 226 exercises much wider discretion than the Supreme Court exercises under Article 32. The High Court have held that they would refuse to exercise jurisdiction, *inter alia,* if there is an adequate alternative remedy, if there are laches, if the conduct of the petitioner is reproachable, if interest of justice does not require a writ to be granted, if the petition involves disputed questions of fact or if granting of the writ would be futile . But it seems that these considerations would apply only when the High Court grant relief "for any other purpose" and not for the enforcement of fundamental rights. Seervai rightly holds the view that it would not be a judicial exercise of the discretion to refuse a write for the enforcement of fundamental rights on a ground on which the Supreme Court could not refuse a write under Article 32.[85]

Existence of Alternative Remedy

The Supreme Court has repeatedly held that the existence of an alternative remedy did not bar the jurisdiction of the court to grant relief under Article 32.[86] However, in some cases the Supreme Court has observed that it might exercise its discretion to refuse to grant relief when an alternative remedy is available, since extraordinary remedies should not replace the ordinary remedies.[87] It is necessary that the alternative remedy is equally convenient, beneficial and effective . It is not so, it cannot be regarded as an adequate alternative remedy. When it is question of enforcement of a fundamental right, it appears that in most cases the alternative remedy is not adequate and therefore the Supreme Court and the High Court rarely refuse to grant relief on the ground of the existence of alternative remedy.[88] When the jurisdiction of the High Court is invoked in other matters, it takes into account the existence of an alternative remedy as a ground for refusing relief.[89] But the rule of existence of alternative remedy is a rule of policy, convenience and discretion rather than of law.[90]

Petition Barred by Laches

No statute of limitation (such as the Indian Limitation Act) applies to petitions under Articles 32 and 226. But this does not mean that relief can be sought under these articles at any time, Hidayatuallah CJ., rightly observed that there was no lower or upper time limit for entertaining petitions under Article

32, but there was the overriding qualification that a party seeking this extraordinary remedy must come to the court with the utmost dispatch.[91] This means that each petition has to be determined on the basis of its own facts and circumstances .But Beyond this , this Supreme Court has expressed conflicting views. In some cases , it has been held that the Limitation Act might be , applied by analogy.[92] In *Kaminikumar v. State of W.B.*,[93] The Court observed that there was no inexorable rule and when justice required there was no period of Limitation . [94] In some cases the period of limitation prescribed for appeals had been suggested, in some cases a view had been expressed that no petition should be allowed after one year. But all these views need not be discussed here as they stand superseded by the Supreme Court decision in *R.S Deodhar v. State of Maharashtra.*[95] The Court observed that the doctrine of laches was not a rule of law , but a rule of practice based on sound and proper exercise of discretion , and there was no inviolable rule that whenever there was delay , the court must necessarily refuse to entertain the petition . "This Court which has been assigned the role of a sentinel on *quil vive* for the protection of fundamental rights cannot easily allow itself to be persuaded to refuse relief on the *de jure* ground laches, delay or the like ," the present writers are in respectful agreement with the view. The implication of this decision is that the court will decide each on its facts and circumstance as to whether or not the petition should be rejected on the ground of unreasonable delay. It is submitted that the rules evolved under section 23(I) (d) , Hindu Marriage Act , 1955 which deals with delay in matrimonial petitions could be a good guide to Articles 32 and 226.[96]

Petition Barred by *res judicata*

It is now established rule that the doctrine of *res judicata* applies to petitions under Articles 32 and 226. The doctrine of *res judicata* seeks to regulate the manner in which the remedial fundamental right can be asserted in a court of law. A petition under Article 32 is not maintainable if the petitioner a decision on merits on the same matter in a petition under Article 226.[97] Like the doctrine of laches the doctrine of *res judicata* is based on considerations of public policy and is not a technical rule of procedure. The public policy requires that the finality should attach to binding decision of court of competent jurisdiction and that the individuals should not be made to suffer the odium of the same kind of litigation to be brought over and over again. The doctrine of *res judicata* lays down that if a matter has been decided on merit between the parties, then the same parties cannot agitate the same question over again. A person cannot move successive write petitions on the same cause of action

Thus where an order assessing a tax was once challenged by a petition and dismissed by the court after considering the case on merits, then the petitioner cannot challenge the assessment of the same tax by another writ petition even through the petition alleges some new grounds of challenge.[98] But if order of assessment by successive writ petitions do not relate to the same years , the petition is maintainable.[99] The doctrine of constructive *res judicata* also applies (constructive *res judicata* means that a ground ought to have been taken but was not in fact taken is tantamount to ground taken).[100] The principle is the same namely , there should be an end to litigation and that a person should not be vexed twice in respect of the same subject matter. This also means that a person must elect as to whether he wants to file a petition under Article 32 or Article 226. If a petition is dismissed, neither another writ petition, nor a suit on the same subject is maintainable.[101]

Withdrawal of a petition has the same effect.[102] A writ petitions is also not maintainable against an order passed by the High Court in a revision petition; in such case even an appeal may not be entertained.[103]

The doctrine of *res judicata* obviously does not apply if the matter is not decided on merit.[104]

The doctrine of *res judicata* obviously does not apply to a writ of *habeas corpus*. Even if the petition is dismissed by the High Court on merit, a fresh petition to the Supreme Court is maintainable.[105]

Petition Barred on Account of Misconduct or Bad Conduct of Petitioner

The equitable principle of one who comes to equity much come with clean hands applies to the writ jurisdiction under Articles 32 and 266. If a petitioner is guilty of bad faith, fraud or improper conduct inspect of matter relating to controversy, the petition may be refused; improper conduct may be precedent or subsequent to the filing of the petition.[106] If the affidavit filed by the petitioner is not candid and does not state the facts fairly but states them in such a way as to mislead and deceive the court the petition may be dismissed.[107] In *Daulat Singh vs. Dy. Commr., Karnal*,[108] where the petition himself unlawfully invoked the jurisdiction of a tribunal, the court observed that they could not be heard to say that the tribunal had no jurisdiction when the self-same jurisdiction is invoked by the opposite party it was held that conduct of the petitioners was such as to disentitle them for any relief under Article 226.[109]

Disputed Question of fact may Bar petition

If a *prima facie* case of violation of a fundamental rights made out, the petition will not be barred, even if its determination involves an inquiry into disputed questions of fact.[110]

A Writ will not be Issued if it would be Futile

The court will not issue a writ, order or direction if its granting will be futile. Thus it would be futile to issue a writ of *mandamus* against a Returning Officer him to accept the nomination paper which he had rejected, since despite the writ , it was open to an election tribunal to take the view that the nomination paper was rightly rejected.

[111] Similarly , It has been held that there was no use granting a writ in respect of a liquor license to a third person without authority of law where the contract would be terminated within days,[112] or to order reinstatement to an office from which the petition could be removed by a higher authority .[113]

Can a Remedy under Article 32 be directly pursued in the Supreme Court?

Before 1989, it was the confirmed view that for the enforcement of any fundamental right a person could approach the Supreme Court . But in *P.N. Kumar v. Municipal Corporation of Delhi*,[114] the Supreme Court expressed the view that the citizen should first go to the High Court and if not satisfied he should approach the Supreme Court. The Supreme Court laid down the following guidelines:

(1) The scope of Article 226 is wider than Article 32. The parties should first seek relief in the High Court and should come to the Supreme Court in appeal only.

(2) Hearing of the case at the level of High Court is move convenient to the parties. It saves of time.

(3) The High Court has its own traditions. They have emient judes, whose capacity should be utilized.

(4) Every High Court has a good Bar. There, eminent lawyers with wide experience, handle different kinds of case . They know history of every legislation in their State.

(5) The Supreme Court has no time to decide case pending before it for the last 10 to 15 years, with the strength of judges it will take more than 15 years to dispose of all pending cases.

(6) If the cases are filed in the High Court , the task of Supreme Court action as an original court which is time –consuming can be avoided.

(7) If case which may be filed in the High Court are filed in this Court it would effect initiative of the High Court. We should preserve the dignity and efficiency of the High Courts. The taking over by the this court the work of High Court may undermine the capacity and efficiency of the High Court and should avoided.

(8) The time saved by this court by not entreating the cases which may be filed before the High Court can be utilized to dispose of old matters in which parties are crying relief.

In our submission , the views expressed by the Supreme Court are not in conformity with the enshrined in constitution and with rule of law .The rationale behind the Supreme Court is that the ever increasing load that is placed on the Supreme Court by arrears of cases would be thereby reduced. In our submission it is not the citizen to be blamed for the mounting arrears of case, but the executive with temples over the rights of citizen with impunity and arrogance. It is hoped that the Supreme Court would confine this judgment to live in archives only.

The Writs

The remedial fundamental rights contained in Article 32 can be brought into action, by what may be compendiously called, the writ jurisdiction of the Supreme Court and High Court. Under Article 226 the High Courts have power to issue order , directions or writs including writs in the nature of *habeas corpus , prohibition, certiorari and quo warranto* for the emforcement of the fundamental rights as well as for "any purpose" , including the enforcement of any other legal rights.[115]

With the enshrinement of a Chapter on Fundamental Rights in the Constitution, it was necessary corollary to provide for a quick and inexpensive remedy for the enforcement of fundamental rights. We drew from the English law and found the prerogative writs were peculiarly suited for the purpose. Article 32 makes it a fundamental right of any person who alleged violation of a fundamental right to seek the remedy through these writs. In the State's sphere similar power was conferred upon the High Courts. Power was conferred upon the High Courts of not merely issuing these writs, etc ., for the enforcement of fundamental rights, but also for the enforcement of any other legal right.[116]

Although these writs have been borrowed from English law , we need not get bogged down by the arid technicalities and precedents of English law , through with a view to having a proper perspective , we may keep in view the broad and fundamental principles of the writ jurisdiction of English law .

Mandamus

In English law, "the writ of *mandamus* is a high prerogative writ of a most extensive remedial nature, and is in form a command issuing from the High Court of Justice directed to any person, corporation, or inferior court, requiring him or them to do some particular thing therein specified which appertains to his or their office and is in the nature of public duty. Its purpose is to supply defects of justice ; and accordingly it will issue, to the end that justice may be done, in all cases where there is a specific legal right and no specific legal remedy for enforcing that right," [117] This description of *mandamus* has been accepted by the Indian Courts. A writ of *mandamus* is in the nature of command issued by a court of law asking a public authority to perform a public duty which it is bound to perform, or to refrain from performing a particular act which is should not perform. For instance, if a tribunal is bound to decide a matter are it refuses to decide, *mandamus* could be issued to it directing it to decided the matter . A *mandamus* lies to compel the performance of an obligatory duty imposed by law. Thus a mandamus would lie to compel an Income - tax Officer to carry out the direction given to him by the Income –tax Appellate Tribunal. [118]

It also lies to restrain an authority which acts without the authority of law or contrary to law or in excess of the authority conferred by law or acts mala fides. Thus *mandamus* was issued to Government restring it from giving effect to a notification cancelling a reference made to an Industrial Tribunal since it had not authorized to do so by law ,[119] or against a court or tribunal which acted in excess of jurisdiction or failed to exercise jurisdiction or committee error apparent on the face of the record . A writ can be issued quashing the order of the tribunal, and directing it to hear determine the matter according to law, or restraining it from giving effect to its order.[120] For issuance of a *mandamus* the following conditions should be fulfilled:

(i) The petitioner must have a legal right to compel the public authority to do or refrain doing something.

(ii) *Mandamus* is ordinarily issued against a public authority and not against a private body or individual but if private body has public duty to perform *mandamus* may be issued against it.

(iii) *Mandamus* is meant to secure the performance of a public or statutory duty in the performance of which the petitioner has sufficient legal interest.

(iv) *Mandamus* does not lie where the performance of the public duty is discretionary. But if the authority is under a duty to exercise discretion, *mandamus* lies to compel the authority to exercise the discretion.

Who can Seek Mandamus

A petition for the issuance of a writ of *mandamus* must show that he has a legal right to compel the authority to do or refrain form doing something. This is subject to what we have stated the head "public interest litigation." In other words, the petitioner must have a right to compel performance of some public duty part of the respondent. Thus, a mandamus will not lie where the petitioner's contention is that a man junior or him in service has been appointed when in fact the junior so appointed was qualified, and the petitioner had no qualifications for the post.[121] A petition will lie against the respondent only when he has a duty of public nature, whether created by the Constitution, statute or common law, and not if the duty is of a private nature even if the respondent is a public body.[122] Contractual obligations cannot be enforced through *mandamus*,[123] but mandamus will lie if the public authority acts in an arbitrary and unlawful manner even where right arises under contract.[124] Mandamus will lie to restrain a public authority from action under a law declared unconstitutional.[125]

Mandamus is not available to enforce purely money obligation under a civil liability, but an order to pay money passed against a public authority if monetary obligation arises under a statute,[126] *Mandamus* would, thus, lie to prevent the authority from realizing illegal tax.[127]

It is necessary that before approaching the court the petitioner must have made a demand on the authority concerned and the latter must have refused to concede it.[128] The refusal to concede the demand may be inferred form the conduct. The demand of the right on the part of the petitioner is not a mere matter of form; it is a matter of substance .An evasion or shelving of a demand is tantamount to denial.[129]

Against Who Mandamus may be Claimed

In *State of J.&K. V. A.R. Jakki,*[130] the Supreme Court said that a writ of *mandamus* cannot be issued to the Legislature to enact a particular legislation . Nor can direction be issued to executive to frame rules as the same is also a legislative action. The ordinary rule is that mandamus lies against a public authority or person holding a public office or a public corporation or inferior court to perform a public or statutory duty imposed upon it by law. In *Sohan Lal v. Union of India,*[131] *mandamus* was issued against the Union of India restore possession to the petitioner when he (a displaced person) was evicted in Contravention of the express provision of the Public Premises (Eviction) Act. At one time this was a strict rule thus, an application for *mandamus* will not lie against a company for an order of reinstatement to an office which is essentially of a private character, nor can such an application be maintained to secure performance of obligations owed by a company towards its workmen or to resolve any private dispute. In *Praga Tool Corporation v. Immanuel ,*[132] Shelat , J., observed that *mandamus* was an order which was made against a person directing him to do some particular thing specified in the other which appertained to his office in the nature of a public of a public duty, and as a company is a non-statutory body incorporated under the Companies Act , had neither a statutory nor a public duty imposed on it by statute in respect of which enforcement could be sough; by a *mandamus*; nor did the workers have any corresponding legal right of enforcement of any such statutory or public duty . This restrictive meaning is no longer tenable. In several cases, it has been held that a writ may be issued against a private body , if the duty cast upon it is of a public nature . Of these cases,[133] *Vaish College Society v. Lakshmi Narain ,*[134] is the most instructive . The main question before the court was: could *mandamus* lie against the Managing Committee of a private college affiliated to a University (statutory body) against its order terminating the service of a teacher? Although teachers were appointed in the college under contract, a statutory duty was cast upon the Managing Committee while appointing a teacher under Meerut University Act . In the worlds of Asthana, J., "when non- statutory bodies perform non-statutory functions their acts will not be subject to judicial review by the court but when they perform stator functions , there is no value reason why it should not be held that their action will be amenable to judicial review by the inasmuch as non- statutory bodies when performing statutory function will be nothing else than instrumentalities acting under the statute which imposes duty upon it affecting the right of third persons and parties".

A writ would lie against a Judge, including the judge of the High Court, against his administrative actions.[135]

Sharif Ahmed v. Regional Transport Authority,[136] takes the law of *mandamus* a step further. It lays down that *mandamus* can be issued against an authority asking it perform its ministerial functions. The shortened facts of the case are: The Transport Appellate Tribunal directed the Regional Transport Authority to issue carriage permit to those persons who complied with all the conditions laid down for the issuance of the permit. The petitioner complied with all the conditions. However, before the permits were issued, the State Government issued notification changing its policy and directed the RTA not issue permits. Subsequently, certain changes were made in the law retrospectively. The Supreme Court observed that once the Transport Appellate Authority had directed the RTA to issue the permit, the consideration of the applications for grant of permit was not longer pending before it ; what remained pending was a mere ministerial act to be performed by the RTA. When the Government changed the law there was nothing pending before the RTA expect "that in the physical sense a paper containing a permit was not actually issued." Since it did not issue the permit, it failed in its legal duty in not implementing the order of the Appellate Tribunal. The court felt it was just and proper to grant the writ to *mandamus*. Untwalia, J., observed that the RTA had merely a ministerial duty to perform and the minor discretionary element given to it for finding out whether the terms of the order has been complied with or not was enough to deter the court from characterizing the function as ministerial.

A writ of *mandamus* does not lie against a legislature or subordinate legislature (like a municipality) to prevent it from enacting a law in violation of the Constitution or asking it to pass a particular law.[137]

When performance of public Duty is Discretionary, no Mandamus Lies

A writ of *mandamus* cannot be issued to compel an authority to perform its discretionary duty. In *State of M. P V. Mandawar*[138], Rule 44 of the Fundamental Rules conferred discretion to grant dearness allowance at a particular rate. The court held *mandamus* could not be issued. The administrative which have no statutory force cannot be enforced by *mandamus*.[139]

But if the authority is bound to exercise its discretion the mandamus lies.[140] A mandamus can be issued to an authority to compel the exercise of discretion through not to compel it in the manner in which it has to be exercised.[141] A *mandamus* lies where the discretion is exercised on irrelevant or extraneous considerations or where the exercise of discretion is delegated to someone else or where it exercises is declined.[142] But where the discretion has been exercised in good faith, the court would not intervene: it is not the function of the court to substitute their wisdom and discretion for that of the persons to whose judgment the matter is entrusted by the law.[143]

Certiorari and prohibition

In the modern law, the horizon of *certiorari* has been much widened. At one time it was the confirmed view that the writs of *certiorari* and prohibition lay only to control judicial or quasi- judicial acts. Today it is established that these write lie to control the administrative act also if there is a duty on the person or authority acting administratively to act fairly. The landmark English decisions propounding this view are *Ridge v. Baldwin*[144] and *in re H.K. (An infant)*,[145] and the leading Indian decision are *A.K. Kraipak v. Union of India*,[146] and *Maneka Gandhi v. Union of India*.[147]

In the modern law certiorari is issued to quash the of a court or quasi-judicial tribunal or an administrative body of having duty to act fairly or in accordance with the principles of natural justice when it has assumed jurisdiction which it does not possess or where the order passed by it contains an error of law apparent on the face of the record . Prohibition issues in similar circumstances to restrain the court tribunal or authority which threatens to assume or has assumed a jurisdiction not vested in it or acts in contravention of any law including the principle of natural justice, before the conclusion of proceedings. The court has often that in *certiorari* jurisdiction the courts do not supplant but only supplement. In *Halsbury's Law of England,* the writ of *certiorari* is defined as the writ which "issues out of a superior court and is directed to the judge or other officer of an inferior court of record. It requires that the record of the proceeding in some cause or matter pending before such inferior court shall be transferred to the superior court to be there dealt with in order to ensure that the applicant for the writ may have a more sure and speedy justice." Prohibition is defined as a write " issuing out of the High Court of Justice and directed to an inferior court which forbids such court to continue proceedings therein excess of its jurisdiction or in contravention of the law of the land." These definitions have been accepted by the Indian Court. Both the writs are issued practically on the same grounds. The maid distinction between the two is that prohibition lies before the curt or tribunal has completed its proceedings or delivered the judgment or passed in order. While *certiorari* lies where proceedings have been completed or a judgment delivered or order passed . Sometimes both the writs lie in the same cause ; a petitioner may pray that inferior court or tribunal should be prohibited from proceeding further in the matter and that the case be transferred to the superior court.

Who can Seek these Writs

Any person who alleged that in his case the inferior court or any other authority or person having the duty to act judicially or the duty to act fairly is acting without jurisdiction , or in excess of jurisdiction or in violating of principles of natural justice or fair play can maintain a petition for the issuance of the writ.

In a petition of *certiorari* or prohibition, the petitioner must state all material facts of the case and should not suppress or mis-state any material facts.

Against whom, Certiorari and Prohibition Lie

In the modern law the writ of certiorari or prohibition lies not only against the inferior court or quasi – judicial tribunals or bodies, but also against any person, body or authority having duty to act judicially or fairly. These writs do not lie against private tribunals or bodies or persons even if they are required to act judicially or fairly. It seems that the writ would lie against an arbitrator appointed under section 10-A, Industrial Disputes Act.[148] *Certiorari* also lies to determine questions affecting the fundamental rights.

In early cases, the Supreme Court stuck to the formulation made in the English case,[149] viz., writ would issue to anybody or person having legal authority to determine questions affecting the rights of an individual and having duty to act in

excess of its legal authority.[150] Kania. CJ. Observed "...When the law under which the authority is making a decision *itself requires a judicial approach,* the decision will be quasi- judicial. " (emphasis author's).The italicised word should be noted .This was further elaborated in *Nagendra Nath Bora v. Commr. of Hill Div.,*[151] where Sinha J., observed that whether and authority had an obligation to act judicially must determine in each on an examination of the relevant statute and the rules framed thereunder.[152]

In the early Indian case, the court considered two questions: (a)whether the authority is a tribunal, and (b) whether authority is required to act judicially. In *Associated Cement Co .v. P.M. Sharma,*[153] the court was concerned with the fact whether the State Government exercising appellate jurisdiction under the Punjab Welfare Officer (Recruitment & Condition of Service) Rules, 1952 was a tribunal, and in *Shri Bhagwan v. Ram Chandra,*[154] whether there was violation of natural justice when Government did not hear the parties in the exercise of its revisional jurisdiction . In both cases court gave an affirmative answer. In *Sadhu Singh v. Delhi Admn .,*[155] the *detenu* challenged his preventive detention on the ground that he was given no opportunity to make a representation against his detention when his case was reviewed under Rule 35-A, Defence of India Rules. The court held the detention its review were purely administrative acts and not subject to *certiorari*. This case has been overruled in *P.L Lakhanpal v. Union of India.*[156] The Supreme Court held that when the authority reviewed a detention case, it was required to act objectively. With this decision the modern trend was set in motion. Then came the crucial decision in *State of Orissa v. Binapani Devi,*[157] which held that the principles of natural justice must be followed even in respect of administrative or executive acts. Shah, J., observed ; "But the decision of the State could be based upon the result of an enquiry in a manner consonant with the basic concept of justice . An order by the State to the prejudice of person in derogation in derogation of his vested right may be made only in accordance with the basic rules of justice or fair-play."[158] The rule that a party to whose prejudice and order is intended to be passed is entitled to a hearing applies alike to judicial tribunals and bodies of persons invested with authority to adjudicate upon matters involving civil consequences. Duty to act judiciously, would, therefore, arise from the very nature of the function intended to be performed; it need not be shown to be superadded, In this case the Department was engaged in the task of determining the age of a Government servant.[159]

The decision in *A.K.Kraipak v. Union of India,*[160] has put a stamp on this view. In this case, person sat on the selection board in which he was a rival with other candidates through at the time of his own selection he withdrew but continued to sit when his rivals were interviewed . He was selected and his rivals were left out. It was a case of violation of the second limb of the principle of natural justice, viz., disqualification by interest and bias (the first requirement of natural justice is that no one3 should be condemned unheard). Hedge, J., Observed:

The dividing line between and administrative power and a quasi-judicial power is quite than is being gradually obliterated. For determining whether a power is an administrative power or a quasi- judicial power, one has to look to the nature of the power conferred, the person or persons on whom it is conferred, the framework of the law conferring that power, the consequences ensuing from the exercise of the power, and the manner in which that power is expected to be exercised. In a welfare state like oursit is inevitable that the State Constitution is regulated and controlled by rule of law. The concept of rule of laws would lose it validity if the instrumentalities of the State are not charged with the duty of discharging their functions in a fair and just manner. The requirement of acting judicially in essence is nothing but a requirement to act justly and fairly and not arbitrarily or capriciously.[161]

The court observed that reaching a just decision was the air of quasi- judicial and administrative enquiries.[162] An unjust decision in an administrative enquiry will have more far- reaching effect than a decision in a quasi- judicial enquiry. The court held that natural justice has more than two rules (as bit was understood in the past). It means:

(i) No one shall be judge in his own cause.

(ii) No one shall be condemned unheard, and

(iii) Inquiries must be held in good faith without bias and not arbitrarily unreasonably.

Modern concept of natural justice has a few more subsidiary rules . Today it is no longer correct to say that principles of natural justice apply only to the authority which is required by the law under which it functioned to act judicially. Often it is not easy to draw the line between administrative enquire and quasi-judicial enquires.[163]

The decision in *Maneka Gandhi v. Union of India*[164] goes a step further. In this case the passport of the petitioner was cancelled without giving her any reasonable opportunity of being heard. Bhagwati, J., observed:

Although there are no positive words in the statute requiring that the party shall be heard yet the justice of the common law will supply the omission of the legislature. The principal of *audi alteram partem* which mandates that no one shall be condemned unheard is part of the rule of natural justice.[165]

His Lordship further observed :

The law must now be taken to be well settled that even in an administrative proceeding , which involves consequence, the doctrine of natural justice must be held to be applicable.[166]

In the civil service examination, candidates were required to write their roll number , on the space provided and at no other place . For the breach of this condition, the PSC decided that answers –book should not be evaluated. No opportunity of hearing need be given to the candidate.[167] The order was quashed.

When does Certiorari or Prohibition Lies

It seems to be now settled that a writ of *certiorari* or prohibition would lie in case where the tribunal or the authority:

(a) Refuse to exercise jurisdiction,

(b) Acts without jurisdiction,

(c) Exercise jurisdiction by erroneously deciding necessary to confer jurisdiction,

(d) Exercise jurisdiction by taking into consideration irrelevant and extraneous matter , or

(e) Makes an effort of law apparent on the face of the record.[168]

Want of jurisdiction may arise on several counts. It may be on account of the fact that the tribunal has no jurisdiction over the subject-matter of the enquiry, or from absence of some preliminary proceedings, Such as omission to serve notice, or the tribunal may not be properly constituted, or the law which conferred jurisdiction of the tribunal is unconstitutional.[169] In *Ambika Mills v. Bhatt*,[170] the court found that the construction placed by the tribunal on the two clauses of the agreement between the Mill- owner's Association and Textile Labor Association was patently and manifestly erroneous. The court observed: "It is not a case where two alternative conclusion are possible; it is a case of plain misreading of the two provisions ignoring altogether the very object with which the two separate provision were made."

"The error apparent on the face of the record" does not mean mere, error of law such an error which is manifest and apparent.[171] *Certiorari* does not lie to correct an error of facts. The *Certiorari* jurisdiction is not an appellate jurisdiction. But finding of fact based on evidence, or where the tribunal erroneously refused to admit admissible evidence or material evidence, or has erroneously admitted inadmissible evidence which led the tribunal to reach conclusion which it had, tantamount to error of law and certiorari lies.[172] But the finding of fact cannot be challenged merely on the ground of inadequacy of the evidence.[173]

The jurisdiction of the *certiorari* has been extended to such an extent that was probably not contemplated originally. The courts now hold that the violation of natural justice includes the violation of duty of act fairly. (The aspect of the matter we have already discussed). The court have repeatedly said that the concept of natural justice is flexible, and what amounts to violation of natural justice, will vary from case to case.[174]

In *Hiranath*,[175] certain student were expelled from the Court after an inquiry . Allegations against them were that they, being quite naked, entered the compound of the Girl's Hostel and even went outside the rooms of some girl student and tried to pull them out. The inquiry was conducted by a Committee of teachers constituted by the Principal of the College , The inquiry was challenged on the ground that the statements of the girl student were recorded in the absence of the accused, the girl student were not called for cross-examination to test their veracity , and a copy of the report of the Inquiry Committee was not supplied to them , Rejecting these contentions, the Supreme Court observed that the requirements of natural justice were not static these vary from case to case . The court observed that inquiry into the incident involved some delicacy , the police could not be called in , because the police investigation would have frightened the girl student and they might not have cooperated; an open inquiry was not feasible as the girl student would not have ventured to make their statement before the accused for fear of future harassment ; (since the college was not in a position to give protection to them outside the college and hostel premises); and for these very reasons a copy of the report was not given to the accused . The court held since the college stood in the capacity of *loco parents* to the girls staying in the hostel, it was necessary to hold the inquiry, and the type of inquiry held and the investigation made was only course open to the college as the accused were informed of the changes against them and were accorded adequate opportunity to defend themselves. There was no violation of natural justice or fairness.

We had already reviewed *A .K. Kraipak v. Union of India,*[176] which is a case of bias. The principals of natural justice require that a prosecutor cannot be a judge; nor can a person be a judge in his own Case; and the adjudicator should have no interest in the subject matter of adjudication either.[177]

It is also part of the principle of natural justice that the accused should be given a fair hearing. It is of repeated that no one should be condemned unheard. But this does not mean that there should be oral hearing or adherence should be made to all the rules and the principles of the Evidence Act. What is required is that the accused should be given adequate opportunity so that can explain his conduct, should be given adequate time to prepare his defiance , and should be allowed to lead evidence in his defence.[178]

Ordinarily, the evidence should be recorded in his presence and he should be allowed to cross-examine the witness.[179] But this is not a hard and fast rule. *Hiranath and State of J&K v . Bakshi Gulam Md,* [180] provides an exception to this rule and illustrates the flexibility of the rules of natural justice. Representation through the lawyer is not part of natural justice.[181]

Habeas Corpus

The fundamental right to personal liberty can be rendered nugatory if there does not exist of *habeas corpus* which secures the instant release of a person detained unlawfully. The writ of *habeas corpus* calling upon the detainee to bring the detenu before the court and to let the court know on what ground he is detained , and if no legal justification is shown the detenu is released forthwith . The writ of *habeas sub jiciendum,* as it was originally named, proved to be very speedy and effective legal remedy to secure personal liberty. The person to whom the writ is directed must, at the return of the writ, produce in open court the body of the party so committed or restrained, and certify the true cause of imprisonment within three days after such return the court must proceed to examine and determine whether the cause of such commitment appearing upon the return is just and legal or not, and must deliver bail or remand the prisoner accordingly , under penalty or treble damages forfeitable to the party aggrieved.[182] In England, the right to *habeas corpus* was secured firmly through several states. The Habes Corpus Acts of 1640, 1679 and 1816 are important landmark status. The Habeas Corpus Act, 1862 laid down that the writ of habeas corpus could be issued out of the jurisdiction.

In India the writ of *Habeas Corpus* is part of the remedial fundamental right under Article 32, and the High Court also has the power to issue it under Article 226. It can be issued for the release of any person who is detained unlawfully. A detention is unlawful if it is not in accordance with law, or the procedure by law has not been complied with, or detention is not under a valid law, (invalidity may be because it infringes a fundamental right or legislature passing it has exceeded its authority or has no authority or has contravened Article 22). A detention would also be unlawful if the detaining authority exceeds its authority or abuses it or exercises it *mala fide.*[183]

Who can Seek Habeas Corpus

The right to seek the writ of *Habeas Corpus* obviously belongs to the person who has been detained unlawfully. But it may happen that a prisoner or detenu is not in a position to make the application. Keeping such a situation in view, the law accords the right to apply for the writ on any of his relation or friend. This happens in those cases where a prisoner is denied the facility to file the writ or is not in position to do so.[184] Thus, a child in unlawful detention may not be in a position of applying for the writ. It may happen that a child so detained has no legal guardian or the legal guardian is not capable of acting or does not act an application may be made by relation of friend.

Against whom Petition for Habeas Corpus Lies

Under Article 32 a petition is maintainable only when a breach of fundamental right is alleged and if question of violation of the fundamental right under Article 21 does not arise petition is not competent.[185] Under Article 32 petition is not available against a private person who is alleged to have unlawfully detained the petitioner. But a petition for *Habeas Corpus* under Article 226 is maintainable in all case of unlawful detention and against any detainee whether a private person or Government or any of its department s or authority. Where conflicting claims for custody of a child are made, the court has power to inquire into them and award the custody to the proper person.[186]

Habeas Corpus Jurisdiction is Remedial and not Punitive

The purpose of the habeas corpus is to secure the release of a detenu from unlawful detention and not to punish the detainee. In *Kedar Nath v. State of Punjab*,[187] the court observed that writ of habeas corpus was meant to determine the legality or illegality of the detention and not for punishing the detainee. This principle has very important consequence. Thus in *habeas corpus* proceeding the court has to consider the legality of the detention on the date of hearing. If on the date of hearing it cannot be said that the aggrieved party has been unlawfully deprived of his personal liberty, and his detention is contrary to law, a writ of *habeas corpus* cannot be issued.[188] In *Tajik Hussian v. State of J&K*[189] a person who was convicted by a court marital for criminal misappropriation of money and sentenced to a term of imprisonment applied for a writ of *habeas corpus* questioning the correctness of sentence. The court observed that in *habeas corpus* proceedings the correctness or otherwise of a conviction could not be questioned; the court go only into the question of jurisdiction of the court martial or whether it was properly constituted or whether some such illegality or irregularly was committee as would go to the root of the jurisdiction or the court. This principle also means that if at the time of the hearing the detaining authority has superseded its earlier unlawful detention order with a fresh order which is free from defects the writ would not lie.[190] In *Anwar v. State J&K*,[191] It was held that a foreigner who had entered India secretly and was detained could not seek the writ of *habeas corpus* as his detention was not illegal. In Kanu Sanyal v. Dist Magistrate,[192] the court observed that in habeas corpus proceedings the court might examine the legality of detention without the detenu's production before it. Bhagwati, J., "…it is not necessary to go through the idle formality of requiring him to be produced before the court and that it would be sufficient and appropriate instead to examine the validity of the detention without having him brought before the court."

Preventive Detention and Habeas Corpus

A preventive detention, too, can be challenged by a writ *habeas corpus* under Article 226. The main question that the court considers in preventive detention cases is whether the detention is prima facie legal or not. But otherwise of the detention order cannot be challenged. This means that a detenu has to establish infringement of Article 21 or 22.[193] In a petition for habeas corpus by a detenu the affidavit in reply to the petition must be that of the District Magistrate who passed the detention order or some responsible officer who had personally dealt with the case.[194]

Successive Application for Habeas Corpus

Under English law before the decision in *In re Hastings* (No .2)and in *In re Hastings* (NO.3) ,[195] a person was free to apply for a writ of *habeas corpus* form judge and from court to court . *In re Hastings(No.2)* and *In re Hastings* (No.3) lay down that successive writ applications could not be moved from one division to another , since there was only one High Court (in England). This view was followed in India, in *In re Prahlad Krishna Khurana,*[196] and court held that once an application was rejected by a judged or division of the High Court , another Application could not be made to another judge or another Bench of the High Court . Chagla, CJ., observed that this would not cause any hardship to the petitioner as he could directly approach the Supreme Court under Article136. Thus, the court applied the doctrine of constructive *res Judicator* to *habeas corpus* proceeding. It is submitted that Seervai rightly says that the doctrine of constructive res judicator should not be applied to the petitions of *habeas corpus*. Thus, a second petition should lie to the same division or judge or to another division or judge of the High Court in case a petition is supported by fresh evidence or it made on some other ground. The petition should not be barred even if these grounds and evidence could have been taken in earlier petition, since "it would be contrary to public policy to apply the principle of constructive *res judicata* to the liberty of the subject and to allow an illegal detention to continue."[197]

The court has power to grant interim bail in *habeas corpus* proceedings. [198]

Appeal

In England no appeal lies against an order granting the writ of *habeas corpus.*[199] But an appeal lies to the Court of Appeal from an order refusing a writ of habeas corpus expect in criminal cause or matter. But this not so in India. Appeal lies against an order granting or refusing the writ of habeas corpus.

Quo Warranto

Till 1938, in English law, *quo warranto* law against the usurpation of any office, whether created by charter, along, or by the Crown with the consent of parliament, provided the office was of public nature, and a substantive office. But no writ if the office was not of a substantive nature, such as where the office was determinable at the will or pleasure of others.[200] In 1238 *Quo Warranto* was abolished and it was laid down that the court might, at the instance of any person who would have been able to apply for *quo warranto* , grant an injunction restraining the usurper of office from so acting and might also declare the office vacant . The Constitution of India retains that writ of *quo warranto* under Articles 32 and 226. In *University of Mysor v. Govin Rao*citizen from being deprived of public office to which he may have a right ....in some cases persons not entitled to public may be allowed to occupy them and to continue to hold them as a result of the connivance of the executive or with its active help , and in such cases, if the jurisdiction of the courts to the issue of *quo warranto* is properly invoked , the usurper can be ousted and the person entitled to the post allowed to occupy it." For the issuance of *quo warranto* the following conditions should be fulfilled:

(a) The office in question should be a public office.

(b) The office should be held by a usurper without legal authority, and

(c) it is not necessary for the petitioner to show that he himself suffered a personal injury; nor is it necessary to show that he is seeking redress of a personal grievance.[202]

It is essential for the issuance of a writ of *quo warranto* that the office held by usurper should be of a substantive character. The holder of the following offices have been holders of public officers of substantive character: Advocate – General, Government pleader, Speaker, the Mayor, Chairman of Municipality, a member of Municipal Board or of any local body, and a member of the University Senate of Syndicate.[203] But a *quo warranto* cannot be issued to quash things already done or to vindicate a private right.[204] A futile *quo warranto* cannot be issued. Thus in P.L. Lakhanpal v. A.N.Roy,[205] The petition sought a *quo warranto* challenging the validity of the appointment of the Hon'ble Mr Justice A.N. Roy, Chief Justice of India on ground that it violated Article 124 (2) and the rule of seniority inherent in it. The petition was dismissed as futile, since after the resignation of Shelat, Hedge and Grover, JJ., Roy J., could again be appointed to the office of the Chief Justice.

The petitioner need not show a personal injury or grievance; but he must act *bona fide*. Obviously, a person having a special interest in the office can also apply. Thus an M.L.A. has *locus standi* to apply for *quo warranto* if he *bona fide* believes that the Speaker held office without legal authority.[206]

The writ of *quo warranto* is discretionary, and the court has discretion to refuse it in the following cases :[207]

(i) when petitioner acquiesced to the nomination or appointment of the respondent,

(ii) the petitioner has an alternative remedy under the statute,

(iv) the petitioner is guilty of laches, and

(v) the petition is barred by *judicata*.

Conclusion

Human Rights are the basic fundamental rights which form the integral part for the overall development of human beings and in absence of which a person cannot live with dignity. The provisions of the Constitution not only protects the fundamental rights or human rights but in fact the Preamble also casts the fundamental freedom and dignity of individuals. For the protection of human rights the Indian Judiciary has also relaxed the rule of locus standi that paves the way for development in the concept of Public Interest Litigation. Its through the system of Public Interest Litigation various instances regarding the human rights violation have been put before the courts. Thus judiciary plays the role of guardian of the human rights of the people so that each individual can live with dignity. Throughout the world, the protection of human rights is an important concern. Thus various international instruments have been incorporated with the sole prospect of protecting the human rights and on such basis various national endeavours have been taken such as the enactment of the of the Protection of Human Rights Act, 1993. Provisions have been made under the Act for establishment of National Human Rights Commission as well as State Human Rights Commission which provides for the establishment of Human Rights Courts at district level to provide speedy justice for people at all levels.

Refrences

[1] Article 28(2).

[2] Article 29(1).

[3] Article 28(1).

[4] Article 30(3).

[5] Article 30(4).

[6] Article 31(1).

[7] Article 31 (2).

[8] Article 32 (1).

[9] Article 32 (2).

[10] Such removal can be effected only id a member has ceased to carry out his functions for any cause other than temporary absence. [Article 33 (1)].

[11] Article 34.

[12] Article 35.

[13] Article 37 (3). The initial meeting is to be convened by the Secretary General of the United Nations.

[14] Article 36.

[15] Article 39(2) (a).

[16] Article 39(2) (b).

[17] Article 39(2).

[18] Article 38.

[19] Article 43.

[20] Article 40.

[21] Article 40(4).

[22] Article 40(5).

[23] Article 2.

[24] Article 3.

[25] Article 4.

[26] Article 5.

[27] Article 6.

[28] The Human Rights Committee has received some complaints, of these some may be noted: Communication by one Ambrosini a Urugnayam national residing in Brazil, about unlawful detentionand torture. Edurado Dente Santulle Veleade's Communication by a Urugnayam national residing in Mexico alleging unlawful detention and torture and violence against his person. Ana Maria Gracia Lanze Netto's, again a Urugnayam national, residing in Mexico. The communication was on behalf of her aunt and uncle about the same matter, i.e., unlawful

detention and torture. In all these cases the Committee did express its "views" on the substance of the matter with the result some relief was obtained by the complaints.

[29] Article 2.

[30] Article 16.

[31] Article 17.

[32] Article 19.

[33] Article 20.

[34] Article 21.

[35] Article 22.

[36] Per Ganjendragadkar, J., in Prem Chand v. Excise Commr., AIR 1963 SC 996.

[37] Per Patanjali Sastri, J., in Romesh Thapar v. State of Mad., AIR 1950 SC 124.

[38] State of Mad. v. V.G. Row, AIR 1952 SC 96.

[39] Darva v. State of U.P., AIR 1961 SC 1457.

[40] State of M.P. v. Peer Md., AIR 1963 SC 645; Kalyan Singh v. State of U.P., AIR 1962 SC 1183; Rameshwar Prasad v. Commr., Land Reform, AIR 1959 SC 498.

[41] Ibid.

[42] T.T. Devasthanams v. Ram Chandra, AIR 1966 AP 112.

[43] Hans Muller v. Supdt. Presidency Jail, AIR 1955 SC 367; Bakoro and Ramgur Ltd. V. State of Bihar, AIR 1963 SC 516.

[44] Chiranji Lal v. Union of India, AIR 1951 SC 42.

[45] R.C. Cooper v. Union of India, (1970) 35 CR 530; Bennet Coleman & Co. v. Union of India, AIR 1973 SC 106.

[46] AIR 1969 SC 783.

[47] Asiad Workers Case, AIR 1982 SC 1976.

[48] Judges Transfer Case, (1981) Supp. SCC 87.

[49] (1981) Supple, SCC 87 at 211.

[50] Ibid., at 213.

[51] AIR 1991 SC 1902.

[52] Subhas Kumar v. State of Bihar, AIR 1991 SC 420.

[53] S.P. Gupta v. UOI, (1981) Suppl, SCC at 507.

[54] Ibid., at 265.

[55] Ibid.

[56] AIR 1982 SC 1976.

[57] (1985) 2 SCC 481.

[58] (1987) 4 SCC 463; see also M.C. Mehta v. UOI, (1988) 2 SCC 421.

[59] (1990) Suppl SCC 37.

[60] AIR 1990 Ker 321.

[61] See for a review of environmental cases Paras Diwan and Peeyushi Diwan: Environmental Administration, Law and Judicial Attitude, Vol. I, 558 – 827.

[62] (1990) Annual Survey of Indian Law 181 – 82.

[64] AIR 1967 SC 1857.

[65] AIR 1971 SC 1820.

[66] AIR 1970 SC 1244.

[67] AIR 1975 SC 1331.

[69] Coffee Board, Bangalore v. Commercial Tax Officer, AIR 1971 SC 870.

[70] Ibid.

[71] AIR 1967 SC 1.

[72] Chranji Lal v. Union of India, AIR 1951 SC 42.

[73] Ram Chandra v. State of Orissa, AIR 1957 SC 298.

[74] Laxminappa v. Union of India, AIR 1955 SC 3; Nain Sukh v. State of U.P., AIR 1953 SC 3 U.P.

[75] DAV College v. State of Punjab, (1971) Supp SCR 688.

[76] Daryao v. State of U.P., AIR 1961 SC 1457.

[77] Prem Chand v. Excise Commr., AIR 1963 SC 996.

[78] K. K. Kochuni v. State of Mad., (1959) Supp 2 SCR 356.

[79] Kharak Singh v. State of U.P., AIR 1963 SC 1295.

[80] K.C. Kochuni v. State of Mad., AIR 1959 SC 725.

[81] T.C. Basappa v. Nagappa, AIR 1954 SC 440.

[82] Trilokchand v. H.B. Munshi, AIR 1970 SC 898.

[83] Daryao v. State of U.P., AIR 1961 SC 1475.

[84] AIR 1950 SC 124.

[85] Seervai, Vol. II, 825.

[86] S.H. Kochuni v. State of Mad., (1959) SCR 725.

[87] Trilok Chand v. H.B. Munshi, (1969) 2 SCR 824.

[88] Veerappa v. Raman, AIR 1952 SC 192; Himmat Lal v. State of M.P., AIR 1954 SC 403.

[89] Veerappa v. Raman, AIR 1952 SC 192; (Motor Vehicle Act is a complete code); P. Basant v. Eugle Rolling Mills, AIR 1964 SC 1260 (Industrial Disputes Act); Champalal v. CIT, AIR 1970 SC 645 (Income Tax Act).

[90] Venkateswaran v. Wadhwan, AIR 1961 SC 1506 (when alternative remedy is burdensome and onerous); NMCS & Weaning Mills v. Ahmedabad Municipality, AIR 1967 SC 1801 (when tribunal acts under ultra vires law).

[91] Trilokchand v. H.B. Munshi, AIR 1979 SC 898.

[92] Ibid., per Nhagwati and Mitter, JJ 73. See also State of M.P. V. Bhailal, AIR 1964 SC 1006. But see E. Bhusan v. Dy. Director Cons., U.P., AIR 1967 SC 1273 where this view has been dissented.

[93] AIR 1972 SC 2062.

[94] Haryana Electricity Board v. State of Punjab, AIR 1974 SC 2060; Nand Kishore v. State of Orissa, AIR 1991 SC 1720 1728.

[95] AIR 1974 SC 259.

[96] See Paras Diwan, Modern Hindu Law, (975 Ed.) 187 – 88.

[97] Amalgamated Coal – fields v. Janapade, AIR 1964 SC 1013; Daryao v. State of U.P., AIR 1961 SC 1457; Govt. of A.P. v. Nersimha, AIR 1991 SC 1732.

[98] Devilal Modi v. STO, AIR 1961 SC 1150.

[99] Amalgamated Coal – fields v. Ranade, AIR 1961 SC 964.

[100] Devilal v. STO, AIR 1965 SC 1150.

[101] Gulab Chand v. State, AIR 1965 SC 1953; Union of India v. Nanak Singh, AIR 1968 SC 1370.

[102] Bishnu Charan v. State, AIR 1973 Orissa 199.

[103] Shankar v. Krishna, AIR 1970 SC 1.

[104] Joseph Pothen v. State of Kerela, AIR 1965 SC1514; A.R. Chaudhary v. Union of India, AIR 1974 SC 532.

[105] Ghulam Sarwar v. Union of India, AIR 1967 SC 1335; Niranjan Singh, AIR 1972 SC 2215.

[106] Gandhinagar Motor Transport Society v. State of Bombay, AIR 1964 Bom. 202.

[107] A. Pillai v. Government of India, AIR 1970 Ker 110 (FB).

[108] AIR 1972 P & H 28.

[109] Mahor Chandru Bhan v. Latafat Ullah, AIR 197 SC 1814.

[110] K.K. Kochuni v. State of Madras, AIR 1959 SC 725.

[111] Shankar v. Returning Officer, AIR 1952 Bom 277.

[112] K.N. Guruswami v. State of Mysore, (1955) 1 SCR 305.

[113] Lekhraj v. Mathur, AIR 1962 Ker 152.

[114] AIR 1989 SC 1285.

[115] Before the coming into force of the Constitution under the Specific Relief Act the power to issue writ was conferred only on three Presidency High Courts, namely, Calcutta, Bombay and Madras.

[116] See Rashid Ahmed v. Municipal Board, Kairana, AIR 1950 SC 163.

[117] Halsbury's Law of England (2nd Edition.), Vol IX, 744.

[118] Bhopal Sugar Industries v. Income Tax Officer, AIR 1961 SC 182.

[119] State of Bihar v. D.N. Ganguly, (1959) SCR 1991.

[120] Ghrita Mohan v. Addl. District Magistrate, AIR 1954 Cal 97.

[121] Umakant v. State of Bihar, AIR 1973 SC 965.

[122] State of M.P. V. Madawar, AIR 1954 SC 493; Rashid Ahmad v. Municipal Board, AIR 1950 SC 610, State of Bombay v. Hospital Mazdoor Sabha, AIR 1960 SC 1960 SC 610; Commr. Of Police v. Gordhandas, AIR 1952 SC 16.

[123] Lekhraj v. Dy. Custodian, AIR 1966 SC 334.

[124] D.F.O. V. Ram Sanehi, AIR 1973 SC 204.

[125] Dwarka Prasad v. State of U.P., AIR 1954 SC 224.

[126] Burmah Construction Company v. State of Orissa, AIR 1962 SC 1320.

[127] Himmat Lal v. State of M.P., AIR 1954 SC 403.

[128] Amrit Lal v. State of W.B., AIR 1972 SC 2060; Amrit Lal v. Collector, AIR 1975 SC 538.

[129] Commr. of Police v. Gordhandas, (1953) SCR 135.

[130] AIR 1992 SC 1546.

[131] AIR 1957 SC 829.

[132] AIR 1969 SC 1306.

[133] Hare Krishna v. Chief Minister, Orissa, AIR 1971 Ori 175; Borhan Kumar v. Boruni Oil Refineries, AIR 1971 Pat 174; Mathew v. Union of India, AIR 1974 Ker 4; R.D. Singh v. Bihar State Small Industries Co., AIR 1974 Pat 212.

[134] AIR 1974 All 1.

[135] Pramatha Nath v. Chief Justice of Calcutta, AIR 1961 Cal 545; Jyoti Prakash v. M.K. Bose, AIR 1963 SC 209.

[136] AIR 1978 SC 209.

[137] Chotey Lal v. State of U.P., AIR1951 All 228; Narinder Chand v. Ly. Governor, H.P., (1971) 2 SCC 743.

[138] AIR 1954 SC 493.

[139] Raman & Raman v. State of Madras, AIR 1959 SC 694; G.J. Fernondez v. State of Mysore, AIR 1967 SC 1753.

[140] Samarth Transport Co. v. RTV, AIR 1961 SC 932.

[141] State of Mysore v. Chandrasekharan, AIR 1965 SC 932

[142] T.G. Goakar v. R.N. Shukla, AIR 1968 SC 1050; Bombay Union of Journalist v. State of Bombay, AIR 1964 SC 1617.

[143] Vice Chancellor, Utkal University v. S. K. Ghosh, (1954) SCR 883.

[144] (1963) 2 WLR 935.

[145] (1967) 2 KB 617.

[146] AIR 1970 SC 150.

[147] AIR 1978 SC 597.

[148] Air Corporation Employees' Union v. D.V. Vyas, 1962 Bom 274; Engineering Mazdoor Sabha v. Hind Cycles, AIR 1963 SC 874.

[149] R.V, Electricy Commissioner, (1924) KB 173, per Atkin, CJ and R. v. Legislative Committee of the Church Assembly (1928) 1KB 411, per Lord Heward, CJ (Lord Heward's gloss over Atkin, CJ's formulation, as it is called).

[150] State of Bombay v. K. S. Advani, AIR 1950 SC 222 where this view was adopted.

[151] AIR 1958 SC 398.

[152] See also Radheshyam v. State of M.P., AIR 1959 SC 107; Gullapalli v. A.O. State Transport Corporation, AIR 1959 SC 388; Raman Ltd v. State of Mad., AIR 1959 SC 694; Board of High School v. Ghanshyam, AIR 1962 SC 1110; Shankar Lal v. Shankar Lal, AIR 1965 SC 507; National Institute v. K.K. Raman, AIR 1992 SC 1809.

[153] AIR 1955 SC 1595.

[154] AIR 1965 SC 176.

[155] AIR 1966 SC 91; See also Union of India v. Win Chadda, AIR 1993 SC 1082.

[156] AIR 1967 SC 1507.

[157] AIR 1967 SC 1269.

[158] Ibid.

[159] See also Bool Chandra v. Chancellor, AIR 1968 SC 292, State of M.P. v. Srikant, AIR 1992 SC 2303.

[160] AIR 1970 SC 150.

[161] Ibid., at 154.

[162] S. N. Mukherjee v. Union of India, AIR 1990 SC 1984.

[163] Suresh Koshy v. University of Kerela, AIR 1969 SC 1998 is an illustration where rules of natural law were followed. See also Kanungo v. Collector of Customs, Calcutta, AIR 1972 SC 2136; Hira Nath v. Rajendra Medical College, Ranchi, AIR 1973 SC 1216 to the same effect.

[164] AIR 1978 SC 597.

[165] Ibid., at 624.

[166] Ibid., 628.

[167] Karnataka Public Service Commission v. B.M. Vijai, AIR 1992 SC 952.

[168] See STO v. Shiv Ratan, AIR 1966 SC 142; CIT v. Raman & Co., AIR 1964 SC 49; Chetkar v. Vishwanath, AIR 1970 SC 1932; Express Newspaper v. Workers, AIR 1963 SC 569; Shanngam v. SRVS, AIE 1963 SC 1963; Prem Sagar v. S.V. Oil Co., AIR 1956 SC 111.

[169] Rajamahundary v. State of A.P., AIR 1954 SC 201.

[170] AIR 1961 SC 970.

[171] C. Shanmugam v. SRVS, AIR 1963 SC 1926; Prem Sagar v. S.V. Oil Mills, AIR 1965 SC 111.

[172] Pioneer Traders v. C.C. Exports & Imports, AIR 1963 SC 734; Subar v. Workmen, AIR 1960 SC; Rukmanand v. State of Bihar, AIR 1971 SC 746; D.C. Works v. State of Saurastra, AIR 1957 SC 164; Sayed Yakoob v. Radhakrishna, AIR 1964 SC 477; Parry & Co. v. Second Industrial Tribunal, AIR 1970 SC 1334; Sahngin Singh v. Desa Singh, AIR 1970 SC 672; State of Orissa v. Murlidhar, AIR 1963 SC 404; Union of India v. Goel, AIR 1964 SC 364; State of Mad. V. Sundaram, AIR, 1964 SC 1103.

[173] See the last three cases in the preceding footnote.

[174] Fedco v. Bilgrani, AIR 1960 SC 415; Hiranath v. Rajendra Medical College, AIR 1973 SC 1260.

[175] AIR 1975 SC 1260.

[176] AIR 1970 SC 150.

[177] Manek Lal v. Prem Chand, AIR 1957 SC 429; State of U.P. v. Nooh, AIR 1958 SC 86. See also Gullapalli I, AIR 1959 SC 308 and Gullapalli II, AIR 1959 SC 1376; T.G. Mudaliar v. State of T.N., AIR 1973 SC 974.

[178] M.P. Industries v. Union of India, AIR 1966 SC 671; D.C. Mills v. Commr. of Income Tax, AIR 1955 SC 65; Union of India v. T. R. Varma, AIR 1957 SC 882; B.E. Supply Co. v. The Workmen, AIR 1972 SC 330; Prem Prakash v. Punjab University, AIR 1972 SC 1408.

[179] State of Orissa v. Murlidhar, AIR 1963 SC 404.

[180] AIR 1967 SC 122.

[181] Kalinadi v. Tata Loco & Engineering Co., AIR 1963 SC 914. But see Subramanium v. Collector of Customs, AIR 1972 SC 2178.

[182] Halsbury, Vol. XI, 28.

[183] G. Sadanandan v. State of Ker., AIR 1966 SC 1952; Ram Manohar Lohia v. State of Bihar, AIR 1966 SC 740.

[184] Raj Bahadur v. Legal Remembrancer, AIR 1952 Cal 522.

[185] Smt. Vidhya Verma v. Shive Narayan Verma, AIR 1956 SC 108.

[186] Gohar Begum v. Suggi, AIR 1960 SC 93.

[187] AIR 1960 Punj 122.

[188] S. Soundarajan v. Union of India, AIR 1970 Del 29.

[189] Talik Hussain v. State of J. & K., AIR 1971 SC 62.

[190] Naranjan Singh v. State of Punj, AIR 1952 SC 1063; Ram Narayan Singh v. State of Delhi, AIR 1953 SC 227; Gopalan v. Government, AIR 1966 SC 816.

[191] AIR 1971 SC 337.

[192] AIR 1973 SC 2684.

[193] Ram Bali v. State of W.B., AIR 1975 SC 623.

[194] Md. Alam v. State of W.B., AIR 1974 SC 917.

[195] 1959 KB 358.

[196] AIR 1951 Bom. 25.

[197] Constitutional Law of India, Vol II, 993. See also in Ghulam Sarwar v. Union of India, AIR 1967 SC 1335.

[198] State of Bihar v. Rambalak Singh, AIR 1966 SC 1441.

[199] Cox v. Hakes, (1890) 15 AC 506.

[200] Desley v. R. (1846)12 CI & F 520, also R. V. Speyar, (1916) 1 KB 595.

[201] AIR 1956 SC 491.

[202] Satish Chandra v. Rajasthan University, AIR 1970 Raj. 184.

[203] G. K. Karkare v. The Shived, AIR 1952 Nag 330; Ramchandaran v. Alagiriswami, AIR 1961 Mad 45; Anand Henal v. Ram Sahav, AIR 1952 MB 31; Rajendra Singh v. N.K. Shejwalkar, AIR 1972 MP 249; Sukhdesh v. Mahadevanand, AIR 1961 AP 250; Vishwanath v. State, AIR 1967 Raj 75; Piara Singh v. State of Punjab, (1969) 1 SCC 379; Venkataya v. Siverama, AIR 1961 AP 250; Satish Chandra v. Rajasthan University, AIR 1970 Raj 148.

[204] Puran Lal v. P. C. Ghosh, AIR 1970 Cal 118.

[205] AIR 1975 Del 66 (FB).

[201] the Supreme Court observed, "...the procedure of *quo warranto* confers jurisdiction and authority on the judiciary to control executive action in the matter of appointment to public office against the relevant statutory provisions; it also protects a

[206] A. Nesamony v. T. M. Vasghose, (1952) Tr Co. 66; Satish Chandra v. Rajasthan University, AIR 1970 Raj 148, a registered graduate has locus standi to challenge election to the Syndicate.

[207] Miss Cama v. Banwari, AIR 1953 Nag 81; Halder v. Misakar, AIR 1973 Ori 132.

Chapter VI

Role Of Judiciary In India

Introduction

The expression of 'Human Rights' was not expressly defined in Indian legal structure till enactment of the Protection of Human Rights Act, 1993. However, one must not construe, directly or indirectly, that the human rights movement was started in post- independent era only after 1993. In the pursuit for a just society, rather than an ordered socio-political society, Indian Constitution, its constitutionalism and Indian Judiciary esp. Supreme Court of India have been advocating enforcement of 'human rights' from its inception. The role of Supreme Court, in this regard, is phenomenal. The concepts involved with the human rights are dynamic per se. The terms "Life", "Liberty", "Equality" and "Dignity" is not defined either in the Constitution of India or Statute. Only through judicial interpretation, we conceive the scope and domain of these ever growing and affluent concepts of human existence. Human emancipation against all forms of subjugation or exploitation of State, society or individual is fought on these concepts. All these concepts are so closely juxtaposed in a human life, it will lose its edge and shine in the absence of others. However, considering the vastness of these concepts, the author confines its venture to the role of SC in the realm of right to life, guaranteed under Art 21 of the Constitution of India, in enforcing Human Rights in India by way of positive assertion of human rights in Indian polity.

The Role of the Supreme Court of India in Enforcing Human Rights

Judiciary in every country has an obligation and a Constitutional role to protect Human Rights of citizens. As per the mandate of the Constitution of India, this function is assigned to the superior judiciary namely the Supreme Court of India and High courts. The Supreme Court of India is perhaps one of the most active courts when it comes into the matter of protection of Human Rights. It has great reputation of independence and credibility. The preamble of the Constitution of India encapsulates the objectives of the Constitution-makers to build a new Socio Economic order where there will be Social, Economic and Political Justice for everyone and equality of status and opportunity for all.

This basic objective of the Constitution mandates every organ of the state, the executive, the legislature and the judiciary working harmoniously to strive to realize the objectives concretized in the Fundamental Rights and Directive Principles of State Policy.

The judiciary must adopt a creative and purposive approach in the interpretation of Fundamental Rights and Directive Principles of State Policy embodied in the Constitution with a view to advancing Human Rights jurisprudence. The promotion and protection of Human Rights is depends upon the strong and independent judiciary. The main study here would be given wide coverage to the functional aspect of the judiciary and see how far the Apex judiciary in India has achieved success in discharging the heavy responsibility of safeguarding Human Rights in the light of our Constitutional mandate. The major contributions of the judiciary to the Human Rights jurisprudence have been twofold: (1) the substantive expansion of the concept of Human Rights under Article 21 of the Constitution, and (2) the procedural innovation of Public Interest Litigation.

In the *Paschim Banga Khet Samity vs. State of West Bengal,* 1996, the petitioner(s) aggrieved by the indifferent and callous attitude on the part of the medical authorities at the various State run hospitals in Kolkata in providing treatment for the serious injuries sustained by the petitioner following a train accident, filed this writ petition.

The Supreme Court held that the Article 21 imposes an obligation on the state to safeguard the right to life of every person. Preservation of human life is thus of paramount importance. The government hospitals run by the State and the medical officers employed therein are duty-bound to extend medical assistance for preserving human life. Failure on the part of a government hospital to provide for timely medical treatment to a person in need of such treatment results in violation of his right to life guaranteed under Article 21. Therefore, the failure of a government run health centre to provide timely treatment is violative of a person's right to life. Further, the court ordered that Primary health care centres be equipped to deal with medical emergencies. It has also been held in this judgment that the lack of financial resources cannot be a reason for the state to shy away from its constitutional obligation.[1]

"The Constitution envisages the establishment of a welfare state... providing adequate medical facilities for the people is an essential part of the obligations undertaken by the government in this respect and discharges this obligation by running hospitals and health centres."

In line with its general approach of frequently offering comprehensive remedies that go beyond merely providing redress for the victim and also laying down the necessary policy and administrative steps to be taken by the state in the wider public interest, the court not only ordered compensation but also directed by the type of facilities that the state government had to provide. This included hospitals and emergency provision (ambulances and communication) by formulating a blueprint for primary health care with particular reference to treatment of patients under an emergency as part of the state's public health obligation under Article 47. Furthermore, the Court ruled that its orders should apply to other states, together with the national government, and that they should be sent a copy of the judgment.[2]

In *Paramanand Katara vs. Union of India,* 1989, a Division Bench of the Supreme Court admitted an application filed under Article 32 by a practicing advocate along with a new item entitle: "Law Helps the Injured to Die" published in The Hindustan Times, New Delhi, as a public interest litigation. The petitioner, through this public interest litigation, had highlighted the difficulties faced by the injured persons in getting medical treatment urgently required to save their lives, in view of the refusal by many doctors and hospitals on the ground that such cases are medico-legal cases. In that case, the petition narrated the unfortunate incident of a person dying due to the non-availability of immediate medical treatment. "The Court extensively death with the professional ethics of the medical profession and issued a number of directions to ensure that an injured person is instantaneously given medical aid, notwithstanding the formalities to be followed under the procedural criminal law. The court declared that the right to medical treatment is a Fundamental Right of the people under Article 21 of the Constitution. The court issued directions to the Union of India, Medical Council of India, and Indian

Medical Association etc. to give wide publicity to the Court's directions in this regard[3]. "The Supreme Court regarding obligation of state to provide emergency medical treatment, said that whether the patient was innocent of criminal, it was the obligation of those in charge of community health to preserve the life of the patient"[4].

Writ Jurisdiction of the Supreme Court and the High Courts

The most significant of the Human Rights is the exclusive right to Constitutional remedies under Articles 32 and 226 of the Constitution of India. Those persons whose rights have been violated have right to directly approach the High Courts and the Supreme Court for judicial rectification, redressal of grievances and enforcement of Fundamental Rights. In such a case the courts are empowered to issue appropriate directions, orders or writs including writs in the nature of Habeas Corpus, Mandamus, Prohibition, Quo-warranto, and Certiorari. By virtue of Article 32, the Supreme Court of India has expanded the ambit of Judicial Review to include review of all those state measures, which either violate the Fundamental Rights or violative of the Basic Structure of the Constitution. The power of Judicial Review exercised by the Supreme Court is intended to keep every organ of the state within its limits laid down by the Constitution and the laws. It is in exercise of the power of Judicial Review that, the Supreme Court has developed the strategy of Public Interest Litigation.

The right to move to the Supreme Court to enforce Fundamental Rights is itself a Fundamental Right under Article 32 of the Constitution of India. This remedial Fundamental Right has been described as "the Cornerstone of the Democratic Edifice" as the protector and guarantor of the Fundamentals Rights. It has been described as an integral part of the Basic Structure of the Constitution. Whenever, the legislative or the executive decision result in a breach of Fundamental Right, the jurisdiction of the Supreme Court can be invoked. Hence the validity of a law can be challenged under Article 32 if it involves a question of enforcement of any Fundamental Rights.

The Right to Constitutional remedy under Article 32 can be suspended as provided under Articles 32(4), 358 and 359 during the period of promulgation emergency. Accordingly, in case of violation of Fundamental Rights, the petitioner under Article 32 for enforcement of such right can not be moved during the period of emergency. However, as soon as the order ceases to be operative, the infringement of rights made either by the legislative enactment or by executive action can be challenged by a citizen in a court of law and the same may have to be tried on merits, on the basis that the rights alleged to have been infringed were in operation even during the pendency of the presidential proclamation of emergency. If, at the expiration of the presidential order, the parliament passes any legislation to protect the executive action taken during the pendency of the presidential order and afford indemnity to the execution in that behalf, the validity and effect of such legislation may have to be carefully scrutinized.

Under Article 226 of the Constitution of India, the High Courts have concurrent jurisdiction with the Supreme Court in the matter granting relief in cases of violation of the Fundamental Rights, though the High Courts exercise jurisdiction in case of any other rights also. The Supreme Court observed that where the High Court dismissed a writ petition under Article 226 after hearing the matter on merits, a subsequent petition in the Supreme Court under Article 32 on the same facts and for the same relief filed by the same parties will be barred by the rule of Resjudicata. The binding character of the judgment of the court of competent jurisdiction is in essence, a part of the rule of law on which, the administration of justice is founded[5]. Thus the judgment of the High Court under Article 226 passed after hearing the parties on merits must bind the parties till set aside in the appeal as provided by the Constitution and can not be permitted to be avoided by a petition under Article 32.

Article 226 contemplates that notwithstanding anything in Article 32, every High Court shall have power, throughout the territorial limits in relation to which it exercises jurisdiction to issue to any person or authority including the appropriate cases, any government, within those territories, direction, orders or writs in the nature of Habeas Corpus, Mandamus, Prohibition, Quo-warranto and Certiorari or any of them for the enforcement of Fundamental Rights conferred by part-III and for "any other purpose". Hence, the jurisdiction of a High Court is not limited to the protection of the Fundamental Rights but also of the other legal rights as is clear from the words "any other purpose". The concurrent jurisdiction conferred on High Courts under Article 226 does not imply that a person who alleges the violation of Fundamental Rights must first approach the High Court, and he can approach the Supreme Court directly. This was held in the very first case *Ramesh Thapper vs. State of Madras*[6].

But in *P.N. Kumar vs. Municipal Corporation of Delhi*[7] the Supreme Court expressed the view that a citizen should first go to the High Court and if not satisfied, he should approach the Supreme Court. Innumerable instances of Human Rights violation were brought before the Supreme Court as well as the High Courts. Supreme Court as the Apex Court devised new tools and innovative methods to give effective redressal.

Rule of Locus Standi vis-à-vis Public Interest Litigation

The traditional rule is that the right to move the Supreme Court is only available to those whose Fundamental Rights are infringed. A person who is not interested in the subject matter of the order has no *Locus Standi* to invoke the jurisdiction of the court. But the Supreme Court has now considerably liberalized the above rule of *Locus Standi*. The court now permits the "public spirited persons to file a writ petition for the enforcement of Constitutional and statutory rights of any other person or a class, if that person or a class is unable to invoke the jurisdiction of the High Court due to poverty or any social and economic disability. The widening of the traditional rule of Locus Standi and the invention of Public Interest Litigation by the Supreme Court was a significant phase in the enforcement of Human Rights.

In *S.P. Gupta vs. Union of India and others*[8], the seven member bench of the Supreme Court held that any member of the public having "sufficient interest" can approach the court for enforcing the Constitutional or legal rights of those, who cannot go to the court because of their poverty or other disabilities. A person need not come to the court personally or through a lawyer. He can simply write a letter directly to the court complaining his sufferings. Speaking for the majority Bhagwathi, J. said that any member of the public can approach the court for redressal where, a specific legal injury has been caused to a determinate class or group of persons when such a class or person are unable to come to the court because of poverty, disability or a socially or economically disadvantageous position. In the instant case, the court upheld the right of lawyers to be heard on matters affecting the judiciary. By this judgement Public Interest Litigation became a potent weapon for the enforcement of "public duties" where executed inaction or misdeed resulted in public inquiry.

While expanding the scope of the *"Locus Standi"*, Bhagwathi, J. expressed a note of caution and observed "but we must be careful to see that the member of the public, who approaches the court in case of this kind, is acting *bonafide* and not for personal gain or private profit or political motivation or other consideration. The court must not allow its process to be abused by politicians and other". Hence the court was aware that this liberal rule of Locus Standi might be misused by vested interests.

As a result of this broad view of *Locus Standi* permitting Public Interest Litigation or Social Action Litigation, the Supreme Court of India has considerably widened the scope of Article 32 of the Constitution. The Supreme Court has jurisdiction to give an appropriate remedy to the aggrieved persons in various situations. Protection of pavement and slum dwellers of Bombay, improvement of conditions in jails, payment of Minimum Wages, protection against Atrocities on Women, Bihar blinding case, Flesh trade in protective home of Agra, Abolition of Bonded Labourers, Protection of Environment and Ecology are the instances where the court has issued appropriate writs, orders and direction on the basis of Public Interest Litigation.

The strategy of Public Interest Litigation has been evolved by this court with a view to bringing justice within the easy reach of the poor and disadvantaged sections of the community[9]. In *Peoples Union for Democratic Rights vs. Union of India*[10], the Supreme Court held that Public Interest Litigation is brought before the court the court not for purpose of enforcing the right of one individual against another as happened in the case of ordinary litigation, but it is intended to promote and vindicate public interest which demands that violations of Constitutional or legal rights of large number of people who are poor, ignorant or in a socially or economically disadvantageous position should not go unnoticed and unredressed.

In *Bandhu Mukti Morcha vs. Union of India*[11], the Apex Court held that the power of the Supreme Court under Article 32 includes the power to appoint Commission for making enquiry into facts relating to the violation of Fundamental Rights. The Apex Court further held that Public Interest Litigation through a letter should be permitted, but expressed the view that, in entertaining such petitions, the court must be cautious so that, it might not be abused. The court suggested that all such letters must be addressed to the entire court and not a particular judge and secondly it should be entertained only after proper verification of materials supplied by the petitioner. This is known as epistolary jurisdiction.

The advent of Public Interest Litigation (here in after referred to as PIL) is one of the key components of the approach of "Judicial Activism" that is attributed to the higher judiciary in India. The verdict of Bhagwati, J. in *M.C.Mehta vs. Union of India*[12], opened the doors of the Apex Court of India for the oppressed, the exploited and the down – trodden in the villages of India or in urban slums. The poor in India can seek enforcement of their Fundamental Rights from the Supreme Court by writing a letter to any judge of the court even without the support of an Affidavit. The court has brought legal aid to the door steps of millions of Indians which the executive has not been able to do despite that, a lot of money is being spent on new legal aid schemes operating at the central and state level.

A study of the notable cases of the Supreme Court speak of the fact that the Indian judiciary has adopted strong sentiments in favour of Public Interest Litigation and the functioning of judiciary reveals that it has exercised its powers in the most creative manner and devised new strategies to ensure the protection of Human Rights to the people. The Supreme Court of India has used the strategy of Public

Interest Litigations as an aid to enforce the rights of prisoners, workers, pensioners, victims of environmental pollution and others. The Public Interest Litigation plays an important role in ensuring the Principle of Rule of Law by making the administration is accountable to the people. The Supreme Court of India *in Narmada Bachao Andolan vs. Union of India*[13] held that Public Interest Litigation was an invention essentially to safeguard and protect the Human Rights of those people who were unable to protect themselves.

In the recent past Public Interest Litigation has acquired a new dimension. Apart from securing several non–justifiable socio–economic rights as guaranteed under the Fundamentals Rights, the Supreme Court has frequently resorted to a novel feature in the field of Human Rights jurisprudence such as compensatory jurisprudence, judicial law making with a view to secure justice to the down–trodden and also to the oppressed people. Public Interest Litigation is a weapon which has to be used with care and caution. The judiciary has to be extremely careful to see that whether it contains public interest or private vested interest. It is to be used as an effective weapon in the armoury of law for delivering social justice to citizens. The strategy of Public Interest Litigation should not be used for suspicious products of mischief. It should be aimed at the redressal of genuine public wrong or public injury and not publicity–oriented or founded on personal vendetta[14].

There have been in recent times, increasingly instances of abuse of Public Interest Litigations. Therefore there is a need to re–emphasize the parameters within which Public Interest Litigation can be resorted to by a petitioner and entertained by the court. It was essentially meant to protect basic Human Rights of week and disadvantaged. Public Interest Litigation has not been moved under disguise with some ulterior motive or some purpose. The courts are now imposing moderate to heavy costs in cases of misuse of Public Interest Litigation which should be an eye opener for non–serious Public Interest Litigation mover.

The greatest contribution of Public Interest Litigation has been to enhance the accountability of the governments towards the Human Rights of the poor. Public Interest Litigation interrogates power and makes the courts as peoples court. The Supreme Court of India in a number of important decisions has significantly expanded the scope and frontier of Human Rights. Public interest matters today focus more and more on the interests of the Indian middle classes rather than on the oppressed classes. PIL seeking order to ban Quran[15] transmission of T.V. Serials[16], implementation of Consumer Protection Law[17] removal of corrupt ministers[18], invalidation of irregular allotment of petrol pumps[19] and government accommodation[20] prosecution of politicians and bureaucrats for accepting bribes and Kickbacks through Hawala transactions[21], better service conditions of the members of lower judiciary[22] or quashing selection of university teachers[23] are some blatant examples espousing middle class interests. Some initial successes of PIL, however cannot certify that it shall always remain an effective instrument for protection of Human Rights. The future of PIL will depend upon who uses it and for whom.

Prisoners and the Human Rights

The Supreme Court of India in the recent past has been very vigilant against encroachments upon the Human Rights of the prisoners. In this area an attempt is made to explain the some of the provisions of the rights of prisoners under the International and National arenas and also as interpreted by the

Supreme Court of India by invoking the Fundamental Rights. Article 21 of the Constitution of India provides that "No person shall be deprived of his life and Personal Liberty except according to procedure established by law". The rights to life and Personal Liberty is the back bone of the Human Rights in India. Through its positive approach and Activism, the Indian judiciary has served as an institution for providing effective remedy against the violations of Human Rights.

By giving a liberal and comprehensive meaning to "life and personal liberty," the courts have formulated and have established plethora of rights. The court gave a very narrow and concrete meaning to the Fundamental Rights enshrined in Article 21. In *A.K.Gopalan"s* Case[24], the court had taken the view that each Article dealt with separate rights and there was no relation with each other i.e. they were mutually exclusive. But this view has been held to be wrong in *Maneka Gandhi* case[25] and held that they are not mutually exclusive but form a single scheme in the Constitution, that they are all parts of an integrated scheme in the Constitution. In the instant case, the court stated that "the ambit of Personal Liberty by Article 21 of the Constitution is wide and comprehensive. It embraces both substantive rights to Personal Liberty and the procedure prescribed for their deprivation" and also opined that the procedures prescribed by law must be fair, just and reasonable.

In the following cases namely *Maneka Gandhi*[26], *Sunil Batra (I)*[27], *M.H. Hoskot*[28] and *Hussainara Khatoon*[29], the Supreme Court has taken the view that the provisions of part III should be given widest possible interpretation. Every activity which facilitates the exercise of the named Fundamental Right may be considered integrated part of the Article 21 of the Constitution. It has been held that right to legal aid, speedy trail, right to have interview with friend, relative and lawyer, protection to prisoners in jail from degrading, inhuman, and barbarous treatment, right to travel abroad, right live with human dignity, right to livelihood, etc. though specifically not mentioned are Fundamental Rights under Article 21 of the Constitution. One of the most powerful dimensions that arose through Public Interest Litigation is the Human Rights of the prisoners.

The Supreme Court of India has considerably widened the scope of Article 21 and has held that its protection will be available for safeguarding the fundamental rights of the prisoners and for effecting prison reforms. The Supreme Court by its progressive interpretation made Article 21, which guarantees the Right to Life and personal liberty, the reservoir of prisoner"s rights. Under the seventh schedule of the Constitution of the India, the prison administration, police and law and order are to be administered by the respective states. The states have generally given low priority to prison administration. In fact, some of the decisions of the Supreme Court on prison administration have served as eye–openers for the administrators and directed the states to modernize prison administration.

The Human Rights saviour Supreme Court has protected the prisoners from all types of torture. Judiciary has taken a lead to widen the ambit of Right to Life and personal liberty. The host of decisions of the Supreme Court on Article 21 of the Constitution after Maneka Gandhis case, through Public Interest Litigation have unfolded the true nature and scope of Article 21. In this thesis, an attempt is made to analyse the new dimensions given by the Supreme Court to Article 21 through Public Interest Litigation to safeguard the fundamental freedom of the individuals who are indigent, illiterate and ignorant. Public Interest Litigation became a focal point to set the judicial process in motion for the protection of the residuary rights of the prisoners.

Judicial conscience recognized that Human Rights of the prisoners because of its reformistic approach and belief that convicts are also human beings and that the purpose of imprisonment is to reform them rather than to make them hardened criminals. Regarding the treatment of prisoners, Article 5 of the Universal Declaration of Human Rights, 1948 says "No one shall be subjected to torture or cruel treatment, in human or degrading treatment or punishment". While Article 6 of the Universal Declaration of Human Rights, 1948 contemplates that "everyone has the right to recognition everywhere as a person before law". Article 10(1) of the International Covenant on Civil and Political Rights lay down that "All persons deprived of their liberty shall be treated with humanity and with respect for the inherent dignity of the human person".

The Supreme Court of India has developed Human Rights jurisprudence for the preservation and protection of Prisoner's Right to Human Dignity. The concern of the Apex judiciary is evident from the various cardinal judicial decisions. The decisions of the Supreme Court in Sunil Batra was a watershed in the development of prison jurisprudence in India.

The courts have strong view against solitary confinement and held that imposition of solitary confinement is highly degrading and dehumanizing effect on the prisoners. The courts have taken the view that it could be imposed only in exceptional cases where the convict was of such a dangerous character that he must be segregated from the other prisoners. The Supreme Court in *Sunil Batra*(1)[30]considered the validity of solitary confinement. The Constitutional validity of solitary confinement prescribed under section 30(2) of the Prisons Act, 1894 was considered. Section 30(2) of the Act provides the solitary confinement when prisoner is under sentence of death, while section 56 of the said Act permits the use of bar fetters for the safe custody of the prisoners.

The Supreme Court while approving section 30(2) of the Prisons Act, 1894 declared that the imposition of solitary confinement on Sunil Batra was illegal on the ground under sentence of death refers to a finally executable death sentence, which means that the sentence of death has become final and conclusive, and cannot be annulled by any judicial or Constitutional authority. Sunil Batra was not considered as a prisoner under sentence of death, since his appeal against the death penalty was pending before the Supreme Court and in the event of its dismissal, he retained the right to appeal for presidential clemency. The court held that Batra was put in statutory confinement and not solitary confinement.

The Supreme Court has also reacted strongly against putting bar fetters to the prisoners. The court observed that continuously keeping a prisoner in fetters day and night reduced the prisoner from human being to an animal and such treatment was so cruel and unusual that the use of bar fetters was against the spirit of the Constitution of India.

On the question of the validity of the use of bar fetters, the court in Sunil Batra (I) observed that subjecting a prisoner to bar fetters for an unusually long period, without due regard to the safety of the prisoner and the security of the prisoner would violate basic Human Dignity and is hence impermissible under the Constitution of India. The court while approving section 56 of the Prisons Act and declared that bar fetters can be used subject to the following procedural safeguards:

a. It must be absolutely necessary to use fetters;

b. The reasons for doing so must be recorded;

c. The basic condition of dangerousness must be well–grounded;

d. Principles of natural justice must be observed;

e. The fetters must be removed at the earliest opportunity;

f. There must a daily review of the absolute need for bar fetters;

g. Continuance of bar fetters beyond a day is subject to the direction of a District Magistrate or Session's Judge[31].

The Supreme Court in Sunil Batra (I) diluted the rigour of solitary confinement and bar fetters to a considerable extent by specifying the procedural norms to be followed when resorting to sections 30 (2) and 56 of the Prisons Act, 1894.

Rights against Hand Cuffing

In *Prem Shanker vs. Delhi Administration*[32] the Supreme Court added yet another projectile in its armoury to be used against the war for prison reform and prisoners rights.

In the instant case the question raised was whether hand–cuffing is Constitutionally valid or not? The Supreme Court discussed in depth the hand cuffing jurisprudence. It is the case placed before the court by way of Public Interest Litigation urging the court to pronounce upon the Constitution validity of the "hand cuffing culture" in the light of Article 21 of the Constitution. In the instant case, the court banned the routine hand cuffing of a prisoners as a Constitutional mandate and declared the distinction between classes of prisoner as obsolete. The court also opined that "hand cuffing is prima-facie inhuman and, therefore, unreasonable, is over harsh and at the first flush, arbitrary. Absent fair procedure and objective monitoring to inflict "irons" is to resort to Zoological strategies repugnant to Article 21 of the Constitution"[33].

While deciding the Constitutional validity of hand cuffing, the Supreme Court specifically referred to Article 5 of the Universal Declaration of Human Rights, 1948[34] and Article 10 of the International Covenant on Civil and Political Rights[35] and held that hand cuffing is impermissible torture and is violate of Article 21. In the instant case justice Krishna Iyer rightly emphasized hand cuffs should not be used in routine and they were to be used in extreme circumstances only, when the prisoner is a security risk, desperate, rowdy or involved in non–bailable offences. But in even such circumstances, the escorting authority must record the reasons for doing so. Otherwise, the court pointed out, under Article 21 of the Constitution the procedure will be unfair and bad in law.

In spite of such clear ruling of the Supreme Court against hand cuffing, the high handedness of the police personnel came to the light in Delhi Judicial Service Association case[36], wherein the Supreme Court held that an extraordinary and the unusual behaviour of police was not proper and the court laid down detailed guidelines which should be followed in case of arrest and detention of judicial officer. The Supreme Court took a serious note of whole incident and it amounts to interference with the administration of justice, lowering of its judicial authority and it amounts to criminal contempt.

It is submitted that wherever any police official acts contrary to the clear directions against hand cuffing as laid down by the Supreme Court and thus violates the basic Human Right to human dignity, he should be made personally liable to pay the compensation and this fact is clearly established in state of Maharashtra vs. Ravikanth S.Patil[37]. Apart from the above the Supreme Court had delivered many cases[38] against hand cuffing and ruled that it is violative of Article 21 of the Constitution. In Citizen for Democracy vs. State of Assam[39], the Supreme Court said that it lays down as a rule that hand cuffs or other fetters shall not be forced on prisoner, convicted or under trail, while lodged in a jail any where in the country or while transporting or in transit from jail to another or from jail to court and back. The police and jail authorities, on their own, shall have no authority to direct transport from one jail to another or from jail to court and back". The court declared that if it is absolutely necessary for the jail or police authorities to hand cuff, permission of Magistrate is to be obtained. The Magistrate may grant the permission to hand cuff the prisoner in rare cases. Violation of the directions given by the Supreme Court by the authorities shall be punishable under the contempt of court Act, 1971.

The Supreme Court directed the Union of India to frame rules or guidelines regarding the circumstances in which hand cuffing of the accused should be resorted to, in conformity with the judgment of the court in Prem Shankar case; and to circulate them among all the Government of the states and Union Territories for strict observance. It is important to mention that so as to put an end to hand–cuffing it is suggested that the parliament may make a suitable amendment to the Indian Penal Code, 1860 and the Code of Criminal Procedure, 1973 where in, hand–cuffing should be made a cognizable offence so as to give effect to the ruling of the Apex Court of the land and also to preserve the right to live with Human Dignity, which is a important facet of personal liability of the individuals.

Rights against Inhuman Treatment of Prisoners

Human Rights are part and parcel of Human Dignity. The Supreme Court of India in various cases has taken a serious note of the inhuman treatment on prisoners and has issued appropriate directions to prison and police authorities for safeguarding the rights of the prisoners and persons in police lock–up[40]. The Supreme Court read the right against torture into Articles 14 and 19 of the Constitution. The court observed that "the treatment of a human being which offends human dignity, imposes avoidable torture and reduces the man to the level of a beast would certainly be arbitrary and can be questioned under Article 14". In the Raghubir Singh v. State of Bihar[41], the Supreme Court expressed its anguish over police torture by upholding the life sentence awarded to a police officer responsible for the death of a suspect due to torture in a police lock – up.

In *Kishore Singh VS. State of Rajasthan*[42] the Supreme Court held that the use of third degree method by police is violative of Article 21. The court also directed the Government to take necessary steps to educate the police so as to inculcate a respect for the human person. In the instant case the Supreme Court brought home the deep concern for Human Rights by observing against police cruelty in the following words: "Nothing is more cowardly and unconscionable than a person in police custody being beaten up and nothing inflicts a deeper wound on our Constitutional culture that a state official running berserk regardless of Human Rights."

It is pertinent to mention that the custodial death is perhaps one of the worst crimes in civilized society governed by the rule of law. The court promptly ruled that the inhuman treatment meted to the accused in police custody is the gross and blatant violation of Human Rights. In the absence of any legislative or executive guidelines the court has undertaken an activist role and ruled in plethora of cases and one such case is D.K.Basu vs. State of West Bengal[43].

The decision of the Supreme Court in the case of D.K. Basu is note worthy. While dealing the case, the court specifically concentrated on the problem of custodial torture and issued a number of directions to eradicate this evil, for better protection and promotion of Human Rights. In the instant case the Supreme Court defined torture and analyzed its implications. The observations of the court on torture are valuable and worth quoting at length. With a view to curbing this menace, the Supreme Court laid down detailed guidelines as preventive measures as follows:

a. The police personnel carrying out the arrest and handling the interrogation of the arrestee should bear accurate, visible and clear identification and name tags with their designations. The particulars of all such police personnel who handle interrogation of the arrestee must be recorded in a register.

b. That the police officer carrying out the arrest of the arrestee shall prepare a memo of arrest at the time of arrest and such memo shall be attested by at least one witness, who may either be a member of the family of arrestee or a respectable person of the locality from where the arrest is made. It shall also be countersigned by the arrestee and shall contain the time and date of arrest.

c. A person who has been arrested or detained and is being held in custody in a police station or interrogation centre or other lock – up shall be entitled to have one friend or relative or other person known to him or having interest in his welfare being informed as soon as practicable that he has been arrested and is being detained at the particular place unless the attesting witness of the memo of arrest is himself such a friend or relative of the arrestee.

d. The time, place of arrest and venue of custody of an arrestee must be notified by the police where the next friend or relative of the arrestee lives outside the district or town through legal aid organizations in the district and the police station of the area concerned telegraphically within a period of 8 to 12 hours after the arrest.

e. The person arrested must be aware of this right to have someone informed of his arrest or detention as soon as he is put under arrest or is detained.

f. An entry must be made in the diary at the place of detention regarding the arrest of the person which shall also disclose the name of the next friend of the person who has been informed of the arrest and the names and particulars of the police officials in whose custody the arrestee is.

g. The arrestee should, where he so requests, be also examined at the time of his arrest and major and minor injuries, if any present on his/her body, must be recorded at that time. "Inspection Memo" must be signed both by the arrestee and the police officer affecting the arrest and its copy provided to the arrestee.

h. The arrestee should be subjected to medical examination by a trained doctor every 48 hours during his detention in custody by a doctor on the panel of approved doctors appointed by Director, Health Services of the State or Union Territory concerned. Director, Health Services should prepare such a panel for all tehsils and districts as well.

i. Copies of all the documents including the memo of arrest, referred to above should be sent to the area Magistrate for his/her record.

j. The arrestee may be permitted to meet his lawyer during interrogation though not throughout the interrogation.

k. A police control room should be provided at all district and state head quarters, where information regarding the arrest and the place of custody of the arrestee shall be communicated by the officer causing the arrest within 12 hours of effecting the arrest and at the police control room it should be displayed on a conspicuous notice board.

In the instant case, the Apex Court made it clear that, custodial violence, including torture and death in the police lock–up, strikes a blow at the rule of law, which demands that the powers of the executive should not only be deprived from the law but also that the same should be limited by the law. The court also made it clear that failure to comply with guidelines should, apart from rendering the official concerned liable for departmental action and also render him liable to contempt of court[44]. The Supreme Court has made it clear beyond doubt that any form of torture of cruel, inhuman or degrading treatment is offensive to Human Dignity and is violative of Article 21 of the Constitution.

Right to have Interview with Friends, Relatives and Lawyers

The horizon of Human Rights is expanding. Prisoner's rights have been recognized not only to protect them from physical discomfort or torture in person, but also to save them from mental torture. The Right to Life and Personal Liberty enshrined in Article 21 cannot be restricted to mere animal existence. It means something much more than just physical survival. The right to have interview with the members of one's family and friends is clearly part of the Personal Liberty embodied in Article 21. Article 22 (I) of the Constitution directs that no person who is arrested shall be denied the right to consult and to be defended by a legal practitioner of his choice. This legal right is also available in the code of criminal procedure under section 304[45]. The court has held that from the time of arrest, this right accrues to the arrested person and he has the right of choice of a lawyer. The accused may refuse to have a lawyer but the court has to provide an Amicus Curie to defend him. When an accused is undefended it is the duty of the court to appoint a counsel on Government expenses for his defence[46]. In a series of cases the Supreme Court of India considered the scope of the right of the prisoners or detainees to have interviews with family members, friends and counsel. In *Dharmbir vs. State of U.P*[47] the court directed the state Government to allow family members to visit the prisoners and for the prisoners, at least once a year, to visit their families, under guarded conditions.

In *Francis Coralie Mullin vs. Administrator, Union Territory of Delhi*[48], the petition under Article 32 of the Constitution raises a question in regard of the right of a detenu under conservation of Foreign Exchange and Prevention of Smuggling Activities Act, to have interview with a lawyer and the members of his family. In the instant case, the court considered the prisoners right to have interviews from the perspective of the Right to Life and Personal Liberty under Article 21. The court also observed that the Right to Life includes the right to live with Human Dignity and with this the right of a detenu to consult a legal advisor of his choice for any purpose not necessary limited to defence in criminal proceeding but also for securing release from preventive detention or filing a writ petition or prosecuting any claim or of any civil and criminal proceeding. In this case, the court also opined that the right to have interviews is clearly part of Personal Liberty and that "Personal Liberty" would include the right to socialize with members of family and friends subject to any valid prison regulations.

Therefore any prison regulation or procedure regulating the prisoners right to have interviews with members of family and friends must be reasonable and non–arbitrary. Otherwise it would be liable to be struck down as invalid, being violative of Articles 14 and 21. From the above analysis, it firmly leads to the conclusion that the rights of the prisoners to have interviews with friends and family members is an integral part of Article 21 of the Constitution.

In *Hussainara Khatoon vs. Home Secretary, Bihar*[49], the Supreme Court has held that it is the Constitutional right of every accused person who is unable to engage a lawyer and secure legal services on account of reasons such as poverty, indigence or incommunicado situation, to have free legal services provided to him by the state and the state is under Constitutional duty to provide a lawyer to such person if the needs of justice so require. If free legal services are not provided the trail itself may be vitiated as contravening the Article 21.

In *Sheela Barse vs. State of Maharashtra*[50] case, the petitioner, a Bombay based freelance journalist had sought permission to interview women prisoners in the Maharashtra jails and the letter of the petitioner was treated as writ petition under Article 32 of the Constitution. In the instant case the Supreme Court relying on Prabhu Dutts case[51], has held that the terms "life" under Article 21 covers the living condition prevailing in jails. The court observed that the citizen does not have any right either under Article 19 (1)(a) or Article 21 to enter into the jails for collection of information, but in order that the guarantee of the Fundamental Right under Article 21 may be available to the citizens detained in jails, it becomes necessary to permit the pressmen as friends of the society and public spirited citizens access to information as also interviews with prisoners. Those citizens who are detained in prisons either as undertrails or as convicts are also entitled to the benefit of the guarantee subject to reasonable restrictions.

In the instant case, the court held that interviews of the prisoners become necessary as otherwise the correct information may not be collected but such access has got to be controlled and regulated. The pressman are not entitled to uncontrolled interview. As and when factual information is collected as a result of interview, the same should usually be cross – checked with the authorities so that a wrong picture of the situation may not be published. Those who receive permission to have interviews will agree to abide by reasonable restrictions.

In *Jogindar Kumar vs. State of U.P*[52], the court opined that the horizon of Human Rights is expanding and at the same time, the crime rate is also increasing and the court has been receiving complaints about violation of Human Rights because of indiscriminate arrests. The court observed that there is the right to have someone informed. That right of the arrested person upon request, to have someone informed and to consult privately with a lawyer was recognized by Sec 56(1) of the Police and Criminal Evidence Act, 1984 in England. For effective enforcement of the Articles 21 and 22 (1) of the Constitution of India which require to be recognized and scrupulously protected, the court issue the following requirements.

a. An arrested person being held in custody is entitled, if he so requests to have one friend, relative or other person who is known to him or likely to take an interest in his welfare told as far as practicable that he has been arrested and where is being detained

b. The police officer shall inform the arrested person of his right when he is brought to the police station.

c. An entry shall be required to be made in the diary as to who was informed of the arrest. These protections from power must be held to flow from Articles 21 and 22 (1) and enforced strictly.

Right to Legal Aid

The main object of the Free Legal Aid scheme is to provide means by which the principle of equality before law on which the edifice of our legal system is based. It also means financial Aid provided to a person in matter of legal disputes. In the absence of Free Legal Aid to the poor and needy, Fundamental Rights and Human Freedoms guaranteed by the respective Constitution and International Human Rights covenants have no value.

Though, the Constitution of India does not expressly provide the Right to Legal Aid, but the judiciary has shown its favour towards poor prisoners because of their poverty and are not in a position to engage the lawyer of their own choice. The 42nd Amendment Act, 1976 has included Free Legal Aid as one of the Directive Principles of State Policy under Article 39A in the Constitution[53]. This is the most important and direct Article of the Constitution which speaks of Free Legal Aid . Though, this Article finds place in part-IV of the Constitution as one of the Directive Principle of State Policy and though this Article is not enforceable by courts, the principle laid down there in are fundamental in the governance of the country. Article 37 of the Constitution casts a duty on the state to apply these principles in making laws[54]. While Article 38 imposes a duty on the state to promote the welfare of the people by securing and protecting as effectively as it many a social order in which justice, social, economic and political, shall inform all the institutions of the national life. The parliament has enacted Legal Services Authorities Act, 1987 under which legal Aid is guaranteed and various state governments had established legal Aid and Advice Board and framed schemes for Free Legal Aid and incidental matter to give effect to the Constitutional mandate of Article 39-A. Under the Indian Human Rights jurisprudence, Legal Aid is of wider amplitude and it is not only available in criminal cases but also in civil, revenue and administrative cases.

Maneka Gandhi vs. Union of India[55] case was a catalyst which laid down a foundation for interpreting Articles 39-A and 21, widely to cover the whole panorama of Free Legal Aid. In the instant case the Supreme Court held that procedure established by law in Article 21 means fair, just and reasonable procedure.

In *Madhav Hayawadan Rao Hosket vs. State of Maharashtra*[56], a three judges bench (V.R.Krishna Iyer, D.A.Desai and O.Chinnappa Reddy, JJ) of the Supreme Court reading Articles 21 and 39-A, along with Article 142 and section 304 of Cr.PC together declared that the Government was under duty to provide legal services to the accused persons. Justice Krishna Iyer observed that Indian socio legal milieu makes free legal services, at trial and higher levels, an imperative procedural piece of criminal justice. The Supreme Court decided the point of Legal Aid in appeal cases as follows "If a prisoner sentenced to imprisonment is virtually unable to exercise his Constitutional and statutory right of appeal, inclusive of special leave to appeal, for want of legal assistance, there is implicit in the court under Article 142 read with Articles 21 and 39 A of the Constitution, power to assign counsel for such imprisoned individual for doing complete justice". The court further added that legal Aid in such cases is state's duty and not Government's charity.

In the words of justice Krishna Iyer, "Where the prisoner is disabled from engaging a lawyer, on reasonable grounds such as indigence of incommunicado situation, the court shall, if the circumstances of the case, the gravity of sentence and the ends of justice so require, assign competent counsel for the prisoners defence, provided the party does not object to that lawyer. The state which prosecuted the prisoner and set in motion the process which deprived him of his liberty shall pay to assigned counsel such sum of as the court may equitably fix".

In *Hussainara Khatoon and others vs. Home Secretary, State of Bihar*[57], the main observations of the Supreme Court are on speedy trail. Bhagwathi and Koshal, JJ observed that the speedy trail, which means reasonably expeditious trial, is an integral and essential part of the Fundamental Right to Life and Liberty enshrined in Article 21. However the Apex Court declared the speedy trial as a constituent of Legal Aid and directed the Government to provide Free Legal Aid service in deserving cases. This case reinforces the principles laid down in M.H .Hoskot"s case.

Justice Bhagwathi observed that Article 39-A of the Constitution also emphasizes that free legal service is an unalienable component of reasonable, fair and just procedure for without it a person suffering from economic or other disabilities would be deprived of the opportunity for securing justice. The right to free legal services is, therefore clearly an essential ingredient of "reasonable, fair and just procedure for a person accused of an offence and it must be held implicit in Article 21 of the Constitution. In the instant case justice Bhagwathi emphasized upon the necessasity of introducing by the central and state Governments, a dynamic and comprehensive legal services programme with a view to reaching justice to the common man. His lordship thought this cause as a mandate of equal justice implicit in Articles 14, 21 and also the compulsion of Constitutional directive embedded in Article 39-A. The concern of his lordship was that such programmes of legal Aid are intended to reach the justice to the common man.

In *Sunil Batra vs. Delhi administration (II)*[58] justice Krishna Iyer observed that the free legal services to the prison programmes shall be promoted by professional organization recognized by the court. His lordship further added that the District Bar Association should keep a cell for prisoner relief.

In *Khatri (I) vs. State of Bihar*[59] a division bench of the Supreme Court held that the state is under Constitutional mandate to provide Free Legal Aid to an accused person who is unable to secure legal services on account of indigence and whatever is necessary for this purpose has to be done by the state.

In Kedra Pahadiya and others vs. state of Bihar[60], the Supreme Court once again reiterated the principles laid down in Hussainara Khatoons and Sunil Batra (I) cases, and observed that the court directed that the petitioners must provided legal representation by a fairly competent lawyer at the cost of the state, since legal aid in a criminal case is a Fundamental Right implicit in Article 21, and the Fundamental Right has merely remained a paper promise and has been grossly violated. In the instant case, the Supreme Court directed the state Government to file a list of undertrial prisoners who have been in jail, for a period of more than 18 months without their trail having commenced before the Courts of Magistrates.

It is submitted that while making the above observations, the Supreme Court was more concerned with Article 39-A and least bothered to Article 21. Right to Free Legal Aid was raised to the status of a Fundamental Right in Hoskot"s case as a part of fair just and reasonable procedure under Article 21 and this premise was reinforced in cases of Hussaniara, Khatra (I). Right of Free Legal Aid was included in under the protective umbrella of Article 21, which is a Fundamental Right under the Constitution. Though Article 39 A, a non – enforceable and non justiciable directive principle became an enforceable Fundamental Right . Hence Free Legal Aid is a Fundamental Right which can be enforced against the state as defined in Article 12 of the Constitution, if Free Legal Aid is denied for whatever reasons.

Right to Speedy Trial

The speedy trial of offences is one of the basic objectives of the criminal justice delivery system. Once the cognizance of the accusation is taken by the court then the trial has to be conducted expeditiously so as to punish the guilty and to absolve the innocent. Everyone is presumed to be innocent until the guilty is proved. So, the quality or innocence of the accused has to be determined as quickly as possible. It is therefore, incumbent on the court to see that no guilty person escapes, it is still more its duty to see that justice is not delayed and the accused persons are not indefinitely harassed. It is pertinent to mention that "delay in trail by itself constitute denial of justice" which is said to be "justice delayed is justice denied". It is absolutely necessary that the persons accused of offences should be speedily tried so that in cases where the bail is refused, the accused persons have not to remain in jail longer than is absolutely necessary.

The right to speedy trial has become a universally recognized human right. In United States of America, the speedy trail is one of the Constitutionally guaranteed rights. In India, the right to speedy trail is not specifically enumerated as one of the Fundamental Rights in the Constitution since 1978, there have been sea - saw changes in the judicial interpretation of the Constitutional provisions. In *Maneka Gandhi vs. Union of India*[61], the Supreme Court has widened the concept of life and Personal Liberty under Article 21 of the Constitution. In this case, the court established that the law and procedure contemplated by Article 21 must answer the test of reasonableness in order to be in conformity with Articles 14 and 19. It also establishes that the procedure established by law within the meaning of Article 21 must be right, just and fair but not arbitrary, fanciful or oppressive.

Taking the principle of fairness and reasonableness evolved in Maneka Gandhis cases, the Supreme Court in *Hussainara Khatoon (I) vs. Home Secretary*[62] case held that "Obviously procedure prescribed by law for depriving a person of his liberty cannot be reasonable, fair, or just unless that procedure ensures a speedy trial for determination of the guilty of such person. No procedure which does not ensure a reasonably quick trial can be regarded as reasonable, fair or just and it would fall foul of Article 21. There can be no doubt that speedy trail and by speedy trail we mean reasonably expeditious trial, is an integral and essential part of the Fundamental Right to Life and Liberty enshrined in Article 21. Thus, the right to speedy trial is implicit in broad sweep and content of Article 21 of the Constitution. Hence any accused who is denied this right of speedy trial is entitled to approach the Supreme Court for the purpose of enforcing such right.

However, the main procedure for investigation and trial of an offence with regard to speedy trial is contained in the code of criminal procedure. The right to speedy trial is contained under section 309 of

Cr.PC[63]. If the provisions of Cr.PC are followed in their letter and spirit, then there would be no question of any grievance. But, these provisions are not properly implemented in their spirit. It is necessary that the Constitutional guarantee of speedy trial emanating from Article 21 should be properly reflected in the provisions of the code. For this purpose in A.R.Antulay vs. R.S.Nayak[64] the Supreme Court has laid down following propositions which will go a long way to protect the Human Rights of the prisoners. The concerns underlying the right to speedy trial from the point of view of the accused are:

a. The period of remand and pre – conviction detention should be as short as possible. In other words, the accused shall not be subjected to unnecessary or unduly long detention point of his conviction.

b. The worry, anxiety, expense and disturbance to his vocation and peace resulting from an unduly prolonged investigation, in query or trial shall be minimal; and.

c. Undue delay may result in impairment of the ability of the accused to defend himself whether on account of death, disappearance or non–availability of witnesses or otherwise.

In the instant case the Apex Court held that the right to speedy trial flowing from Article 21 of the Constitution is available to accused at all stages like investigation, inquiry, trial, appeal, revision and retrial. The court said that the accused cannot be denied the right to speedy trial merely on the ground that he had failed to demand a speedy trial.

From the above cases and principles of the Supreme Court, it can be concluded that the right to speedy trial is implicit under Article 21 of the Constitution. In the words of justice Bhagwathi that it is the Constitutional obligation of the state to provide a procedure which would ensure speedy trial to the accused. The state cannot be permitted to deny the Constitutional rights of speedy trial to the accused on the ground that the state has no adequate financial resources to incur the necessary expenditure needed for improving the administrative and judicial apparatus with a view to ensuring speed trial.

A close examination of the judicial action reveals that the Supreme Court has devised new strategies and tools to ensure the protection of Human Rights to the people. The courts are innovating new methods for the purpose of providing access to justice to large masses of people who were denied their basic Human Rights. The Supreme Court has enlarged the ambit and scope of the Right to Life and Personal Liberty in Article 21 in very wide and comprehensive terms. The crucial right in Article 21 is greatly enlarged in magnitude and dimension to include the rights of prisoners.

Care and Treatment in Mental Health Institutions

Since mental health takes a back seal and is largely ignored, public litigation and media exposure plays a role in highlighting gross violations of human rights Judiciary therefore, plays a specific role in addressing some of the critical mental health care needs of the country. Supreme court and state high court decisions have tried to address the issues pertaining to denial of right to mentally ill people.

The courts in India have held in a number of cases that mental health is an integral and inseparable part of health and have repeatedly extended that there lies a positive duty on the part of the Government to promote health and rights to live with human dignity which are fundamental rights enshrined in

Article 21 of the constitution of India. The guiding principles enunciated by the Apex Court in some of these judgments are referred as under:-

- In Hussainara Khatoon (No.1) vs. Home Secretary, Bihar it was held by the Apex Court that "right to a speedy trial, a fundamental right, is implicit in the guarantee of life and personal liberty enshrined in Article 21 of the Constitution". Speedy trial is the essence of criminal justice. These principles were reiterated in Abdul Rehman Antuley vs. R. S. Nayak in which detailed guidelines for speedy trial of an accused were laid down even though not time limit was fixed for trial of offences.

- In a public interest litigation (PIL), involving Veena Sethi vs. State of Bihar case in 1982, the court was informed through a letter that some prisoners who had been insane at the time of trial but had subsequently been declared sane had not been released due to inaction of the state authorities and had remained in jail for 20 to

   30 years. The court directed them to be released forthwith, considering the requirement of protection of right to life and liberty of the citizen against the lawlessness of the state.

- In a public interest petition *Dr. Upendra Baxi vs. State of Uttar Pradesh & others* was filed before the Hon'ble Court (1981) to enforce human rights of protective home inmates at Agra, UP, who were kept in abject dehumanized living conditions, the Hon'ble court issued various appropriate directions from time to time in order to ensure that the inmates of the Protective home at Agra do not continue to live in inhumane and degrading conditions and that the right to life with dignity enshrined in Article 21 of the Constitution is made real and meaningful for them.

- In a set of Public Interest Petitions *B. R. Kapoor & others vs. Union of India* and others (1983) and PUCL & Others vs union of India & others (1983), filed before the Hon'ble Court regarding Shahdara Mental hospital, Delhi, Hon'ble court observed that the Mental hospital located at the capital of the country should be run by the Union of India and not by Delhi Administration. The Hon'ble court directed that the Mental hospital located at Shahdara should be modeled on the lines of similar psychiatric specialty obtaining at the institution run by NIMHAS at Bangalore, and also directed to examine as to whether the hospital could be attached to a teaching institution which has post graduation specialization in Psychiatry, neurology and neuron Psychiatry. This led to the formation of the Institute of human Behaviour and Allied Sciences, IHBAS.

   In the case of *Chandan kumar Bhanik vs. State of West Bengal* (1988) the apex Court observed: "Management of an institution like the mental hospital requires flow of human love and affection, understanding and consideration for mentally ill persons these aspects are far more important than a reutilized, stereotyped and bureaucratic approach to mental health issues".

- In the case of *Sheela Barse vs. union of Indian and others* (1993) the apex Court observed that admission of non-criminal mentally ill persons in jails is illegal and unconstitutional; All mentally ill persons kept in various central, district and sub jails must be medically examined immediately after admission; Specialized psychiatric help must be made available to all inmates who have been lodged in various jails/subs jails; Each and every patient must receive review or revaluation of developing mental problems; a mental health team comprising clinical psychologists, psychiatric nurses and psychiatric social workers must be in place in every mental health hospital.

- The apex Court in its judgment in *Rakesh Chandra Narayan vs. State of Bihar (1986)* had laid down certain cardinal principles. These are: Right of a mentally ill person to food, water, personal hygiene, sanitation and recreation is an extension of the right to life as in Article 21 of the Constitution: Quality norms and standards in mental Health are non- negotiable; Treatment, teaching training and research must be integrated to produce the desired results; Obligation of the State in providing undiluted care and attention to mentally ill persons is fundamental to the recognition of their human right and is irreversible.

The apex Court in *Rakesh Chandra Narayan vs. State of Bihar* case requested the National human Rights Commission (NHRC) to be involved in the supervision of mental health hospitals at Agra, Ranchi and Gwalior w.e.f. 11.11.1997. it stated as under:

"Having death with this matter for some time, we have formed the opinion that a better method for supervision of the functioning of Agra Protective Home is necessary. Now that the benefit of the National Human Rights Commission (NHRC) with statutory powers under the Protection of Human Rights Act, 1993 is available and since most of the problems associated with the functioning of Agra Protective Home are such that they can be better dealt with by NHRC we consider it expedient to make this order to involve the NHRC in the exercise. It is likely that the pendency of this matter and the directions made by this court may have to some extent inhibited the NHRC in exercise of its ordinary functions relating to Agra Protective Home so far.

The Hon'ble court further observed "This matter pertains to the functioning of the Agra, Gwalior and Ranchi mental Asylums. We have today November 11th 1997 *in Dr. Upendra Baxi v. State of Uttar Pradesh & Others* requested the NHRC to be involved in the supervision of the functioning of Agra Protective home in the manner indicated in the order. We are of the opinion that the same kind of order needs to be made in this matter also relating to Agra, Ranchi and Gwalior asylums. Accordingly, we request the NHRC to perform this exercise in the same manner"

The Hon'ble court vide order dated 12.5.2000 disposed of the Writ Petition (Dr. Upendra Baxi, observing "Now that the National human Rights Commission is seized of the matter it will not be appropriate for this court to proceed any further in this writ petition. The petition is accordingly consigned to the records if and when the Commission requires any help or assistance from the court it is at liberty to make an appropriate application. The writ petitions are disposed of".

Compensatory Jurisprudence and Human Rights

A significant contribution of judicial activism in the post Maneka Gandhi[65] period has been the development of compensatory jurisdiction of the Supreme Court and the High Courts under Articles 32 and 226 of the Constitution. The scope of writ jurisdiction has also been expanded to uphold the Human Dignity and other Fundamental Human Rights. Consequent upon the expansion of writ jurisdiction, the Compensation as a mode of redressel of violation of Human Rights gained importance. The Supreme Court made a departure from the ordinary civil law, where the right to claim compensation is only through a civil suit instituted by the aggrieved party before the court of first instance.

Currently, the writ jurisdiction of higher judiciary and the original jurisdiction of the civil court regarding the award of compensation invoked upon infraction of Human Rights are based upon distinct Constitutional and legal principles. Judicially, it is well established that doctrine of sovereign immunity is not applicable against the Constitutional remedy under Articles 32 and 226 of the Constitution. The development of the remedy of monetary compensation as to Constitutional and civil law remedies for violation of Human Rights is analysed through the judicial pronouncements expanding their respective nature, extent and limitations.

Monetary Compensation and Human Rights

It is internationally recognized principle that right to compensation is not alien to the concept of enforcement of guaranteed right[66]. The development of the remedy of monetary compensation for the enforcement of Human Rights may be discussed with reference to writ jurisdiction of the higher judiciary and the ordinary original jurisdiction of the civil court. Compensation through writs is a recent development and an extension of the prerogatives of the Supreme Court and High Courts in the field of Constitutional remedies. Even though, there was much criticism on the payment of compensation under Article 32 of the Constitution, because of this Article as such itself does not expressly empowers the courts to award such relief. It is important to mention here that the seed of compensation for the violation of the rights implicit in Article 21 is first sowed in Veena *Sethi vs. State of Bihar*[67] and Khatri *vs. State of Bihar (II)*[68]. In both the cases, one of the questions raised was if the state deprives a person of his life or Personal Liberty on violation of the right guaranteed by Article 21, is the court helpless to grant relief to the persons who has suffered such deprivation? To this question, Bhaghawathi, J *in Veena Sethi* case observed that "the question would still remain to be considered whether these prisoners are entitled to compensation from state Government for their illegal detention in contravention of Article 21 of the Constitution.

Where in Khatri"s case, the Supreme Court initiated the jurisdiction of payment of monetary compensation under Public Interest Litigation to the victims on violation of their life and personal liberty. Therefore a question of great Constitutional importance as to what relief could be given for violation of Constitutional rights was before the court. Bhagwathi .J., speaking for the court observed: "the court can certainly inject the state for depriving a person of his life or Personal Liberty except in accordance with the procedure established by law but, if life or Personal Liberty is violated otherwise than in accordance with such procedure, is the court helpless to grant relief to the person who has suffered such deprivation? Why should the court not be prepared to forge new and devise new remedies for the purpose of vindicating the most precious Fundamental Right to life and Personal Liberty? Otherwise Article 21 would be reduced to a nullity, a "mere rope of sand". The court described this issue as of gravest Constitutional importance involving exploration of new dimension of the Right to Life and personal liberty[69].

The jurisdiction to award compensation for deprivation of Fundamental Rights of a person through writs was recognised by the Supreme Court in *Rudal Shah VS. State of Bihar*[70] case, wherein the petitioner was detained illegally in the prison for over fourteen years after his acquittal in full dressed trial. He challenged the said act in the court by filing habeas corpus petition and contended that he was entitled to be compensated for his illegal detention and that the court ought to pass an appropriate order for the payment of compensation. The Supreme Court in this case explained the jurisdiction to award compensation under Article 32 of the Constitution by observing; "It is true that Article 32 cannot be used as a substitute for enforcement of rights and obligations which can be enforced efficaciously through the ordinary process of courts, civil and criminal. A money claim has therefore, to be agitated in and adjudicated upon the suit instituted in a court of lowest grade competent to try it. In the exercise of its jurisdiction under Article 32, the Supreme Court can pass an order for the payment of money in the nature of compensation consequential upon the deprivation of a Fundamental Right to Life and Liberty of the petitioner".

The decision of the Supreme Court in *Rudul Shah case* made it clear that, through the exercise of writ jurisdiction, the Supreme Court or the High Courts have powers to award compensation for the violation of Fundamental Rights and this decision has been followed in a number of decisions by the Supreme Court and the High court"s in the similar situations of violation of the Right to Life and liberty of a person.

The Supreme Court in *Sebastian M. Hongray v Union of India*[71] case, through a writ petition of habeas corpus awarded exemplary costs on failure of the detaining authority to produce two missing persons, on assumption that they were not alive and had met unnatural deaths at the hands of security forces. In the instant case D.A.Desai and O.Chinnappa Reddy JJ. Observed that the respondents would be guilty of civil contempt because of their wilful disobedience to the writ. The Supreme Court keeping in view the torture, the agony and mental oppression through which the wives of the persons directed to be produced has to pass, instead of imposing a fine, directed that as a measure of exemplary cost of Rs. 1,00,000/- to each of the wives of the persons.

Subsequently, in the case of Bhim Singh vs. state of Jammu & Kashmir[72], the Apex Court followed *Rudul Shah and Sebastian* cases, by observing that "when a person comes to the Supreme Court with the complaint that he has been arrested and imprisoned with mischievous or malicious intent and that his Constitutional legal rights were invaded, the mischief or malice and invasion may not be washed away or wished away by his being set free. In appropriate cases, the court has the jurisdiction to compensate the victim by awarding suitable monetary compensation. In this case, the illegal detention of the petitioner was held to constitute violation of rights under Articles 21 and 22 (2) of the Constitution by the Supreme Court. O. Chinnappa Reddy and V.Khalid, JJ. stated that police officers who are the custodians of law and order should have the greater respect for the Personal Liberty of citizens and should not flout the laws by stooping to the bizarre acts of lawlessness. Custodians of law and order should not become depredators of civil liberties. The duty of the police officers is only to protect and not to abduct. Exercising its power to award compensation under Article 32, the court directed the state to pay monetary compensation of Rs. 50,000/- to the petitioner for violation of his Constitutional right by way of exemplary costs.

In Saheli, A Women's Resource Centre vs. Commissioner of Police, Delhi[73] case, the police officers raided the house of Mrs. Kamalesh Kumari. The Victim was staying in a house with her three children. The landlord of that house took the help of police to forcibly evict them from the house. During the police raid, the police trampled upon nine years child of Kamalesh Kumari resulting the death of the child. It is well settled that the state is responsible for the tortious acts of its employees. In the instant case court observed that "in the matter of liability state is liable for tortious acts committed by its employees in the course of their employment. On these facts, the Supreme Court ordered for payment of Rs. 75,000/- as compensation to the mother of the deceased child. In this case, the court ordered to recover the amount of compensation from the concerned police officer.

In *Nilabeti Behara vs. state of Orissa and others*[74] case, the Supreme Court struck down the doctrine of sovereign immunity in the arena of public law. This is the case of the custodial death of a person. In the instant case one youth by name Suman Behara was taken into police custody in connection with the investigation of a theft on 1 st December, 1987, and on the next day, his dead body was found on the railway track. There were multiple injuries on the body of Suman Behara. The petitioner Nilabati Behara, addressed a letter to the Supreme Court under Article 32 of the Constitution of India. The police took the plea that the deceased was taken to custody but he managed to escape from the custody and that they could not trace him. The police denied the custodial death. It this context, the Supreme Court ordered enquiry by the District Judge of Sundergarh, Orissa. The report of the District Judge reveals that there is a torture of the deceased with eleven external injuries and as a result of these injuries inflicted by the police, the report confirmed that the death is in the nature of custodial death. The Supreme Court awarded Rs. 1,50,000/- as compensation to the mother of the deceased.

In the instant case, the court further held and clarified that "public law proceedings" are different from private law proceedings" and the award of compensation in proceedings for the enforcement of Fundamental Rights under Article 32 and 226 of the Constitution is a remedy available in public law. It was rightly observed: "the court is not helpless and wide powers given to the Supreme Court by Article 32, which itself is a Fundamental Rights, imposes a Constitutional obligation on the court to invent such new tools, which may be necessary for during complete justice and enforcing the Fundamental Rights guaranteed in the Constitution which enable the ward of monetary compensation in appropriate cases".

To support the above observation, the court rightly referred to Article 9 of the International Covenant on Civil and Political Rights, 1966 and held that the state is liable to pay compensation for police atrocities. The court further held that the said provision indicates that an enforceable right to compensation is not alien to the concept of a guaranteed right. It is also pertinent to mention that the provision of compensation to the crime victims is crying need of the honour. The International Covenant on Civil and Political Rights, 1966 indicates that an enforceable right to compensation is conceptually integral to Human Rights.

It would suffice to state that the provisions of the covenant which elucidate and go to effectuate the Fundamental Rights guaranteed by the Constitution under part III can certainly be relied upon by courts as facets of those Fundamental Rights and hence enforceable as such. It is doubtful whether it was right on the part of the court to reach such a conclusion without ensuring authority of such covenants and leaving it for the decisions of a later forum. It is also to be noted that the covenant on civil and political rights, 1966 was ratified by India with a reservation that Article 9 (5) of the said covenant is not applicable in India. Hence it is submitted that reading of the covenant into the Indian law is not correct.

Nature of the Constitutional Remedy

A perusal of the above judicial panorama in the foregoing discussion makes it clear that, at present, the power to grant compensation through the writs is an established remedy. Compensation has been awarded by the Supreme Court by referring to its different concept like "Exemplary costs", "palliative measures", solarium or "exemplary damages".

On the basis of the above discussion it can be inferred that the development of Constitutional remedy affords an effective remedy in the form of monetary compensation on infraction of Human Rights. However this remedy is a distinct remedy and not a substitute of the remedy under civil law. The Constitutional remedy is only an additional remedy and an aggrieved person avail other remedy available to him under law. In Nilabetis case, a distinction is made between the remedy of compensation available under the public law i.e., Constitution and the private law, i.e. civil law of Tort. In this case Anand J, in his concurring judgment further explained the distinction by observing that "the payment of compensation in such cases not to be understood, as it is generally understood in a civil action for damage under the private law, but in the broader sense of providing relief by an order of making "monetary amends", under public law for the wrong done due to breach of public duty of not protecting the Fundamental Rights of the citizen. The compensation is in the nature of exemplary damages awarded against the wrongdoer for the breach of its public law duty and it is independent of the rights available to the aggrieved party to claim compensation under the private law in action based on tort through a suit instituted in a court of competent jurisdiction or to prosecute the offender under the penal law.

Therefore, the monetary compensation through the writs for violation of Human Rights and fundamental freedoms is an acknowledged remedy to uphold the Constitutional guarantee unlike civil law remedy, though Constitutional remedy is not in the nature of damages, for the loss suffered, yet affords monetary relief to an aggrieved person. The very nature of the Constitutional remedy suggests that it is subject to certain inherent limitations viz., precise amount of compensation to make good the loss and Personal Liberty of the concerned officials are the issues which can only be properly adjudicated in a civil suit. The Constitutional and civil law remedies being supplementary to each other also require a discussion on the question of applicability of doctrine of sovereign immunity in their respective forums.

Sovereign Immunity and Violation of Human Rights

The Indian History reveals that the concept of sovereign immunity did not exist in any point of time. In ancient times also the king was subjected to the rule of law and the will of the people. In India, the absolutism of king was never accepted. It was the primary duty of the king to protect the people, administer justice and there by maintain order and protecting people in enjoyment of their property. While discharging this mandatory duty, the king was not immune from liability to compensate his subjects. It is note worthy that the obligation on the part of the king was entirely absent under the English system. During the British rule in India neither section 65 of the Government of India Act, 1858[75] nor Sec 176 of the Government of India Act, 1935 extended immunity to the company or the secretary of state which the Crown in England enjoyed in respect of Torts committed by its servants.

In India, the doctrine of Sovereign Immunity is purely a judicial creation having its origin in Judicial pronouncements which can be traced back to 1861 when the question of state liability in tort came before the Supreme Court of Calcutta in peninsular and oriental steam Navigation Company vs. The Secretary of State for India[76], in this case, Lord Peacock made a distinction between sovereign and non sovereign function of the state to determine the tortuous liability. The only point for consideration was whether in case of a tort committed in the conduct of business, the secretary of state was liable to pay compensation. It is evident that the court intended to include only acts of state within the ambit of sovereign power.

The law relating to the liability of the state for the wrongs committed by its servants is laid down in Article 300 of the Constitution[77]. The theory of sovereign Immunity with regard to the liability of state was applied in India by virtue of Article 300 propounded.

In many cases, the Supreme Court rejected the compensation on the ground that discharge of police functions are sovereign functions and the state is not liable for the wrongful acts of its servants while discharging the sovereign functions.

Subsequent to the attainment of Independence, the Supreme Court of India got an opportunity for discussing the liability of the State in case of tortious acts committed by its servants in *State of Rajasthan vs. Vidhyawathi case*[78], in which the court held that the state was liable for the torts committed by its servants. On the question of sovereign immunity of state in paying compensation of the tort of negligence of its servants, the court observed that after adoption of republican Government under the Constitution there is no justification for granting immunities to the state and held the state is vicariously liable for the acts of its servants and refused to concede the defence of sovereign immunity. Though the court criticized sovereign immunity, it never clarified whether the defence of immunity is available now in India or not. This paved the way for the unfortunate decision in the case of Kasturilal vs. State of U.P.[79]

In Kasturilals case the Apex Court approved the distinction made in the steam navigation case between sovereign and non-sovereign functions of the state. Gajendragadkar, C.J said: "If a tortious act committed by a public servant gives rise to a claim for damages, the question to ask is: was the tortious act committed by a public servant in discharge of statutory function which is referable to, and ultimately based on the delegation of the sovereign powers of the state to such public servant. If the answer is in the affirmative the action for damages will not lie. On the other hand, if the tortious act has been committed by a public servant in the discharge of duties assigned to him not by virtue of the delegation of any sovereign powers, and action for damages would lie. The court held that the tortious act of the police officers was committed by them in discharge of sovereign powers and the state was therefore not liable for the damage caused to the appellant. The Apex Court however made a strong plea for enactment of a legislation to regulate and control the claim of the state for immunity on the lines of the Crown proceedings Act of England.

In Nilabeti's case, the Supreme Court made observations regarding the applicability of doctrine of sovereign immunity in a Constitutional remedy under law of torts as "Award of compensation in proceedings under Article 32 by this court or by the High Courts under Article 226 of the Constitution is a remedy available in public law based on strict liability for contravention of Fundamental Rights to which the principle of Sovereign immunity does not apply, even though, it may be available as a defence in private law in an action based on tort". In the instant case, the Supreme Court made reference to its earlier decision in Sahelis case as "the state was held liable to pay compensation payable to the mother of the deceased who dies as a result of beating and assault by the police. However the principle indicated there in was that the state is responsible for the tortious acts of its employees". In Sahelis case no reference has been made to the decision of Kasturi Lal"s case, wherein, the sovereign immunity was upheld in the case of vicarious liability of the state for tort of its employees. The decision is therefore more in accord with the principles indicated in Rudul Shah Case.

The Supreme Court through this reference appears to have pointed out that doctrine of sovereign immunity is still applicable in law of tort but not available, where the remedy is sought through the writ as a Constitutional remedy. This distinction does not appear proper. The question for applicability or non-applicability of doctrine of sovereign immunity should be with reference to the nature of the right violated, but not from the forum of remedy.

However in state of A.P Vs. Challa Rama Krishna Reddy[80] case, the Supreme Court held that in the process of Judicial advancement Kastuilal"s case has placed into insignificance and no longer of any binding value. In this case a prisoner who had a informed the jail authorities that he apprehended danger to his life but no action was taken on this information and no measures were taken for his safety and he was killed the prisoner which was hatched in prison. The court held that in case of violation of Fundamental Right the defence of Sovereign immunity which is an old and archaic defence cannot be accepted and the government and the police are liable to compensate the victim. The Apex Court held that the personal liability should be given Supremacy over sovereign Immunity.

There are catena of cases delivered by the Supreme Court and the High Courts with regard to the payment of compensation concerning custodial violence. Thus, the courts adopted the technique of giving a narrow interpretation to the concept of Sovereign functions while granting the compensation in the interest of justice. In recent past, the Supreme Court started awarding compensation whenever the Human Rights are violated and thus developed a new compensatory jurisprudence.

It is universally recognized that right to life, liberty and dignity are inherent in the human nature. These basic Human Rights are enforceable rights in every civilized and welfare state. Monetary compensation as a mode of redressal and enforcement of Human Rights , in the event of their violation, is an established remedy of great significance. In India, the Constitution ensures the Right to Life and Personal Liberty to every person as a Fundamental Right . The activist approach of the Supreme Court not only added to the list of Human Rights guaranteed under the Constitution, but also expanded the jurisdiction of the court to grant monetary relief on their infraction.

A significant contribution of Judicial Activism in the post – Maneka Gandhi period has been the development of compensatory jurisdiction of the Supreme Court and the High Courts under Article 32 (2) and 226(1) of the Constitution and these courts have ample powers to grant monetary compensation in appropriate cases. The law relating to award of compensation in writ petitions is a new development in Constitutional law of India, which should be based on the well accepted principles of administrative law. As a result of this development, which was set in Rudul Shah principle, that the compensation has been awarded in writ petitions in number of cases. Most of these cases related to custodial death, torture, rape, illegal detention and other similar areas. It is also to be noted that besides the above cases, compensation has been awarded in a few cases where illegality or ultravires nature of administrative action was not patent or visible on the face.

The doctrine of sovereign immunity should have no application in a case in which the remedy of compensation for violation of Right to Life or liberty is sought even through a civil suit for damages. In the present day this doctrine does not find place in a welfare state. It is high time that this immunity should be legislatively abolished in India for giving full enforcement and protection of Human Rights of an individual. Even though, a plethora of cases has been decided by the court in awarding the compensation, the court has constantly failed to evolve any definite criterion as to the computation of the quantum of compensation. It is pertinent to mention that since the development of law based on public law for the violation of Fundamental Rights, where the judicial discretion play a major role, the court fails to produce any jurisprudence as to the liability of the state.

Environmental Protection and Human Rights

The protection and improvement of human environment has become a world wide concern. A clean and healthy environment is the basic need of the existence of life. The ecological imbalance contributes to the environmental hazards like acid rains, noise pollution, air pollution, water pollution. The depletion of ozone layer causes skin cancer, cataracts, damage to body"s immunity system, mutation, loss of productivity. Environmental law is an instrument to protect and improve the environment and to control or prevent any acts or omissions likely to pollute the environment. There are hundreds of environmental laws in India, directly or indirectly dealing with the subject of environment. In the world the Constitution of India is the first which made provisions for the protection of environment which are Articles 21, 47, 48-A, 51 (A)(g) and sections

227 and 278 of Indian Penal Code, sections 133 and 134 of the code of Criminal Procedure. These provisions contain clear mandate on the state and to the citizens to protect and improve the environment.

Though, India was a party to the Stockholm declaration, had initiated legislative measures for the prevention of the pollution of environment by enacting specific legislation and also incorporated the Stockholm principles by an amendment to the

Constitutions of India in 1976. It incorporated Article 48A and 51 A (g). It is to be noted that these provisions though not enforceable in court of law, directs the state to enact legislations and frame policies towards the promotion and protection of Environment. Thus the state is under a moral duty to take measures to prevent ecological imbalances resulting from modern industrialization. The Constitution has also cast a duty on the citizen to take steps for maintaining ecological balance.

In accordance with the mandate of the Stockholm Declaration, the government of India enacted the Water (Prevention and Control of Pollution) Act, 1974 Air (Prevention and Control) Act 1981, and Environmental (Protection) Act, 1986, Public liability Insurance Act, 1991, National Environmental Tribunal Act, 1995 and National Environment Appellate Authority Act, 1997.

Judicial Contribution to Protection of Environment

The Apex judiciary in India has been demonstrating its commitment for the protection of environment from time to time and it has given prime importance to the environmental promotion and protection through a serious of trend setting judgments. The Supreme Court is also trying to bring an awareness of the massive problems of pollution and filling the gap between the legislation and its implementation by using its extraordinary powers. The higher Judiciary in India delivered many environmental conscious judgments. By constructive interpretation of various provisions of the law, the Supreme Court in particular has supplemented and strengthened the environmental law. The cases relating to each and every aspect of environment have come up before the Supreme Court of India. The court has relaxed rigid and purely technical rules in admitting many cases involving the protection of the environment.

The Supreme Court has played an activist and creative role in protecting the environment. Most of the actions in the environmental cases are brought under Articles 32 and 226 of the Constitution. The environmental litigations are generally based on the notions of violation of Fundamental Rights.

The Supreme Court widened the horizons of environmental protection. It is a new innovation of Indian judiciary was of Judicial Activism. The Apex judiciary made it clear that Public Interest Litigation is maintainable for ensuring pollution free water and air which is involved in right to live under the Article 21 of the Constitution. The higher judiciary has always endeavoured to strike a balance between conservation of environment on one hand and the economic development on the other hand. The adverse effect of industrialisation on human life has caught the attention of Indian judiciary and it is perhaps with this view, in mind it has shown deep concern for prevention of pollution of environment and asked the authorities concerned to take immediate necessary steps to safeguard the society against the illeffects of industrialization.

The expansive and creative judicial interpretation of the word "life" in Article 21 has lead to the salutary development of an environmental jurisprudence in India. The Right to Life is a Fundamental Right under Article 21 and since the Right to Life connotes "quality of life" a person has a right to the enjoyment of pollution free water and air to enjoy life fully. According to many environmentalists and jurists "The latest and most encouraging of all developments in India is the "Right to a clean and wholesome environment" and the "Right to clean air and water". These rights have been included in the Right to Life under Article 21 of the Constitution. The boundaries of the Fundamental Right to life and Personal Liberty guaranteed in Article 21 were expanded elevating it, to a position of brooding omnipresence and converting it into a sanctuary of human values for more environmental protection.

In *Ratlam Municipality vs. Vardhichand*[81] case, the Supreme Court for the first time treated an environmental problem differently from and ordinary Tort or public nuisance. In the instant cases the Apex Court compelled the M.P. Municipality to provide sanitation and drainage despite the budgetary constraints, there by enabling the "poor to live with dignity". The Supreme Court expanded the principle of "Locus Standi" in environmental cases and observed that environment related issues must be considered in a different perspective. This development in judicial delivery system brought a new dimension and is considered as a silent "legal revolution" and it has cast away all the shackles of technical rules of procedure and encouraged the litigation from public spirited person. The Court not only complemented petitioners who filed environment protection litigation but also awarded money to the petitioners. This development has paved the way for Social Interest Litigation, Class Action Litigation and Common Cause Litigation and so on. The court made it clear and stated that the dynamics of the judicial process had a new enforcement dimension.

The Supreme Court gave an expansive meaning to right to environment in *Rural Litigation and Entitlement Kendra, Deharadun vs. State of UP*[82]. In the instant case, the representatives of the rural litigation and entitlement Kendra, Dehradun wrote a letter to the Supreme Court alleging that heat illegal limestone quarries in the Mussore – Dehraddun region was devastating the fragile ecosystem in the area. The court treated the letter as a writ petition under Article 32 of the Constitution. In the instant case the court presupposes the violation of Fundamental Right. The court ordered the closure of certain lime stone quarries on the ground as that there were serious deficiencies regarding safety and hazards in them. The court stated "the right of the people to live in healthy environment with minimum disturbance of ecological balance and without avoidable hazard to them and to their cattle, house and agriculture, land and pollution of air, water and environment".

In *Govind Singh vs. Shanthi Swarup*[83] case, the Supreme Court has taken microscopic view on the contours of the law of public nuisance. In the instant case the Supreme Court held that the effect of running bakery was injurious to the people, as it was polluting the environment by emitting smoke from chimney and ordered the closure of Bakery. The court said that "in a matter of this nature what is involved is not merely the right of a private individual but the health, safety and convenience of the public at large".

In *M.C. Mehta vs. Union of India*[84], the Supreme Court observed "The Precautionary Principle" and "polluter pays Principle" have been accepted as part of the law of the land". In this case, a Public Interest Litigation was filed alleging that due to environmental pollution, there is degradation of the Taj Mahal, a monument of International reputation. According to the opinion of the expert committees, the use of coke/coal by the industries situated within the Taj Trapezium Zone (TTZ) were emitting pollution and causing damage to the Taj Mahal, as also people living in that area. In the instant case the court ordered the re-location of polluting industries.

In Consumer Education and Research Centre vs. Union of India[85] the Supreme Court has delivered a historic judgment and held that the right to health and medical care is a Fundamental Right under Article 21 of the Constitution, as it is essential for making the life of the workmen meaningful and purposeful with dignity of persons. In M.C. Mehta

(II) vs. Union of India[86] the Supreme Court directed all the Municipalities located on the banks of the river Ganga to take preventive measures for water pollution. The Court held that the Municipality was primarily responsible for the pollution in the river and was not only obliged but also bound to take steps to decrease as well as control the pollution.

The Supreme Court in *M.C. Mehta vs. Union of India*[87] had given direction to the Delhi city authorities to take effective steps for streamlining vehicular pollution in the city. The order of the Supreme Court prohibiting the use of twenty years old vehicles in the city roads of Delhi and its implementation is a welcome step in prevention of the vehicular pollution, avoiding the accident and protecting health of the Delhi Police.

While treading the path of judicial innovation, the Supreme Court has invented an impressive range of concepts and principles. The principles of Strict and Absolute liability, the principle of Sustainable Development, the Polluter Pays principles, the Precautionary principle and the Public Trust doctrine have thus found firm footing in Indian Jurisprudence.

The Supreme Court has firmly held the view that law should not remain static and that it has to evolve to meet the changes arising out of new situations. Law has to grow in order to satisfy the needs of the fast changing society and to keep abreast with the economic development taking place in the country. Finding the rule of strict liability as laid down in Rylands vs. Fletcher[88] to be unsuitable for dealing with enterprises engaged in hazardous or inherently dangerous activities in the country, the Supreme Court unanimously held in

M.C Mehta and other vs. Shriram Food and Fertilizers industries and Union of India[89] case that "where an enterprise is engaged in a hazardous or inherently dangerous activity and harm results to anyone on account of an accident in operation of such hazardous or inherently dangerous activity resulting, for example, in escape of toxic gas the enterprise is strictly and absolutely liable to compensate to all those who are effected by the accident and such liability is not subject to any of the exceptions which operate vis-à-vis the tortious principle of Strict Liability under the rule in Rylands vs. Fletcher".

Thus, the Apex court, by departing from the rule of strict liability as laid down in Ryland vs. Fletcher, took an epoch-making decision having wide ramifications. It is to be noted that this judgment opened a new frontier in the Indian jurisprudence by a new concept of Absolute liability standard, which is not subject to any exception, for industries engaged in hazard activities.

In series of path-breaking judgements towards the end of 1996, the Supreme Court incorporated some of the important environmental norms notably principle of sustainable development, the polluter-pays principle and the precautionary principle as part of the land. While rejecting the old notion that development and environmental protection cannot go together, the Apex Court held the view that sustainable development has now come to be accepted as "a viable concept to eradicate poverty and improve the quality of human life while living within the carrying capacity of the supporting ecosystems". Thus pollution be commensurate with the carrying capacity of our ecosystem. Thus the court further held that the polluter-pays principle and the pre cautionary principle are essential features of sustainable development[90].

It is to be noted that the practice adopted so far by the Supreme Court and the High Courts in Judicial Review of complex issues relating to the protection of Environment has been conspicuous. Before taking a decision they used to refer the matters to professional and technical bodies or commissions for advice. In A.P Pollution Control Board vs. Prof M.V. Naidu (Retd.,) and others[91], the Supreme Court held that monitoring of such investigation process may also be difficult, Formulation of alternative procedure, expeditious, scientific and adequate is necessary and the court thought that "National Environmental Appellate Authority (NEAA) with adequate combination of both Judicial and Technical expertise is the appropriate authority to go into the question in the instant case.

The National Environmental Appellate Authority is the creature of the statute. The question is whether the statutory limitation can tie the hands of the Supreme Court. The jurisdiction is confined to hearing appeals filed by a person aggrieved by an order of environmental clearance. The court relied on *Paramjith Kaur vs. State of Punjab case*[92] wherein though barred by limitation under the law, the National Human Rights Commission could be directed under Article 32 to probe into Human Rights Violations alleged to have occurred long before. The powers of the Supreme Court under Article 32 of the Constitution of India to issue direction to a statutory authority can never be curtailed by statuary limitations. Thus, the NHRC can act sui Juris, free from, any conditions circumscribed by the statute that created the commission.

The emerging environmental Jurisprudence should take all aspects into consideration in order to render Justice and ensure sustainable development. For this prupose, the court can refer to scientific and technical aspects for investigation and opinion by such expert bodies as the National Environmental Appellate Authority whose investigation, analyses of facts and opinion, on objections raised by parties, could give adequate help to the Supreme Court or the High Courts for adjudication.

It is pertinent to mention that the right to access to drinking water is fundamental to life and there is a duty on the State under Article 21 to provide clean Drinking Water to its Citizens. In APPCB vs. M.V. Naidu[93], the court ruled that "Drinking water is of Primary importance in any country. In fact India is a partly to the resolution of the UNO passed during the United Nations water conference in 1977 as "All people", whatever their stage of development and their social and economic conditions, have the right to have access to drinking water in quantum and of quality equal to their basic needs". The court observed that "water is the basic need for the survival of human beings and is part of the Right to Life and Human Rights as enshrined in Article 21 of the Constitution of India.

From the foregoing decisions, it is clear that the Supreme Court has made significant contribution in giving fill up to the rights of the citizen to a hygienic environment but the exercise of their discretionary powers in environmental matters is yet to take a concrete form. The courts have time and again faced the difficulties in respect of investigative machinery required for the citizen"s suits in environmental matters. To overcome this, the courts have resorted to appointing distinguished persons as experts or commissions to investigate and report to it. It is also suggested that the environmental courts on a regional basis, with one professional judge and two experts drawn from Ecological Sciences Research Group, should be setup.

It is to be noted that the right to environment is a comprehensive right like any other basic right at both National and International levels. The Supreme Court has interpreted the various Constitutional and legal provisions relating to environment in an appropriate direction by promoting ecological balance and sustainable development.

The judiciary reasserted the right to pollution free environment as an integral part of the Right to Life under Article 21 asserting that Human Rights are to be respected. The Supreme Court has during the course of various decisions emphasized that the protection of environment is a Constitutional objective. The growing menace of environmental pollution is a formidable challenge to the human race since it affects the lives of billions of people across the world.

Response of the Judiciary on Child Labour

The evil of employment of children in agriculture and industrial sectors in India is a product of economic, social and among others, inadequate legislative measures. The founding fathers of the Constitution, being aware of the likely exploitation by different profit makers for their personal gain specifically prohibited employment of children in certain employment. Article 24 of the Constitution deals with the Child Labour directly, where as Articles 15(3), 21A, 39 (e), 39 (f) and 47 deal with Child Labour indirectly.

Article 24 of the Constitution prohibits the employment of children below the age of Fourteen years in any factory or mine or engaged in any other hazardous employment. Article 15(3) of the Constitution enables the State to make special provisions for the welfare of children. The directive principle of State policy contained in Article 38 (e) directs the state to safeguard the tender age of children from entering into jobs unsuited to their age and strength forced by economic necessity. Article 38(f) imposes a duty on the state to secure facilities for the healthy development of children, and to protect childhood and youth against exploitation as well as moral and material abandonment. Where as Article 21 A directs the state shall provide free and compulsory education to all children of the age of 6 to 14 years. Article 47 imposes a duty upon the state to raise the levels of nutrition and standard of living of its people and improve public health. The government of India has enacted various welfare legislation for the working children from time to time. The basic aim of the legislation is to prohibit the employment of children in certain employments and regulate the conduct of the employers of child workers in such a way that, these poor innocent child are not exploited any more. The protective provisions of the enactments do not cover children employed in smaller establishment. However, the Government of India enacted the Child Labour (Prohibition and Regulation) Act, 1986 which prohibits the employment of children in hazardous work and also regulates the conditions of work in certain other employment where the employment is not prohibited. The Act has many provisions to be welcomed, but at the same time, it has lacunas and its own limitations.

The role and concern of the Supreme Court of India has been a profound concern in making better the lives of children, who were objects of exploitation. The Supreme Court in Bandhua *Mukthi Morcha vs. Union of India*[94] held that "The right to live with Human Dignity enshrined in Article 21 derives its life breath from the Directive Principles of State Policy and particularly Article 39(e)(f) and Articles 41 and 42 and at the least, therefore it must include protection of health and strength of workers, men and women and of tender age of children against abuse, opportunities and facilities for children to develop in a healthy manner and in conditions of freedom and dignity, educational facilities, just and human conditions of work and maternity relief. These are the minimum requirements which must exist in order to enable a person to live with human dignity.

In *Sheela Barse vs. Union of India*[95] the Supreme Court found that though several states have enacted children Acts for the fulfilment of Constitutional obligations for the welfare of children under Article 39(f), yet it is not enforced in some states. In view of this it directed that such beneficial legislation be brought into force and administered without delay. Justice Bhaghawathi made a suggestion to formulate and implement a national policy for the welfare of children. Further, the Hon"ble justice observed that the children"s programmes should find a prominent part in our plans for the development of resources, so that our children grow up to become citizen, physically fit, mentally alert and morally healthy, endowed with the skill and motivations needed by society.

Then the Supreme Court in *L.K. Pandey vs. Union of India*[96] observed that welfare of the entire community, its growth and development depends upon the health and well- being of its children and that children need special protection because of their tender age and physique, mental immaturity and incapacity to look after themselves. Further the Supreme Court in Vishal Jeet vs. Union of India[97] held that it is the duty of the state to see that Article 39(e) and Article 23 of the Constitution are strictly adhered to and every step is ensured to safe guard the interest of the child worker and save them against all forms of exploitation.

In *Peoples Union for Democratic Rights vs. Union of India*[98] case, the Supreme Court held that the employment of children below 14 years of age was being hazardous, ultra- vires of the Article 24 of the Constitution. The court took a serious note of the construction industry being kept out of the ambit of employment of Children Act, 1938. Expressing concern about the "sad and deplorable omission" the court advised the state Government to take immediate steps for the inclusion of construction works in the schedule of the Act and to ensure that the Constitutional mandate of Article 24 is not violated in any part of the country.

The aforesaid view was reiterated in labourers working on *Salal Hydro-Project vs. State of Jammu and Kashmir*[99] case, where the Supreme Court held that construction work being hazardous employment, no children below the age of 14 can be employed in such work because of Constitutional prohibition contained in Article 24. In the instant case the Supreme Court has travelled beyond its traditional job, that is directing the central government to persuade the workmen to send their children to nearby schools ad arrange not only for schools but also provide free of charge, books and other facilities such as transportation etc.,

There are numerous cases where the judiciary has made significant contribution to the cause of child workers. The Apex Court has given a new dimension to several areas such as Locus Standi, Minimum Wages, and Employment of Children, the glaring decision that deal with the payment of Minimum Wages to the children and the protection in flesh trade, employment of children in hazardous occupation, reflect the judicial creativity in the field of the welfare of the children including child workers. The court also expressed its hope that the state Government would direct its policy towards securing that the children are given opportunities and facilities to develop in a better manner and in condition of freedom and dignity, exploitation and against moral and material abandonment.

The Constitution of India provides Dignity, Equality, Liberty and Freedom and the International law through conventions and declaration has tried to stop the abuse of violation of rights of the child exists at various levels unless a vibrant social movement along with the liberal legal culture is built up, the plight of the children and flagrant violation of their rights can not be stopped. A radical change in the social outlook coupled wider dissemination of legal literary is required to promote the Human Rights of the child.

For, the promotion and protection of child rights, the National Commission for protection of child rights, and State Commissions for Protection of Child Rights and children"s courts were constituted in accordance with mandate of the commissions for protection of Child Rights Act, 2005[100].

India has the largest Child Labour force in the world. Since independence, the state has be come fully conscious of its welfare functions and its responsibilities towards children and consequently codified number of enactments in consonance with Directive Principles of State Policy as enshrined in the India Constitution and the ILO conventions and recommendations and adopted various measures for the protection and welfare of children, nevertheless the Child Labour is increasing day by day indicating ambiguities and deficiencies in the present legislative measures.It is unfortunate to point out here that child welfare legislations, Child Labour still have an ugly face in India. It appears that, there is no improvement in the working condition of the child labour. Despite an active role played by the judiciary, there seems hardly any improvement in the working conditions of Child Labour in India. The Supreme Court has introduced a new method in the form of PIL to provide Justice to the children, poor and weaker sections of the society. In number of cases, the Supreme Court directed the government to carry out the measures for the welfare of the child workers but those pronouncements seem to have made a little alert on the working conditions of children.

In the context of the present socio-economic conditions, the evil of Child Labour can not be totally eliminated but only be regulated. The Government should take serious steps to overcome the difficulties in implementing the law and ensure effective implementation of prohibition of child labour. Despite the fact that many commissions and committees have been brought into vogue, the harsh reality is that the problems of Child Labour in India is persisting on its full swing and still remain as a strong menace.

In India, the implementation of prohibition of Child Labour is very ineffective. The main reasons for this are lack of adequate enforcement machinery, lack of political will, deliberate attempt of employers to flout the legal provisions and lack of consciousness within the minds of parents themselves, who obtain false age and medical certificate to enable their children to work. The problems of Child Labour continue to pose a challenge before the Nation. The government has been taking various pro-active measures to tackle this problem. However, considering the magnitude and extent of the problems and that it is essentially a socio-economic problem inextricably linked to poverty and illiteracy, it required concerted efforts from all sections of the society to eradicate this problem.

The Government had formed first committee known as Gurupadswamy committee in the year 1979 to study the issue of Child Labour and to suggest measures to tackle it. The above said committee examined the problem in various dimensions and made some far- reaching recommendations. It observed that as long as poverty continues, it would be difficult to eliminate Child Labour totally and hence, any attempt to abolish it through legal recourse would not be a practical proposition. The committee felt that in the circumstances, the only alternative left was to ban Child Labour in hazardous areas and to regulate and ameliorate the conditions of work in other areas. It recommended that a multiple policy approach was required in dealing with the problems of working children. Indian judiciary has shown a deep concern towards the protection and welfare of the Child Labour in India.

Judicial Response on Bonded Labour System

This is unfortunate that even after so many years of independence and more, certain obnoxious practices like caste system, untouchability, bonded labour and forced labour continue in the Indian Society. They are now been questioned and challenged by the present day society in the changed context of the social order in the welfare society, where rational and sophisticated thinking, Human Dignity, liberty and equality are considered more important than ever before.

In India the Bonded labour system continues to be the most pernicious form of human bondage. under such system a worker continues to serve his master in consideration of debt obtained by him or his ancestors. Bonded labour can be intergenerational or child bondage or loyalty bondage or bondage through land allotment. Most of these labourers come from lowest strata of the society such as the untouchbles, Adivasis, or agricultural labourers. Bonded labour became a mere play thing in the hands of few privileged persons. Attempts have been made both at National and International Level from time to time to eradicate forced labour. Every International instrument dealing with the Human Rights has prohibited the use of Forced or Compulsory Labour.

The Constitution of India guarantees Fundamental Rights against exploitation. Article 23 of the Constitution of India prohibits "Traffic in human beings and begar and other similar forms of forced labour. The contravention of this Constitutional provision is made an offence punishable in accordance with the law. To give effect to this Constitutional mandate parliament has enacted Bonded Labour System (Abolition) Act, 1976. Efforts were thereafter initiated for identification, release and rehabilitation of bonded labourers in different states. The rehabilitation of Bonded labour has been included as one of the important items in the 20 point Economic programme. The system however is still prevailing in some other many parts of India. Keeping in view the seriousness of the problems of Bonded Labour System in India, the Supreme Court has endeavoured to play an important role in recognising the right to live with human dignity, a reality for millions of Indians and has protected them from exploitation. The court has not only given the widest possible meaning to the Fundamental Rights enshrined in Articles 21 and 23, but also taken into its consideration, the various factors which were responsible for the failure of various other social welfare legislations. In People"s Union for Democratic Rights vs. Union of India[101] case and Bandhua Mukthi

Morcha vs. Union of India[102] case the Supreme Court of India recognised the value of field work and socio-legal research by social scientists and social action groups as the basis of factual data for the exercise of its writ jurisdiction under Article 32 of the Constitution for effective enforcement of Fundamental Rights of Socially and economically disadvantaged group of the society.

The latest judicial trend reveals that Indian courts are quite enthusiastic in using the law as a tool of social revolution. The judiciary is expected to act as catalytic agent of social control. In India higher judiciary have been endeavouring to shield the cause of poor, Bonded labour and other deprived sections of the society. A number of writ petitions were filed before the Supreme Court by way of Public Interest Litigation for the enforcement of Article 23 of the Constitution and the Bonded labour system (Abolition) Act, 1976.

Most of the Public Interest Litigation proceedings on the bonded labour seek to implement the Bonded Labour System (Abolition) Act, 1976. The first major Public Interest Litigation on this issue was *"Bandhua Mukti Morcha v. Union of India*[103] filed in 1981. In the instant case the action was brought for the identification, release, and rehabilitation of hundreds of Bonded labours working in the stone quarries of Haryana. The opinion of Justice P.N. Bhagawati going beyond the said Act, defined Bonded labour was forced by economic hardship. The Supreme Court issued 21 directions and appointed member of commissions of inquiry. Unfortunately, most of the direction remained unimplemented for many years. The court acknowledged its limited capacity in monitoring the schemes or rehabilitation. Ultimately, in 1992 the court recounted the history of the case and was shocked that there was not the slightest improvement in the conditions of the workers of the stone quarries[104]. This litigation ended up with one more warning to the government to be responsive to judicial directions.

In *Neeraja Choudhary vs. State of M.P*[105], case the Supreme Court felt that it is not enough merely to identify and release of bonded labourers but it is equally, perhaps more important that after identification and release they must be rehabilitated because without rehabilitation, they could be driven by poverty and helplessness and they may once again turn to Bonded labour. It is the plainest requirement of Article s 21 and 23 of the Constitution that the bonded labourers must be identified and released and on release they must be suitably rehabilitated. The Bonded labour system (Abolition) Act, 1976 has been enacted pursuant to the mandate of the Constitutional spirit with a view to ensuring basic Human Dignity to the bonded labourers and any failure of action on the part of the state Government in implementing the provisions of this legislation would be the clearest violation of Article 21 apart form Article 23 of the Constitutions.

The decisions of the Supreme Court in the above cases set a new trend to ameliorate the plight of Bonded labourers. In these, the Supreme Court highlighted the importance of the involvement of voluntary agencies in the process of identification and release of bonded labourers. While finally reposing confidence in social action groups, the Apex Court in both the cases observed "it is primarily through social actions groups and voluntary agencies alone that it will be possible to eradicate the Bonded labour system". In both the cases the court expressed its faith in the inclusion of the members of voluntary groups in the vigilance committees as a remedy for identification of Bonded labourers. However their achievement can not be much unless the states create the proper climate for this purpose.

The decision of the Supreme Court in Bandhua Mukthi Morcha recognised the right of the Bonded labourers to live with basic human dignity. The court derived this right from Article 21 of the Constitution, which is a sanctuary of human values after much celebrated decision of the Supreme Court in Maneka Gandhi. The Supreme Court used expressions "bonded labour" and "forced labour" in Article 21 to "right to live with human dignity". The rights and benefits guaranteed to the labourers under various labour laws were made parts of basic Human Dignity and raised to the status of Fundamental Rights.

The Public Interest Litigation has been invented with an intention to bring Justice within the reach of the poor masses which constitute the law visibility area of humanity. A close observation of a series of cases shows that the courts in India are earnestly busy to actualise the dream of Human Rights philosophy and make Indian Constitution a workable proposition for the poor people in India. It has reprimanded the labour enforcement Agencies of the Governments for the non-enforcement of Minimum Wages Act, 1948, Employment Of Children Act, 1938, the Contract Labour (Regulation and Abolition) Act, 1972 the Inter-State Migrant workmen (Regulation of Employment and Conditions of Service) Act, 1979 and the various Constitutional provisions namely Articles 21 and 24 intended to secure monetary benefits as well as Human Dignity to the workman. The Supreme Court has quite successfully elaborated the meaning of „begar" and held that Article 23 of the Constitution is designed not only to protect the individuals against state but also against other private citizens.

It is submitted that the observations of the Supreme Court in Bandhua Mukti Morcha and Neeraja Chaudary created new Constitutionalism to secure the implementation of social or labour welfare legislations through judicial process. The judiciary has certainly brought into limelight, the administrative lapses and a sense of awakening in the public. It is high time the administration took serious note of the direction of the Supreme Court in a positive manner. Indeed there is a greater need not only to identify and release bonded labourers but to effectively and adequately rehabilitate the released bonded labourers. Then only it can be considered that Human Rights of the Bonded labourers are well protected in India, in the welfare state established under the Constitution with long cherished goals.

Conclusion

The right to enforce Human Rights as provided under the Constitution of India is Constitutionally protected. Article 226 empowers the High Courts to issue writs for enforcement of such rights. Similarly Article 32 of the Constitution gives the same powers to the Supreme Court. A new approach has emerged in the form of Public Interest Litigation (PIL) with the objective to bring justice with in the reach of the poor and the disadvantageous section of the society. In the recent past the judges of the High Courts and the Supreme Court have from time to time given far reaching and innovative judgements to protect the Human Rights. Public Interest Litigation has heralded a new era of Human Rights promotion and protection in India.

The greatest contribution of Public Interest Litigation has been to enhance the accountability of the Governments towards the Human Rights of the poor. Public Interest Litigation has undoubtedly produced astonishing results which were unthinkable two decades ago. Public Interest Litigation has rendered a signal service in the areas of Prisoner"s Rights, development of compensatory jurisprudence for Human Rights violation, Environmental protection, Bonded labour eradication and prohibition of Child Labour and many others.

A review of the decisions of the Indian Judiciary regarding the protection of Human Rights indicates that the judiciary has been playing a role of saviour in situations where the executive and legislature have failed to address the problems of the people. The Supreme Court has come forward to take corrective measures and provide necessary directions to the executive and legislature,. However while taking note of the contributions of judiciary one must not forget that the judicial pronouncements can not be a protective umbrella for inefficiency and laxity of executive and legislature. It is the foremost duty of the society and all its organs to provide justice and correct institutional and human errors affecting basic needs, dignity and liberty of human beings. Fortunately India has pro-active judiciary. It can thus be aspired that in the times ahead, people's right to live, as a true human beings will further be strengthened.

From the perusal of the above contribution it is evident that the Indian Judiciary has been very sensitive and alive to the protection of the Human Rights of the people. It has, through judicial activism forged new tools and devised new remedies for the purpose of vindicating the most precious of the precious Human Right to Life and Personal Liberty.

Refrences

[1] www.cehat.org/rthc

[2] Byrne, Iain (2005) Making the Right to Health a reality: Legal Strategies for Effective Implementations, Commonwealth Law Officer, Inter rights Visiting Fellow, Human Rights Centre, Essex University

[3] Justice A. S. Anand, in M.C. Bhandari Memorial Lecture Public Interest Litigation as Aid to Protection of Human Rights, www.ebc-india.com

[4] Justice Anand (2003) Inaugural Address, National Consultation on Health Care as a Human Right, Jan Swasthya Abhiyan and NHRC

[5] Daryao Vs. State of U.P (AIR 1961 SC 1457)

[6] AIR 1950 SC 124

[7] AIR 1989 SC 1285

[8] AIR 1982 SC 149

[9] Bihar Legal Support Society vs. Chief Justice of India (1986) 4 SCC 767

[10] AIR 1982 SC 1473

[11] AIR 1984 SC 803

[12] AIR 1987 SC 1087

[13] (2000) 4 SCJ 261

[14] Ashok Kumar Pandey vs. State of West Bengal (2004) 3 SCC 349

[15] Chandanmal Chopra VS. State of West Bengal AIR 1986 Cal 104

[16] Oddessey Lok Vidyayana Sanghatan vs. Union of India (1988) ISCC 168

[17] Common Cause vs. union of India (1996) 2 SCC 752

[18] D.Satyanarayana vs. N.T.Rama Rao AIR 1988 AP 144

[19] Centre for Public Interest Litigation vs. Union of India (1995) (supp) 3 SCC 382

[20] Shiv Sagar tiwari vs. union of India (1996) 2 SCC 558

[21] Vineet Narayan vs. union of India (1996) 2 SCC 199

[22] All India judges association vs. Union of India AIR 1992 SC 165

[23] Bishwajeet serisha vs. Dibrugarh University AIR 1991 GAU. 27

[24] A.K. Gopalan vs. State of Madras A.I.R 1950 SC P.27

[25] Maneka Gandhi vs. Union of India A.I.R 1978 SC P.597

[26] Maneka Gandhi vs. Union of India AIR 1978 SC P.597

[27] Sunil Batra (I) vs. Delhi administration AIR 1978 SC 1675

[28] M.H.Hoskot vs. State of Maharashtra AIR 1978 SC 1548

[29] Hussainara Khatoons NO. I vs. Home Secretary, State of Bihar AIR 1979 SC 1360

[30] Sunil Batra (I) vs. Delhi administration AIR 1978 SC 1675

[31] ibid at P 1719

[32] AIR 1980 SC 1535

[33] ibid at P 1541

[34] Article 5 of the Universal Declaration of Human Rights, 1948 provides that "No one shall be subjected to torture or to cruel, inhuman or degrading treatment or punishment.

[35] Article 10 of the International Covenant on Civil and Political Rights stipulates that "All persons deprived of their liberty shall be treated with humanity and with respect for the inherent dignity of the human person"

[36] Delhi Judicial Service Association vs. State of Gujarath (1991) 4 SCC 406

[37] (1991) 2 SCC 373

[38] Sunil Gupta vs. State of M.P. 1990 (3) S.CC 119; Citizen for Democracy VS. State of Assam, 1995 (3) SCC 743; Khedat Mazdoor chetna sangath VS. State of M.P. AIR 1995 SC 31

[39] 1995 (3) SCC 743

[40] Ramana Murthy V. State of Karnataka AIR 1997 SC 1739; Munna VS. State of U.P AIR 1982 SC 806; Rakesh VS. Suptd. Central prison, New Delhi, AIR 1981 SC 760; D.K.Basu VS. State of West Bengal (1997 I SCC 416; Sheela Barse VS. State of Maharashtra AIR 1983 SC 378; Khedat Mazdoor Chetna Sangtham V. State of M.P. AIR 1995 SC 31

[41] (1986) 4 SCC 481

[42] AIR 1981 SC 625

[43] AIR 1997 SC 610

[44] proceedings under the contempt of courts Act, 1971 can be started in any high court.

[45] Sec 304 (1) of criminal procedure code, 1973 stipulates that "where, in a trail before the court of session, the accused is not represented by a pleader and where it appears to the court that the accused has not sufficient means to engage a pleader, the court shall assign a pleader for his defence at the expense of the state

[46] Tara Singh vs. State AIR 1951SC 441

[47] AIR 1979 SC 1595

[48] (1981) 1 SCC 608

[49] AIR 1979 SC 1377

[50] (1987) 4 SCC 373

[51] Prubhu Datt vs. union of India (1982) 1 SCC 1, In this case, the court was considered the claim of a journalist to interview two condemned prisoners awaiting execution

[52] AIR 1994 SC 1349

[53] Article 39-A provides that "the state shall secure that the operation of the legal system promotes justice, on a basis of equal opportunity and shall in particular, provides Free Legal Aid by suitable legislation or scheme or in any other way to ensure that opportunities for securing justice are not denied to any citizen by reason of economic or other disabilities.

[54] Article 37 of the Constitution of India reads as "the previsions contained in part IV shall not be enforceable by any court but the principles there in laid down are nevertheless fundamental in the governance of the country and it shall be the duty of the state to apply these principles in making laws.

[55] AIR 1978 SC P597

[56] AIR 1978 SC 1548

[57] AIR 1979 SC 1360

[58] AIR 1980 SC 1579

[59] AIR 1981 SC 928

[60] (1981) 3 SCC 671

[65] AIR 1978 SC 597

[66] Article 9(5) of the International Covenant on Civil and Political Rights states that "Anyone who has been the victim of unlawful arrest or detention shall have an enforceable right to compensation".

[67] AIR 1983 SC 339

[68] 1981SC 928

[61] AIR 1978 SC 597

[62] (1980) I SCC 81

[63] Section 309 (1) of Cr.PC contemplates "In every inquiry or trial the proceedings shall be held as expeditiously as possible, and in particular, when the examination of witnesses has once begun, the same shall be continued from day to day until all the witnesses in attendance have been examined, unless the court finds that the adjournment of the same beyond the following day to be necessary for reasons to be recorded.

[64] AIR 1992 SC 1701

[69] Ibid at P 930 Para 3

[70] AIR 1983 SC 1086

[71] AIR 1984 SC 1026

[72] AIR 1986 SC 494

[73] AIR 1990 SC 513

[74] AIR 1993 SC 1960

[75] Sec. 65 of the Government of Indian Act, 1858 reads as follows: the secretary of state in council shall and may sue and be sued as well in India as in England by the name of the secretary of State in council as a body corporate and all persons and bodies politic shall, and may have and take the same suits, remedies and proceedings, legal and equitable, against the secretary of state in council of India as a they could have done against the East India company.

[76] 1868-1869 5 Bom HC Reports;

[77] Article 300 of the Constitution of India contemplates: Suits and proceedings (1) the Government of India may sue or be sued by the name of the Union of India and the Government of a State may sue or be sued by the name of the State and may, subject to any provisions which may be made by Act of parliament or of the legislature of such state enacted by virtue of powers conferred by this Constitution, sue or be sued in relation to their respective

affairs in the like cases as the dominion of India and the corresponding provinces or the corresponding Indian states might have sued or been sued if this Constitution had not been enacted.

(2) If at commencement of this Constitution-

(a) any legal proceedings are pending to which the Dominion of India is a party, the union of India shall be deemed to be substituted for the dominion in those proceedings; and

(b) any legal proceedings are pending to which a province or an Indian state is a party, the corresponding state shall be deemed to be substituted for the province or the Indian State in those proceedings.

[78] AIR 1962 SC 933

[79] AIR 1965 SC 1039

[80] AIR 2000 SC 2083

[82] (1986) 2 SCC 431

[83] AIR 1979 SC 143

[85] (1995) 3 SCC 42

[86] (1998) 1 SCC 471

[87] AIR 1991 SC 1132

[88] (1886) LR 3 HL 330

[89] AIR 1987 SC 965

[90] Vellore Citizens Welfare Forum vs Union of India (1996) 5 SCC 650

[91] AIR 1999 SC 812

[92] AIR 1999 SC 430

[93] 2001 (2) SCC 62.

[94] (1984) 3 SCC 161

[95] AIR 1986 SC 1773

[96] (1984) 2 SCC 244 at 249

[97] 1990 Sc 1412

[98] AIR 1982 SC 1473

[99] AIR 1984 SC 177

[100] Act No. 4 of 2006 – Received assent of the President on January 20, 2006 and published in the Gazette of India extra; Part II, section 1, dated 20.1.2006.

[101] AIR 1982 SC 1473

[102] AIR 1984 SC 802

[103] (1984) 4 SCC 161

[104] Bandhua Mukthi Morcha vs. Union of India, AIR 1992 SC 38

[105] AIR 1984 SC 1099

www.ingramcontent.com/pod-product-compliance
Lightning Source LLC
LaVergne TN
LVHW070530070526
838199LV00075B/6744